D0073478

THE ARMY OF THE
FRENCH REVOLUTION

The Army of the French Revolution

. . .

FROM CITIZEN-SOLDIERS
TO INSTRUMENT OF POWER

Jean-Paul Bertaud

TRANSLATED BY

R. R. Palmer

PRINCETON UNIVERSITY PRESS

Copyright © 1988 by Princeton University Press
Translated from Jean-Paul Bertaud, *La Révolution armée:*
Les soldate-citoyens et la Révolution française.
Paris, © Editions Robert Laffont, 1979

Published by Princeton University Press,
41 William Street, Princeton, New Jersey 08540
In the United Kingdom:
Princeton University Press, Guildford, Surrey

This book has been composed in Linotron Galliard
Clothbound editions of Princeton University Press books are
printed on acid-free paper, and binding materials are chosen
for strength and durability.
Paperbacks, although satisfactory for personal collections,
are not usually suitable for library rebinding

Printed in the United States of America
by Princeton University Press, Princeton, New Jersey

Library of Congress Cataloging-in-Publication Data
Bertaud, Jean Paul.
The army of the French Revolution.
Translation of: La révolution armée.
Bibliography: p.
Includes index.
1. France—History, Military—1789–1815.
2. France. Armée—History—Revolution, 1789–1799.
3. France—History—Revolution, 1789–1799—Influence.
I. Title.
DC151.B4313 1988   944.04   88–15098
ISBN 0–691–05537–8 (alk. paper)

I was a child in 1810, when on the Emperor's birthday the draperies hiding the monument at the Place Vendôme were let fall, and the column appeared. I admired it like everyone else. Only I would have liked to know more about the figures in bronze on the bas-reliefs. "And all those men climbing up the column," I said, "what were their names?"

—JULES MICHELET

A great stirring of valorous poverty . . . which to save the Revolution expanded it and opened its heart to a larger dream.

—JEAN JAURÈS

CONTENTS

• • •

CONTENTS

CONTENTS

PART THREE

From the National and Revolutionary Army
to the Army of the Coup d'État of Fructidor
(Year III to Year V)

TRANSLATOR'S PREFACE

• • •

Jean-Paul Bertaud is Professor of Modern History at the University of Paris I, still commonly called the Sorbonne. He has published widely in France on aspects of the French Revolution, mainly though not exclusively on the military problems faced by the Revolutionary leadership and on the experience of common soldiers in the Revolutionary wars. The present volume is Professor Bertaud's most substantial work, and is likely to remain for a long time the most authoritative treatment of the subject.

Its theme is suggested by its title, which in French is *La Révolution armée*, "the Revolution armed." That is, the book is primarily about the Revolution, and specifically the Revolution in its relation to armed force. The book first reviews the role of the army during the overthrow of the preceding regime. Then it considers the need of the new regime to control the army; the need of mobilization against intervention by foreign powers; and the conduct of a war, which passed from defense against invasion to the invasion and occupation of neighboring countries, followed by a loss of civilian control as the army proved victorious outside of France. The book concludes by examining the climactic transfer of power to one of the Revolutionary generals, Napoleon Bonaparte. The means used for these purposes, as shown in the subtitles of both the original and this translation, was to activate the idea of the citizen-soldier. It was an idea exemplified in the ancient classical republics, and favored by Jean-Jacques Rousseau and other eighteenth-century thinkers, but until then never realized so fully on so large and portentous a scale as in France in the 1790s.

The book is thus also a work of military history in a broad sense. Military history is no longer a story of battles and campaigns, and no particular battle or campaign is recounted here. Military history now embraces the social, economic, political, psychological, technological, and organizational conditions under which a society can exert armed force, either to maintain authority over its own population or to exert power against outsiders. In the present case, we examine these conditions from the fall of the Bastille to the rise of Bonaparte. We see how conditions in the old royal army helped to advance rather than retard the original revolutionary movement in 1789. We then note the spread of revolutionary enthusiasm and mass excitement, of spontaneous activism roughly organized by central planning, the formation of national guards and waves of volunteering, eventuating in the "democracy in arms" of the Year II of the Republic. The tensions within all this agitation are made clear, between professional army men and popular soldiering, between liberty and discipline, equality and subordination, personal interest and patriotic self-sacrifice. The author brings a new and detailed analysis to the famous *levée en masse* of 1793, which produced the largest army ever seen in Europe until that time; he shows how it was actually carried out locally in practice, the resistance it met with, and its failures as well as its successes. And we have a new realization of the difficulties in maintaining an army of over 700,000 men in the face of the shortages, breakdowns, inefficiencies and cross-purposes that were inseparable from revolution.

There is much also on military history in a stricter sense. Although there is no narrative of any one battle, the innovations in battlefield tactics are explored. These include the combined use of infantry, cavalry, and artillery; the training and deployment of infantry in column and line; the way in which muskets were fired;

and how individual skirmishers and sharpshooters operated alongside more massive formations. The importance of organization is also stressed: how battalions were formed, and why; the introduction of the infantry "demi-brigades"; and the putting of units of the combat arms along with supply and administrative services into "divisions." We see how appointment and promotion were shifted from the old basis of social status and favoritism to a new basis of qualification by talent and merit.

A major organizational problem, likely to occur in any revolution, was the unification of armed forces. The potential distrust between career soldiers, volunteers and conscripts had to be overcome. The expertise of professionals of the Old Regime (sometimes nobles who accepted the Revolution, sometimes pre-Revolutionary enlisted men who became officers and even generals in the 1790s) had to be combined with the raw enthusiasm of many (and the reluctance of others) who had been agricultural laborers, artisans, white-collar workers, or students a few weeks before. The author distinguishes between the incorporation of individuals, the juxtaposition of units, and "amalgamation" or what we would call integration—that is, the placing of men of diverse background side by side in the smallest tactical units. This was one of the many processes of nation building ("fraternity") in which the Revolutionary governments engaged.

We have here social history also, in the sense of history "from below," or a concern with what happened to the inarticulate, sparsely documented, and very numerous common people. This approach is evident in the use of computer-assisted quantitative methods where possible, admittedly of the simplest kind; documentation includes the frequent reference to the height of soldiers as measured by army examiners and to average values that tell us something of their age and physique; and the recurrent use of percentages to show the relative importance of social classes in the army at different times, or among officers of grades from lieutenant to general. For the same reason, to reveal the everyday experience of ordinary people, the author draws more fully than his predecessors on the available archival material to offer us unusually frequent and long quotations. He quotes from reports of inspectors on the state of mind of the troops, the petitions and addresses to the government drawn up by battalions and other units, and especially from the letters written by soldiers in their camps and on their campaigns to their mothers, fathers, and wives at home. Fortunately for the historian, the army of the French Revolution, recruited from all social classes, had in all probability a higher literacy rate than any of the armies arrayed against it. Social history is evident also in the author's emphasis on the social policy of the revolutionary governments, as in their efforts to extend the property rights of peasants and to support the dependents of soldiers. It was understood that hundreds of thousands of men could not be expected to fight for their country, especially under a banner of liberty and equality, unless they had reason to believe in their cause, and to feel that their parents, wives, and children would not fall into poverty in their absence.

The author has found the evidence on such matters by long and diligent search in unpublished papers in the French archives. The original of this book contains no less than 762 footnote references, almost all of them citing materials in the Archives Nationales and the Archives de la Guerre. These notes are omitted from the present translation, on the ground that anyone able to consult such sources must know enough of the French language to prefer to use the book in the original. A discussion of these archival materials, which appears in the original after the Historiographical Introduction, is presented in this translation as Appendix I.

Professor Bertaud also refers to a good many monographs and specialized articles, mostly in French, but he is aware also of the considerable work on his subject published in English, chiefly in recent years by American scholars. In the present translation references to publications in French are omitted, but references to those in English are retained. In general, all footnotes in this translation, except the ones on pages 136, 239 and 349, have been added by the translator. Also omitted are an extensive bibliography and five pages of tabulated data annexed to the original. In the present volume Appendix III lists a dozen books written in English on military history in which the French Revolution is of importance, including several published since the publication of *La Révolution armée* in 1979.

The reader may ask himself, at the close of the book, whether the French Revolution ended in a militarization of France. Did a revolution begun by announcing liberal and constitutional principles, and generating a democracy in arms, lead to the dictatorship that some had predicted, and to the "Caesarism" that so many had warned against? The author is troubled by the same questions. His answer is qualified and guarded. Yes, France was reorganized by Napoleon along lines suggested by the military model, a kind of regimentation, subordination and hierarchy, as well as rationalization and national uniformity, applied to the institutions of civilian life. It was a model that stressed also personal abilities, honor, unselfishness, and service to the state, with the state seen as the vehicle of the public interest. But no: it was not simply a suppression of other values by armed force. The Revolution was not crushed. The counter-revolution did not prevail. The old institutions were not restored. The army, in the years of war against the combined governments of Europe, had "secreted" a power of its own; it became an autonomous force apart from civilian government and society; but it saw itself as, and indeed was, the carrier of the revolutionary message, the bearer of the legacy of the Year II. It was still arrayed against the old society of rank and birth, upholding a kind of equality, pitted against everything royal, aristocratic, ecclesiastical, or "feudal" in France and in Europe. And so, as Tocqueville and others believed, the Revolution remained as a continuing force under Napoleon, and even later.

If I may conclude on a personal note, I should like to say that translating this book has been a source of unusual pleasure by recalling to me my own younger days. It is almost fifty years since I wrote a book called *Twelve Who Ruled: The Committee of Public Safety in the French Revolution*. It was not nearly as scholarly or original as the present work, and was less concentrated on military questions, but it made me live vicariously for a while in the Year II of the French Republic. Then for two years and more, during World War II, it was my fate to work with the Historical Section of the old Army Ground Forces, under Kent Roberts Greenfield, housed in what is now the National War College in Washington, D.C. Our task was to write a current history of the organization and training of ground combat troops. It was a lesson in the problems of raising a citizen army, or a mass army, in time of war. It perhaps gave me a feeling for similar problems as they arose in France during its Revolution.

I have benefited throughout from the helpful cooperation of Professor Bertaud. Though he has an excellent knowledge of English, he has not seen the translation, but he has cordially replied to a few questions that I put to him, and he has slightly rewritten a few passages, including the closing paragraphs of the book. I am greatly indebted to him, and to the editors and others at the Princeton University Press. We are all glad to see an English version of this book contribute to the bicentennial observance of the French Revolution.

R. R. PALMER
Princeton, N.J.
January 1988

THE ARMY OF THE
FRENCH REVOLUTION

A HISTORIOGRAPHICAL
INTRODUCTION
• • •

The Army without the Revolution?
or
The Army in and of the Revolution?

The Revolution was the war. For eight years, with musket raised or pike held high, the Frenchman was a fighting man. What was he fighting for? Was it as in the days of the monarchy, when he wished only to defend his home and family from the fury of a murderous soldiery? Or was he a man of the New City, fighting first of all to preserve and extend the rights won on the Night of the 4th of August? Or did he become a pretorian, blindly obeying the orders of chiefs engaged in a struggle for power? What *was* the army at the time of the French Revolution?

In reply to these questions many historians have said that the army soon became separated from the Revolution. In their accounts three images are mingled. In one, we see a troop of men who think only of defending the land of their ancestors. In another, the army is a society serving as a "refuge for decent people" who "by preserving traditional values contributed to the restoration of France after the revolutionary tempest." In a third, it is an army kept going by professional soldiers who won their victories by experience gained before the Revolution in the camps of the king.

At the origin of such views we find the apostasy of some who had served the Revolution, men who had in fact fought for the Great Nation. After participating in the epic struggle, and now wishing to integrate themselves into the new society of "notables," they repudiated the critical phase of the Year II by calling it anarchical. Thus A. Liger, in 1798, in his *Histoire des campagnes des Français pendant la Révolution*, made a sharp distinction between the history of the rulers and the history of the soldiers. The latter, he said, responded to "the cry of honor"; they found the excesses of the Revolution repugnant, but were unable to oppose them and sought at least to save France from invasion. General Latrille developed the same theme during the Consulate, in his book of 1804, *Considérations sur la guerre et particulièrement sur la dernière guerre*. The French, he explained, were so indignant at the insolence of foreigners that they rushed to the frontiers to avenge themselves, while forgetting "the monstrous tyranny" that installed itself at home.

A new kind of distrust came with the Restoration in 1815. The military were now suspected of having served as the right arm of terrorist democracy in the Year II. They produced ingenious justifications of their past actions. To obtain grace from the ultras, they multiplied their disavowals. Were the volunteers of 1792 accused of being *septembriseurs*, perpetrators of the massacres of September? They described themselves as men of "generous courage who, revolted by the cruel spectacle of civil discord, escaped from the troubles and from popular excesses into their camps." "There was a rush to find in the military uniform an honor to be seen nowhere else," according to Colonel Carrion-Nisas in his *Essai sur l'histoire générale de l'art militaire*.

So on one side stood a France "perverted by tyrants and their extravagant cruelties" (Charles Lacretelle), and on the other, the army. All good citizens met in it and upheld the principles of order that the country had forgotten. In the general disintegration of France only the army remained a viable society, unpolluted by politics. Becoming again as in former times the elite of the civic body, the army could react upon it, suppress anarchy, and make possible a return to order. As a conservative force it carried on the work of regeneration, according to an anonymous work of 1827, *Observations sur l'ouvrage de M. le Lieutenant Général Lamarque, De l'esprit militaire en France.*

So the parade of conquerors ended up by doing homage to the Old Regime. The France of the kings, they said, was the source of a military glory unaffected by the crimes of the Revolution. From the time of the Consulate some officers, along with nobles who had rallied to the new regime, insisted, rightly enough, on the efforts of the monarchy before the Revolution to improve the art of war. Knowledge of this art had then been transmitted to the Revolution by old servants of the king, such as sergeants who rose to be officers. That was true enough, but in these military circles, as well as for historians like Toulongeon who took over their ideas (*Histoire de France depuis la Révolution de 1789*, Paris, 1806), the net effect was to see in the victory of the Republic no more than the experience gained in the army of Louis XVI.

The generation of nationalist historians born in the defeat of 1870 brought together and completed these images, making a myth of them that has lasted until our own time. Their myth served at first for military education in the Third Republic. It was diffused in the courses in history given in regimental schools. In these courses, "the consoling spectacle of victories abroad" was contrasted with "internal dissensions." The triumphs of the armies of the Republic were presented as "a cloud of glory rising above our frontiers to prevent the enemy from seeing the strife within." The historian Albert Vandal used similar language in addressing students at the military school of Saint-Cyr in 1898. He admitted that the revolutionary spirit had produced sublime outbursts, but only at a monstrous price. It had created nothing consistent or lasting and had rapidly subsided. In the wreckage of all beliefs and institutions, abysses of immorality had opened up. Shame, baseness, and villainy were everywhere; an age of filth followed an age of iron. Around this France in decomposition there was a fringe of heroism—the army. Strong and forceful, its moral spring lay in "the sentiment of honor that, as has been rightly said, took refuge in the camps during the Revolution."

All forms of nationalism were to draw on this picture of a military society that, throughout the upheaval, remained sane enough to restore and preserve the principles of order and authority, of the unity and continuity of the nation. The army was presented as the most visible and tangible manifestation of the idea of one's country, *la Patrie*. But this word received a content that was far from what it meant to the citizen-soldiers of the Year II.

For many nationalists the *Patrie* was above all "the land and the dead." This theme was developed by journalists well before Barrès. Thus in an article in the *Revue des Deux Mondes* for November 15, 1871, E. Montégut called the democracy born in 1789 the first step in "an adventurist democracy which in the nineteenth century still declares its opposition to the true idea of *la Patrie*. The *Patrie* is the land of our fathers, the country where we were born, its hearths, its altars, and its tombs." The revolutionaries, according to him, had cleverly woven these ideas into their propaganda, but in fact they had rejected them. They had wiped the slate clean of the past without which there is no *Patrie*. The army alone had preserved the heritage, which nourished its heroism and justified its actions although these were unfortunately directed by "tyrants."

This opinion was shared by the military men who came forward in the nineteenth century as historians of the army of the Revolution. For Captain Quarré du Verneuil, for example, in his *La France militaire pendant la Révolution* (1878), the Revolution had become the enemy of the *Patrie* by outraging and denouncing the past, while the army, in which the soul of the Old Regime still lived, preserved *la Patrie* and bequeathed its true image to the French of the future. By this myth the revolutionary nation was mutilated, deprived of the army that it had created and brought to life. The emotional charge carried by the democracy of the Year II faded out in the collective consciousness of the French.

Yet it did not disappear. Nationalist historians in the Jacobin tradition were still impregnated with it at the close of the nineteenth century. To describe the "vast wars of friendship" undertaken by the Great Nation, they recovered the accents of Michelet in portraying the soldiers of the Revolution. "By so many heroic actions in the utmost struggles for liberty, they magnified human nature." Drawing on memoirs, such as those of Gouvion de Saint-Cyr, or on the letters and marching journals that were published in increasing numbers as the centenary approached, these historians recaptured a truer sense of the motivations of the citizen-soldiers in combat. Indeed, some like Albert Sorel, continued to see a dichotomy between soldiers "who faced forward toward enemies bent on dismembering their country" and a rear area "where factions were destroying it." But most understood the union between the military and the rear area of a whole nation that had risen to support them. This union, they argued, was made possible by a shared demand for liberty and national independence. They overlooked the fact that the democracy in arms was the bearer also of another message—equality. Reflecting the outlook of the Radical party of the late nineteenth century, these historians put their main emphasis on only the first term in the republican motto. For them, the armies of Kellermann or Jourdan were missionaries carrying the citizens' decalogue of 1789 to oppressed peoples. It was the sacred tablets of the Republic that the Third Republic had a mission to propagate and to defend. In schools and barracks thousands of Frenchmen learned that the cannonade of Valmy was the first salvo in a struggle still to be carried on. In the collective psychology the reconquest of territories lost in 1870 became part of a crusade for Liberty.

After about 1900 Jean Jaurès gave a new interpretation to the Revolution and its army. In his *Histoire socialiste de la Révolution française*, he urged his reader to see in the army of the Revolution the projection of a society in crisis. In 1910, arguing against a proposed law that would make the army into a body of professional soldiers, he denounced the danger of infeudation to a military caste; instead, he called for a national army in his book, *L'ar-*

mée nouvelle, thus drawing lessons for his own time from the revolutionary tradition.

Jaurès saw a contrast between two periods of the Revolution. In the first, during the constitutional monarchy of 1789–1791, the army was torn, like the country itself, between revolution and counter-revolution. The second began when France went to war in 1792. There now appeared on the political stage, and also in the regular regiments and the volunteer battalions, "a great stirring of valorous poverty, which to save the Revolution expanded it and opened its heart to a larger dream." The army was victorious because it carried on the people's struggle, because it defended, not the old *Patrie* "of aristocrats, priests, speculators and the selfish rich," but a new *Patrie* "of producers, brave citizens, poor and honest, raised up from the servile resignation in which they had lain for ages." The more the Revolution enlarged its appeal the more it was bound to stress its equalitarian aspects, "the social promise contained in its idea." In the army as in the Revolution itself, there were popular masses struggling for the annihilation of privilege and a total destruction of the seigneurial regime. Upon all privileges, "of the political order, the social order, the military order, the lightning struck all at once." It was a threefold indivisible action.

Patrie and Revolution were thus united. The army was the people rising up to destroy the despotism and feudalism of the Old Regime. With archives opened, and files examined, this became the lesson of the Year II. Albert Mathiez learned it, and set it forth in his *Victoire en l'an II*, which he saw as the "victory of Justice, Equality, and Liberty." This work appeared in 1916, during the great national drama of World War I. Jaurès had defended the cause of a new army as a guarantor of peace; he had regretted the perversion of a revolutionary war that began in defense of liberty but then became a war of rapine that led to a military coup against the State. Mathiez, in the midst of the Great War, at a moment when the outcome was uncertain, wished to dispel doubt and discouragement, especially among his students who had become soldiers. His history was in part the product of learned research, but how can we not see it also as a piece of psychological activism?

After Mathiez, historical thinking on the army of the Revolution took place again in a context of democracy in peril. Against those who favored a professional army, historians such as J. Leverrier, in his *La naissance de l'Armée nationale* (1939), again expounded the lesson of the Year II. After World War II the debate over a professional as against a national army was resumed. Georges Lefebvre used it to clarify his views on the army of the Revolution. Comparing the amalgamation of forces born of the Resistance and the Free French in the 1940s with the military *amalgame* effected in 1794, he argued that the latter was the best safeguard of the republican ideal. In articles in *La Pensée* (1944) and *Libertés* (1944), Lefebvre emphasized that the national war was inseparable from a social ideal. Following Jaurès and Mathiez, he analyzed the threefold aspects of the army of the Revolution.

As a national army, it recruited without distinction from all regions and all social classes, and so had large numbers at its disposal. As a national and revolutionary army, in the view stressed by Albert Soboul in *Les soldats de l'An II* (1959), it was composed of citizen soldiers who fought to defend their families and free their land from the "feudal" yoke. Their struggle could not be separated from that of the popular masses that wanted recognition of their right to existence and an "equality of enjoyments." And finally, as an army with a new principle of organization, it fused the soldiers of the Old Regime with the new national volunteers. The latter brought in a revolutionary enthusiasm, the former a science of combat. A freely accepted discipline was not oppressive to the legitimate democratic aspirations of the troops. Attacking in columns, with bayonets raised, and the revolutionary song on their lips, these men embodied the "leveling and conquering Revolution" (M. Reinhard).

This army from 1792 to the autumn of 1793 was also a "deliberating" army. The soldiers considered themselves to be citizens, retaining their rights and applying the direct democracy of the sans-culottes in their encampments. Electing their own chiefs, they intended to control them, to discuss their orders, and to intervene with the "representatives of the people" sent out by the National Convention, whom they regarded as their "mandatories." Against this the Revolutionary Government reacted.[1] From the soldiers it demanded acceptance of discipline as the pledge of victory, and on the generals it imposed a strict subordination to the civilian power. To both, and to others, it taught the principles of Jacobinism.

What were the effects of this policy? Was it not that the Revolution secreted a new kind of power, the power of an army ready to overthrow the state, even if not called upon by certain politicians, as soon as it considered the state unable to preserve the legacy of the revolutionary people of the Year II, of which the army regarded itself as the legatee?

Apart from questions of ideology, either of the Revolutionaries themselves or of historians, a review of histories of the Revolutionary army reveals two weaknesses. On the recruitment and organization of the troops their interest is centered almost entirely on the volunteers of 1791 and 1792. Many of these writings have in any case a tone more of hagiography than of true historical research. The former royal army is studied only superficially, except indeed in a recent American book.[2] We find a repetition of what contemporaries said about the crisis that struck the royal army in 1792 but no attempt to study it in its depths during the preceding years since 1789. Lists are given of officers who emigrated, without attention to those who remained. On the requisition under the *levée en masse* of the Year II, which is less studied than the conscription of the Year VI, the ringing summons of August 23, 1793, is repeatedly quoted, but nothing is said of how the country responded to it, or at most we have generalizations on the attitude

---

[1] For the meaning of Revolutionary Government, see the first paragraph of Chapter VII.

[2] Samuel F. Scott, *The Response of the Royal Army to the French Revolution: The Role and Development of the Line Army, 1787–1793* (Oxford, 1978).

in one of two departments. Only a quarter of the books and articles published from 1886 to 1910, which were the years of greatest production, relate to the *levée en masse*, and even in those there is hardly more than the publication of a few letters. There is no social analysis, with a few exceptions that seldom attempt a synthesis for more than a single department. Many works provide only lists of names like those that were posted on the walls of municipal assembly rooms and which, from 1794, anticipate our monuments to the dead in the twentieth century.

As for the organization of the army, and more precisely the "amalgamation," the researchers only repeat what we learn from speeches in the assemblies, notably the speeches of men like Dubois-Crancé, who took a leading part in the reorganization. Once certain measures were adopted, their application and the reactions they aroused seem of no further interest to our historians. They fail to distinguish the processes of incorporation, brigade forming, and amalgamation, and they confuse deserters with draft evaders when they study them at all. Finally, virtually all these books deal only with the period from 1789 to 1794; they pass over the Directory until Bonaparte plays a role.

To answer all such questions it is not enough to study French society from above, at the level of the debates and decrees of assemblies or the correspondence and memoirs of leading persons. It is necessary to probe the military society more deeply—to count its members, find out their age and physical capacity, judge their talent, and recover their state of mind as revealed in their origin. For a knowledge of such matters the sources are innumerable and difficult to deal with in quantitative terms. Their volume, and above all their dispersion in departmental archives, for a long time made the task impossible, and historians of the past may be excused for not having undertaken it. As long ago as 1907, however, the ministry of war established a historical commission to bring together these scattered materials. New methods of investigation make it possible to master them. A description of these materials and a method for using them may be found in Appendix I.

PART ONE

From the Royal Army
to the Democracy in Arms
(1789 to Summer 1793)

The army presented a problem for the Revolution from the very beginning, first for the Estates General and then for the Constituent Assembly. The new powers had to prevent it from rising against them, and then to unite it with themselves. In fact—though the fact was not then known—the army was divided by the same contradictions and experiencing the same crises as civilian society. The revolutionary spirit already stirred among its members. Far from opposing the Revolution, the army, in its great majority, assisted in its course.

The bourgeoisie saw in the army the bearers of the chains of despotism. It was their aim to control it, to bind it to the new order by reforms reflecting their compromise with liberals among the nobility. After the king's attempted escape from Paris, in 1791, the Constituent Assembly, fearful of royalist bayonets, organized a new military force of its own, using the battalions of volunteers that took form spontaneously. This new army, drawn from the national guard, was in the image of the new society in that it contained both moderates who wished to put an end to the Revolution and Jacobins eager to carry it farther. The army of national volunteers, like the royal army, might become the stake for which opposing political coteries had to contend.

War with Austria began on April 20, 1792, and with Prussia a little later. The army would determine the outcome. If it lost a battle, the Revolution would be overturned and the king restored to his former powers. If it won, its success might give disturbing ideas to some general. Caesarism might result from the war; and Lafayette came under suspicion, by Robespierre first of all. But though at first defeated, both the royal army and the volunteers remained faithful to the Revolution and accepted the fall of the monarchy.

On July 12, 1792, the Legislative Assembly ordered the raising of new battalions. The popular masses who made the Revolution of Equality by the uprising of August 10 responded to the call of *la Patrie en danger*. A third army took form, this time of the "sansculottes." It, too, might be tempted to intervene on the political scene, impose economic controls, demand the pursuit of suspects, and insist on its own domination over elected deputies.

In September 1792, when the National Convention first met, the Girondins were afraid of a *sans-culottisation* of the army. While agreeing to the levy of new battalions, they resisted the amalgamation of the royal and volunteer armies as demanded by the Montagnards, who wanted the army democratized. Both sought to gain control of the army's spirit.

CHAPTER I

• • •

The Royal Army
and the Revolution
(1789–1791)

"Bread and dignity!" This cry of the people in 1789 was heard also among the troops. "Places for talent and merit!" "Equality! Equality!" The demands of the Third Estate ran through the army, especially among the noncommissioned officers and the "officers of fortune," as officers who were not nobles were called. The conflicts in civilian society appeared also in the regiments, and made it impossible for the authorities to use the army as a force of repression.

1. THE SOCIAL CRISIS AND THE ARMY CRISIS

The royal army was composed of three elements: the Royal Household Troops, the regular forces, and the militia. The Royal Household Troops consisted of the Bodyguard, the Hundred Swiss, the regiment of French Guards (3,600 men), and the regiment of Swiss Guards (2,300 men), for a total of 7,278. The Bodyguard assured the service of honor at the Château de Versailles; they were recruited from the nobility, and a simple guardsman enjoyed the rank of lieutenant. The French Guards were commanded by members of the higher nobility and charged with the external service at the château. Hoche and Lefebvre, later general and marshal respectively, began as noncommissioned officers in the French Guards.

The regular forces formed the French army properly speaking. Grouped in 102 regiments of which 79 were French, they numbered about 113,000 men. These regiments bore the name of a person, such as Turenne or Condé, or of a province, such as Provence or Champagne. The latter names no longer signified the regional composition of the unit. For a long time in the eighteenth century the Auvergne regiment had been recruited only in the Cévennes, because it included captains from that region who preferred to enroll men from their own place of origin. To these infantry regiments were added the cavalry regiments (32,000 men) and those of artillery (less than 10,000). The Household and regular forces, which on paper numbered over 160,000, could not in fact have had more than 150,000 men.

The militia was a provincial reserve recruited in rural areas, by lot, from among unmarried men from eighteen to forty years old. In time of peace the militia regiments assembled at irregular intervals for two weeks of training. In wartime they were used to protect storage depots, forts, and coasts. They numbered about 75,000 men.

The regular forces were most often recruited by a kind of impressment. We may take the example of the 18th infantry, commanded by a Colonel Tourville and stationed near Calais. When one of its lieutenants, Poncet, was going on leave to his home in the Franche-Comté, his colonel called him in and asked him to raise a few recruits during his visit. He should find men of good stature, 5 feet 6 inches tall (1.78 meters),[1] which was a considerable height at that time, and accept them only after they had been seen by a surgeon. He might take shorter men if they were "young and good looking" and showed promise of further growth. There

---

[1] About 5 feet 10 inches in Anglo-American measurement, in which the feet and inches are somewhat smaller than the *pieds* and *pouces* of the French Old Regime.

were two incentives for young peasants to enlist—publicity and money. As for publicity, Poncet would take with him a corporal from his village, who would wear a new uniform and be supplied with money to buy drinks for his acquaintances, to whom he would boast of the regiment and the good times to be had in it. As for money, the recruits would receive from 90 to 120 livres according to age and height. It was a temptation in the off season, while the land was resting and the farmer had little to do, for 100 livres was more than could be earned by an agricultural laborer in a year.

Recruiting sometimes therefore had a "feudal" character. An officer found in his own seigneurie or those of his relatives the sons of peasants who were accustomed to the gestures of submission required by seigneurial law. But was a company or a battalion made up only of such dependents?

The army, composed of native Frenchmen by an overwhelming majority, did not recruit only in the home provinces of its commanders, or exclusively among peasants. Stationed at the frontiers, its soldiers came especially from the provinces of the north and east. They were young men; 50 percent of the soldiers of the line infantry were from eighteen to twenty-five years old, and 90 percent of those of all arms were under thirty-five. In the line army 60 percent had served for four years or more, and 20 percent ten years or more. One-eighth were recent recruits. Many were not yet instilled with the automatism that the authorities had tried to impose on their comrades for more than a decade.

A second piece of information: 35 percent of soldiers of the line infantry came from places with a population of 2,000 or more, and 20 percent from towns of over 10,000. In proportion to civilian society, which is estimated to have been 80 or 85 percent rural, town dwellers were overrepresented in the army.

A third point: Men of artisan background who, whether originating in the towns or in the countryside, had a less limited outlook than the peasants, outnumbered the latter and accounted for three-fifths of the soldiers. A small number were the sons of rentiers, officeholders, or members of liberal professions. The army was thus not recruited exclusively from the clientele of minor nobles who were the company and battalion chiefs. In bourgeois circles and among the elite of the populace, there were now men who regarded the profession of arms as an occupation like any other. Less than ever did the army recruit ne'er-do-wells and indigents. The signs at the entrance to public gardens forbidding them to "dogs, loose women, and soldiers" were bound to be all the more insulting.

The French army came also from a generation that had experienced economic difficulty, a generation that, especially since 1770, had known the high cost of bread and unemployment, but which also had formed the habit of discussing the injustices of the times in the cabaret or under the village elm. Who could believe that such men would be willing to contain an insurgent populace moved by hunger, fear, and hope? People and soldiers were joined in the same lot—poverty and humiliation.

Poverty? The common soldier received 6 *sous* 8 *deniers* a day, from which he was charged 2 *sous* 6 *deniers* for army bread. With what was left he had to pay for supplementary food, linen, and shoes. He could not do it. On the small farm or in the little shop that he had left behind, his parents only rarely dipped a morsel of fat in their soup; in the camps the fare was equally sparse. As for lodging, one might have a straw mattress at home; in the barracks as built in the eighteenth century the men slept several in the same bed.

Humiliation? Of course, in the second half of the century, as we know from the work of Lee Kennett,[2] there were officers who were concerned to improve the condition of their men. They should no longer be addressed by the familiar *tu*, or subjected to degrading punishments; they should be regarded as men who had freely accepted a contract, with definite purposes and limits. If

---

[2] *The French Armies in the Seven Years War: A Study of Military Organization and Administration* (Durham, N.C., 1967).

they were treated abjectly, they had a right to break the contract. But most officers, stung by the defeat at Rossbach, had taken a leaf from the Prussian book and wished to transform the soldier into an automaton. It was unfortunate for the man who failed to obey an order instantly, or who broke cadence on the march. Stripped of his insignia, he was made to run the gauntlet while his comrades struck him with rods or the flat of the sword. Often the soldier had no contact with his officer except to be punished. Hence there were many deserters, in the 1780s averaging about 3,000 a year.

Poverty, humiliation, and contempt. The common soldier was scorned by his officers, and sometimes by the bourgeois, many of whom shut their doors and fastened their shutters on hearing of the approach of the military. Yet this was not the general attitude. During his hours of liberty the soldier might offer to work for civilians at small jobs to supplement his wage. He might sometimes go on leave. Frequent and sometimes friendly contact existed between the troops and the inhabitants of villages and towns.

If there was discord within the ranks there were also disagreements and struggles within the officer corps. Between nobles "by race" and nobles of recent date, as between nobles and commoners, there was open war.

The French army was officered mainly by nobles. They constituted 90 percent of its command structure. They were mostly members of the lesser provincial nobility, who came from manor houses hung with portraits displaying their ancestors in corselet and sabre. These nobles were not rich, but they had long used their small incomes to serve the king in his armies. They were among cousins in battalions commanded by fathers or uncles. They knew their trade well, and were ambitious to know it better so as to reach posts of greater responsibility. But "the time of the vile bourgeoisie" had arrived; men from the Third Estate, by purchase of office or letters of ennoblement, had penetrated the ranks of the nobility; they had obtained military grades with money, and deprived the immemorial old nobility of the hope of advancement in their careers. Against these *anoblis* the old nobles rose up; they were the soul of an aristocratic reaction within the army.

Under this pressure the ministry of war, in 1758, had published an order requiring army inspectors to refuse officer appointments to those who could not furnish certificates of nobility. The king took over the property rights in his regiments and companies in 1762, and gradually suppressed the salability of military appointments (1776). Back in 1756 the chevalier d'Arc, in a famous book (*La noblesse militaire, ou Le patriote français*), having demanded practically all posts as officers for the nobility of race, had at the same time urged that they receive a careful military education. The issue was birth and talent combined. Military instruction at a very high level as desired by the nobility was granted to it, and to it alone, in the Ecole militaire founded in 1751. In 1772 it became necessary to show four degrees of nobility to enter the engineering school at Mézières, as for the Ecole militaire. The same was true of the artillery schools. Until 1781 a few were able to circumvent this aristocratic reaction by obtaining courtesy certificates. That was no longer possible after the Ségur edict of 1781, which required any future officer (unless rising from the ranks) to present original documents attesting to his nobility.

From 1781 to 1789 only 46 men became officers by promotion from the ranks. In 1789, of 10,000 officers in the French army, hardly 1,000 were commoners. In the learned or technical arms, the proportion of commoners was higher, but here also the educated bourgeois saw his advancement blocked by the presence of ever more numerous and competent young nobles. Henceforth young commoners, such as Carnot, knew that whatever their intelligence their careers would be limited to the grades of lieutenant or captain at best. As for the non-coms, issuing from the peasantry or lower bourgeoisie, they learned that whatever their merit they could at most, and by exception, become "officers of fortune." The military society thus reflected the antagonism found in the society as a whole between nobles and members of the Third Estate.

Yet the nobility in the army formed no unbroken front against the Third. Nobles of race who had led the aristocratic reaction against new nobles and commoners still found the hoped for positions beyond their reach. The highest nobility manipulated advancements in their own interest. An edict of 1761 made a distinction for those nobles who were "presented at court," who alone could be admitted to the grade of colonel. At the end of the Old Regime, of 11 marshals 5 were dukes, 4 were marquises, 1 a prince, and 1 a count. Of 196 lieutenant generals only 9 were untitled nobles. Of 950 other generals only a fifth were nobles without titles.

It was in a pugnacious mood that the noble who wanted high commands reserved for him on grounds of military knowledge saw the coveted position monopolized by a courtier:

> He gets into his coach and goes to show himself to his regiment, and after twenty years, whatever his efforts to make himself unworthy, he becomes a *maréchal de camp*. In twenty years of service he has served three months a year, and in these three months has spent six weeks amusing himself in the neighborhood of the garrison, so that after twenty years the strictest colonel has served for five years effectively, and in five years after leaving the court he has inevitably become a general officer. What can he know? Nothing, while those condemned to remain his subordinates know what is needed.

There were thus dissensions in 1789 within the body of noble officers. But there was no complete cohesion on the other side, among commoners, soldiers, noncommissioned officers, and officers of fortune. The soldiers were well acquainted with these last-named officers, on whom the nobles usually unloaded the burden of training in the use of arms and simple maneuvers. But the commoner of modest rank was often as brutal as his noble colleague in his attitude toward the soldier. Whether common or noble, those who occupied responsible posts and thought of themselves as military professionals all wished to produce a professional army, thoroughly trained and ready for revenge against Prussia. Hence there was sometimes animosity among commoners of different military rank. But in this military society so full of contradiction, there were also factors making for union, of which one of the strongest was the esprit de corps animating each regiment. The men of a regiment often came mainly from the same part of France, or at least they had lived together so long that their regimental flag became a kind of village bell and their company or battalion a small country. They took pride in belonging to a particular regiment that had won glory in the past. Anyone bringing dishonor on the regiment had to suffer. If he was a fellow member, he was punished severely and, many of the old soldiers thought, very justly. If he was from outside the regiment, he was challenged to a duel and could be badly mauled.

These group solidarities explain in part why the crisis in the army came a year later, sometimes more, than the crisis in civilian society. But if esprit de corps modified or masked the antagonisms between nobles and commoners, these nevertheless remained fundamental.

2. The Army and the Revolution of 1789

It is well known that the Revolution was preceded by a revolt of the aristocracy, and more precisely by the nobility of the robe that sat in the Parlement. These magistrates, after the failure of the Assembly of Notables, opposed the reforms envisaged by Louis XVI as a means of dealing with the financial crisis. To break the opposition, the royal government put restrictions on the powers of the Parlements. These bodies then denounced the measures taken against them as illegal, and claimed to be defending not only their own prerogatives but French "liberties" in the face of despotism. In the towns where Parlements sat, many inhabitants, such as clerks and ushers of the court, were linked to these nobles of the robe, either commercially or by occupation. Revolts broke out in the spring and summer of 1788 in support of the Parlements against the royal authority. The army was called upon to maintain order.

In the military as in civilian society the nobles gave examples of disobedience to their subordinates. Some officers in Brittany, for example, refused to participate in repressive actions at Rennes and submitted their resignations. At Grenoble in June 1788, when a crowd demonstrated in support of the Parlementaires who had been put under arrest, various attitudes were displayed among the troops; the Royal Marine fired without hesitation, but the officers of the Austrasie-Infanterie were very slow in sending their men into action. At Toulouse, at Besançon, and in Béarn there were resignations of officers, and some of them, like the marquis de Langeron, protested by saying it was not the business of the army to attack citizens.

The spring of 1789 was marked by food shortages in the countryside. The preceding year's harvest had been bad, and with the next year's not yet in, the interval between them was a period of numerous revolts. Poor peasants and famished artisans besieged the markets, demanding grain at low prices. For several months much of the army was used to protect the grain convoys and the warehouses, shops, and displays of the dealers. Regiments were broken up into small detachments; the sergeants and corporals who commanded them were as harassed as their men by marches and countermarches across the country. Food was short for them, too, and sometimes no lodging was arranged in advance. Discipline was hard to maintain among men who were fatigued and who, in contact with rebellious crowds, had doubts about their mission.

In Paris the military commander, baron de Besenval, nervously expected a riot by workers and journeymen. It came on April 27, 1789, in the faubourg Saint-Antoine, but the French Guards put it down. In April and May troop reinforcements began to move from the frontiers toward the Ile-de-France. Events rushed on with the meeting of the Estates General at Versailles; the bourgeoisie of the Third Estate brought about a "juridical revolution" by declaring itself the National Assembly and refusing to disband before giving France a constitution. The king, after rejecting most of the reforms at the session of June 23, appeared to yield to the Third Estate on the 27th. But troops continued to surround Paris, and in less than a week, at the beginning of July, the strength of the line units rose from 4,000 to almost 17,000 men. In Paris, rumor had it that the troops were 25,000, 30,000, or even 36,000 strong, and that the king meant to use them to control the deputies at Versailles or the people of Paris if they tried to support them.

These troops arrived after long journeys to settle in encampments where nothing had been prepared. Food was dear and other necessities were lacking. Pamphlets were distributed among the soldiers, not only reminding them of proposals to improve their lot in the *cahiers des doléances* but also inviting them to disobey their officers by refusing to oppose the people. In one such pamphlet, called "Advice to the grenadiers and soldiers of the Third Estate by a former comrade of the French Guards," its anonymous author asserted, "We are citizens before being soldiers; we are Frenchmen and not slaves." The French Guards began to fraternize with the people—some deserted, others were imprisoned but were then freed by a crowd of 40,000 Parisians on June 30. On July 6 the people of Versailles came to the aid of some French Guards who quarreled with troops of German origin. Six days later the French Guards used force to assist the Parisians against the Royal German cavalry regiment. On the 14th, the day of the fall of the Bastille, five of the six battalions of French Guards went over to the insurrectionists.

Nor was the army command, on the eve of the taking of the Bastille, any more sure of the other regiments under its orders. On July 13 the officer commanding the Royal-Cravattes informed his superiors that he could no longer answer for his men. During the second week in July some dragoons told their officer that if he ordered them to fire on citizens they would kill him.

Of the 17,000 men surrounding Paris more than 12,000 were

French. A minority took active part along with the Parisians in the attack on the Bastille. This was especially true of the French Guards, but in the days before and after the event 760 soldiers deserted, and by the end of the year the desertions from the same units reached a figure of 1,600, or 9 percent of the effective force, a far higher percentage than ever recorded before. Many of these deserters joined the National Guard, then in process of formation. Such pronounced opposition to the royal policy served as a warning to Louis XVI. In the royal entourage both Besenval and de Broglie emphasized the impossibility of using the army against the people. The king could not even be assured of a sufficiently loyal guard to escort him to the frontier through a disaffected country.

In the provinces, troops relied upon to maintain order sometimes refused to obey. At Rennes on July 17, when their leader summoned them to disperse a crowd of rioters, the soldiers of the Artois and Lorraine Infantry responded with cries of "Long live the Third Estate!" The same attitude appeared in the La Fère artillery regiment at Auxonne on July 19. At Strasbourg on the 21st, elements of the units charged with containing the rebels joined them instead. Orders for repression met with the same reaction at Thionville, Bordeaux, and Caen, where the regimental adjutant, Belsunce, was murdered by a party of citizens. Agitation and insubordination gained even the regiments farthest removed from the revolutionary centers, such as the Austrasie-Infanterie at Briançon.

In October 1789 the political crisis was aggravated by the food crisis. The king was dilatory in signing the recent decisions of the Assembly, and the people of Paris were hungry. It was said that the hunger was provoked by an aristocratic conspiracy designed to bring the people to their knees and block the reforms. It was learned in Paris that the Bodyguard, at a reception for officers of the Flanders regiment that had just arrived at Versailles from Douai, had trampled the tricolor cockade underfoot, with the king and queen in attendance. On October 5 the women of Paris went to Versailles, looking for "the baker, his wife, and boy," as they called the royal family. They met men from the Flanders regiment stationed at the Palace gates. The regiment had preserved good discipline until this moment, but many of its soldiers had been born in the Ile-de-France and some even in Paris. More than one of them had been seen drinking with patriots in the preceding days. When the Parisians arrived, the officers could do nothing; many of the men simply laid down their arms, declared they were members of the Nation, and placed themselves under Lafayette, commander of the National Guard, which was joined by 106 deserters.

The attitude of the army was thus important for the success of the Revolution in the summer and fall of 1789. Yet in accumulating examples of desertion, passivity toward insurgents, and refusal of obedience to their chiefs, we may forget that there also remained obedient regiments, notably the foreign regiments composed of Germans but also those of Alsace and Lorraine that were separated from the crowds by language and so could not fraternize with them. But there were also some obedient regiments that were strictly French. Thus the Saintonge Infantry, in Paris in July, had very few deserters and followed orders. Or some regiments—for example, the Bourbon Infantry—at first made common cause with the people but changed their attitude as the year 1789 went on and came again under control by their officers. The return to discipline often depended on the noncommissioned officers and officers of fortune, who after at first doing nothing, or even inciting their company, then changed their minds when they saw noble officers ready to compromise on the promotion of commoners. The army had its little "nights of the 4th of August" before and after the famous night on which the inequality of access to office was abolished.

In 1788 and at the beginning of 1789 the French had spoken. They had expressed their wishes in thousands of *cahiers des doléances* at the time of elections to the Estates General. A few months later the army spoke.

Noble officers sought alliance with officers of fortune and non-coms, not only to restore order among the troops but also to carry forward their plans, dating from the mid-century, for a professional army from which courtiers and recent nobles, unsuited for command, should be excluded. In addresses to the king they declared once again that the only valid criteria for military positions should be talent and merit. They thus gave up their privileges of birth and accepted equality. But was their position so clear and straightforward? In fact, when their various proposals are examined, it becomes clear that the places available to commoners would be subject to conditions. Moreover, who would select the new officers from among the meritorious non-coms? It would be the existing officers, and hence nobles. The officer's career would be regulated by the same appearance of liberalism, granting equality for all commands including the highest, but the noble officers made seniority in grade a criterion for advancement. Who then would monopolize the highest grades for decades to come, if not the nobles who for years had been the senior captains and lieutenants?

In the face of the aristocracy, the noncommissioned officers might seem timid in their claims during this summer of 1789 while commoners in civilian society were struggling for full equality. The most assertive, those of the Lille garrison, or of the Languedoc Infantry or Limousin Infantry, asked for no more than one in six or one in nine of the officer vacancies. But they wanted to have sole control over promotion to corporal and sergeant. To have a free hand in these matters would strengthen their own esprit de corps as non-coms, and make it easier when the time came to overcome the barriers that still blocked them. They knew that they were "the backbone of the army," and that some day, perhaps, they might supplant the nobles and enjoy the rank corresponding to responsibilities that they already carried. They wanted a new evaluation of their status. They would get rid of the term *bas-officier* ("lower" officer, as non-coms were called in French), and be known as "under officers" (*sous officiers*) instead. They would no longer pay the external marks of respect due to

officers, which, they said, put them in the position of servants addressing their masters. They wanted distinctive emblems on their
uniforms so that their rank could be easily recognized.

The insubordination of the common soldiers was thus helpful
to the non-coms in their demands with respect to the nobility. Yet
it is surprising to see how limited these demands were. Some sergeants probably feared that if confrontation within the army went
too far, it would overflow the bounds of a nobility-versus-com-
moner contest and bring their own authority into question. But if
they were to obtain more, and eventually supplant the nobles, they
had to maintain close ties with their men. Hence, they asked for
the abolition of degrading punishments. To keep control of the
men, they said, it was enough to prevent too much idleness by
keeping them busy with continual training. The non-coms also
echoed the soldiers in their demands for a decent existence.

To assure the security of the soldier, it was not enough to give
him better pay, or to be more concerned for his clothing and
equipment and the salubrity of his camp. Other realities must also
be considered. The soldier was often a family man who had to
support a wife and children. At times he had to be absent from
camp for tasks unsuited to his military status. Under pressure from
their men, the sergeants had formed the habit of recording in the
troop register the names of children born to men in the regiment.
The non-coms now asked that the practice be institutionalized and
that the birth of a child should be reflected in the soldier's pay.
The officers could not oppose such demands and sometimes
joined the non-coms in urging improvement in the soldier's condition. As those of the Aunis Infantry wrote in September 1789:

> Every French citizen is born free. In becoming a soldier he
> sacrifices his liberty, and possibly his life, for the freedom of
> all, for the safety of their lives and property, and for the glory
> of the country. From that moment the country contracts ob-
> ligations toward him and these obligations bear on his per-
> sonal existence and the consideration that is due him. These

two essential points have been almost ignored until now. It is time for a remedy to let him repossess his rights.

As for these rights, the soldiers would demand them themselves, and seize them by force in the years 1790 to 1792.

3. The Spread of Conflict within the Army (1790–1791)

The disintegration of the royal army began not in 1791, as some historians have claimed, but in 1790. What had been episodic cases of insubordination became chronic in 1790 and sometimes grew into open revolts, which were no sooner extinguished than they flared up again and passed from one unit to its neighbor. Most often, the mutinies began over questions of the regimental funds. Financial management in each regiment had been left to an administrative council made up of officers. Soldiers accused the officers of irregularities or dishonesty in the accounts. In fact the demand to see the accounts was often only a pretext to make life impossible for noble officers and force them to resign.

Beyond the question of regimental funds lay the great question: Are you a patriot or an aristocrat? The noble was obliged to rally clearly to the Revolution and even preach it, if necessary, to those about him. There were said to be units gangrened with aristocratism, and brawls erupted between different regiments. Soldiers of the Royal-Vaisseaux and the Couronne-Infanterie, considering the Normandie-Chasseurs to be a nest of counter-revolutionaries, challenged its men to a duel. The duel became a pitched battle and lasted for nine days in April 1790.

In the same month, at Hesdin, when a soldier was penalized by an officer, another officer, a noble who had been won over to the Revolution, the future marshal Davout, took the side of the soldier, aroused the sergeants and enlisted men against what he regarded as an injustice and, with popular assistance, went and took the man out of his cell.

In May, at Perpignan, soldiers of the Touraine Infantry drove their adjutant and several officers away. Those of the Vermandois Infantry, brought in to suppress the mutineers, refused to act. In July and August more mutinies broke out at Saint-Servan, Epinal, Stenay, Brest, Longwy, Metz, Sarrelouis, Compiègne, and Hesdin. The culmination of those revolts was the "Nancy affair." In this town were stationed the Du Roi Infantry, the Swiss Châteauvieux regiment, and the Mestre de Camp General Cavalry regiment. The soldiers of the Du Roi Infantry were avowed patriots who wore the tricolor cockade and had organized an action committee. In early August, after blockading the officers' quarters, they arrested the quartermaster-treasurer and forced him to turn over a sum of 150,000 livres.

The example of the Du Roi Infantry incited the Châteauvieux Swiss, who sent a delegation to their officers to protest against the regimental discipline and administration. The two French regiments gave armed assistance to the Swiss, who obtained a distribution of 27,000 livres. The cavalrymen of Mestre de Camp Général extorted 48,000 livres from their officers. A deputation was sent to the National Assembly in Paris. We have a number of testimonies to this rebellion, including one originating with the officers of the Mestre de Camp Général:

> The [soldiers'] committee ordered the [regimental] council to meet, and at the same time sent a detachment to guard the door of the riding hall where the officers were confined, and called upon the rest of the regiment to assemble there unarmed. They demanded ball cartridges from the adjutant, who refused them, saying he had no orders from his superiors, to whom he went off to report. On their explicit order to deliver them he returned to his office and let them be taken.
>
> The first session of the council began at eight o'clock in the morning and lasted until two in the afternoon. During all this time the council members insisted on the invalidity of the demands made. We thought that the regimental ordinances and

regulations gave weight to our case. The men would not listen to the sound arguments that we presented. They had the insolence to tell some members to speak more softly, and others more loudly, and when the officer supposed to be commanding the regiment wished to make himself heard he was told to await his turn and let the man who had the floor continue speaking. The officer in charge of clothing and other stores turned over his accounts.

What strikes the reader is not only the rejection of all traditional hierarchy but the kind of direct democracy instituted by the soldiers. Their superiors, when recognized at all, were regarded as agents or mandatories who were obliged to render their accounts and take their turn in speaking in a soldiers' assembly. This "military democracy" was not to the liking of either the aristocrats who were still present in the war ministry or those of the bourgeoisie who were trying to reach a compromise with men of the Old Regime. Lafayette himself recommended to General Bouillé that he make a stern example to stop the dissolution of the army. A veritable battle ensued between the rebellious regiments and Bouillé's troops, among whom numerous foreigners were to be seen. The rebels were defeated and punished. One soldier, a member of the insurgent committee, was broken on the wheel. Twenty-two were hanged, and forty-one were condemned to the galleys for thirty years.

The repression did not end the revolts, which went on into 1791. In that year there were mutinies, among others, in the 15th cavalry regiment, the Royal-Picardie at Angers, the 17th of the line, the 2nd battalion of the 58th at Saint-Pol-de Léon, and the 16th at Saintes. The flight of the king produced more agitation in such garrison towns as Montpellier, Blois, Perpignan, Wissembourg, and Landrecies.

These revolts, revealing the conflict between aristocrats and commoners within the units, showed how far the politicization of the army had gone beyond what it had been in the preceding year.

The agents of politicization were often military men themselves or, more exactly, the noncommissioned officers who now gave up their understanding with the officers of the year before, and formed or assisted in forming soldier committees. The conflict was radicalized in the camps as in the towns and open country. But there were civilian as well as military agents of the Revolution. The Jacobins lent powerful aid in raising the political consciousness of the troops.

Hardly was a regiment stationed in a town when the network of Friends of the Constitution (the "Jacobins") went into action, warning their "brothers" against its aristocratic chiefs and letting them know of the attitude of the rank and file. Thus in 1791 when the 58th regiment (the Rouergue regiment) departed from Quimper for Blois, the Jacobins of Blois learned from their brothers in Brittany that the officers had an "indecent" attitude toward the constitutional bishop, which the enlisted men found shocking. The Jacobins of Blois in turn informed those of Versailles and Tours of the views of men in the 58th when it left their town.

As soon as a regiment arrived the Jacobins sent a committee to invite its members to attend the meetings of their society. The men of the Du Roi Infantry at Nancy had mixed with Jacobins before they mutinied. Soldiers accepting the Jacobin invitation, as the ministry finally permitted them to do, had no voice in the deliberations of the society, which however allowed them to address it, gave them ribbons to wear with its colors, took action on their complaints against officers, and wrote to the ministry or the military committee of the National Assembly demanding justice against officers who had imposed penalties. The Jacobins instructed the soldier on his rights. Thus, on April 10, 1791, the society at Blois, on receiving some troops from Rousillon, made haste to read to them from the decrees on military organization, and explain the means available for the expulsion of counter-revolutionary officers. In February 1792 the 51st infantry regiment, in garrison at Niort, was visited by the Jacobins of Perpignan before its departure for that town. Their spokesman developed three themes: the need for union between soldier and citizen, the need for a reasoned obedience to the law and to proper chiefs, and the usefulness of political education among the troops. Dumouriez, who was present and caught up in the excitement, declared:

> By reading the public press and the acts of the National Assembly you will come to know your rights, reason on your duties, obey promptly according to your rank, . . . distinguish true honor, . . . understand a sublime Constitution that provides immense advantages for the military.

Soldiers attending meetings of Jacobin clubs all affirmed their civic ardor. Those of the 10th regiment announced in an address to the Jacobins of Vendôme:

> It is with a sense of fraternity that we come to live among you and know you; we are as French as you are; to march at your side is our only wish. Do we have different interests because we fight on foot or on horseback or wear clothes of a different color? Are we any the less *enfants de la Patrie*?

Festivals of "federation" offered another way of penetrating the army. Communities exchanged pacts of union in 1790 in a manifestation of national unity, culminating in the *fête de la Fédération* of July 14, 1790, on the Champ-de Mars. Pacts of friendship and fraternity were exchanged between the army and the National Guard, the former seeing themselves as soldier-citizens, the latter as citizen-soldiers. The Languedoc Infantry sealed its union with the National Guard of Montauban in the course of a festival; the National Guard of Toulouse also adhered. The National Guards of Franche-Comté did the same with the Royal Foreign Cavalry regiment, the Conti Infantry with the National Guard of Amiens, the Royal Comtois with that of Orléans, and the Anjou Infantry with that of Tours. Soldiers also fraternized with each other from one army unit to another. The Beauce and Normandy infantry swore the oath of fraternity and invited other regiments to do likewise. For the great Federation of July 14 in Paris, each regiment sent an officer, a noncommissioned officer, and four soldiers. We may imagine how these missionaries returned to their units deeply touched by this festival of Liberty, Equality, and French Unity.

The effects of such military democracy were significant both within the army and outside it. Within it, the noble officers felt obliged to resign in greater numbers, and many of these *ci-devants* joined the emigration. It is estimated that 6,000 officers, by the end of 1791, preferred to abandon their flag and country rather than serve in a revolutionary army. Such cases, known to the troops, only increased their animosity against noble officers. Rebellions against them continued in the regiments through 1791 and 1792.

But it was not only officers that left the ranks. Ordinary soldiers were expelled from their regiment, or deserted. Officers witnessing the first mutinies thought it possible to separate the good grain from the chaff by eliminating the most subversive elements. For example, Colonel Tourville, commanding the 18th Infantry, wrote during the summer of 1791: "We are very quiet here, doing well, and at least partially disciplined, things are all right." But he added, "We have expelled thirty bad characters since you left" (three months before). A few weeks later he wrote: "We are having no trouble, we are very quiet, thanks to having twenty or thirty troublemakers locked up; though we have sent away about ten, others remain." Tourville told his recruiting officer to take only reliable men unspoiled by the revolutionary spirit. He wrote on March 28:

> As for your man from the Du Roi regiment, just thank him for his zeal; if he were six inches taller I wouldn't have him. He would no sooner be here than he would tell what they did in his regiment to get around discipline, and his stories would cause us nothing but fermentation. I would rather have a wholly new recruit.

As in 1789, soldiers showed their opposition to their chiefs by deserting. Where desertion in the line infantry had been 1.87 percent in 1788, it rose to 3.62 in 1789 and to 4.88 in 1790. In 1788 the average strength of a regiment was 1,104 men; in 1790 it was only 908. Recruitment increased in 1791, when average strength rose from 908 to 1,051, and then to 1,409 in the first half of 1792. The regular troops were thus renewed in part, as they took in citizens from a people in revolution in the towns and rural areas. This happened despite the formation of national volunteer battalions, which induced some professional soldiers to desert and join the bourgeois army where the pay was higher and promotion more rapid.

Outside the army the effects of its politicization were also of the greatest importance. Soldiers often refused to turn their bayonets upon patriots, insurgent peasants, or hunger rioters. The years of the Constituent Assembly were in fact a period of crisis and permanent tension. Both patriots and aristocrats took decrees of the Assembly—for example, the one imposing an oath on priests—as a pretext for confrontation. Sometimes political antagonism reflected differences of religion; Protestant patriots opposed Catholic counter-revolutionaries in the southeast, where troubles broke out at Montauban in May 1790, at Nîmes in May–June, and at Uzès in February 1791.

Many provinces and regions—Brittany, Limousin, Périgord and Quercy, Rouergue, Agenais, Albigeois, and part of Haute-Auvergne—during the winter of 1789–1790 saw outbursts of peasant fury against the required repurchase of seigneurial rights, as decided upon by the Assembly. From November 1790 to February 1791 there were revolts in the departments of the Somme, the Côtes-du-Nord, the Ille-et-Vilaine, and the Charente-Inférieure, and again in Quercy and Agenais. Antiseigneurial uprisings continued through the summer of 1791 in the Paris Basin and the Massif Central.

The *guerre aux châteaux* broke out with renewed violence in the winter of 1791–1792 and on into the summer of 1792 in departments of the Center and the South. The war against the seigneurs was soon accompanied by peasant resistance to the combining of farms—that is, against capitalistic concentration in the country-side. In addition, in both town and country the popular masses took arms to prevent the free movement of grain from one region to another. Each year the renewed fear of shortage led to rioting from north to south.

Shaken by such troubles, the municipal and departmental authorities had no force at their disposal to restore order except the national guards, who were few in number, badly armed, and disinclined to combat. They appealed to the minister of war. A law of August 10, 1789, permitted the local authorities to requisition troops of the line.

The army was unable to take firm action. At Aix, for example, in December 1790, a fracas arose between some patriot "clubbists" and counter-revolutionaries. Among the latter were a few officers of the Lyonnais Infantry, who were arrested by the national guard. Other officers of the regiment tried to get their men to free the captives. A sub-lieutenant, Ferriol, who from a common soldier had risen by merit since 1757 through the successive grades, refused to obey; he demanded that the town officials should come themselves and give the order. Word passed through the ranks, and the soldiers would not move.

At Marseille on March 20, 1790, a Colonel d'Ambert who had insulted the national guard was reprimanded by his own men. At Lyon in November 1790, the men of the Guyenne Infantry fraternized with the populace. At Arles in 1791, the 28th regiment sided with the patriots.

Sometimes the troops called upon to repress food disturbances actually joined with the rioters; such was the case at Douai in March 1791 and at Dunkirk in February 1792. On February 2, 1792, Lieutenant-General Victinghoff notified the minister that troops of the line stationed near Paris had allied with the volunteer battalion of the Yonne to aid rioters determined to prevent the movement of grain.

To control insurrection, it was necessary to divide companies into squads of a few dozen men, who, stationed in villages, came into close contact with the people. Recognizing that high prices were a problem that they shared with the people, and that pursuit of aristocrats and monopolizers was a common duty, the soldiers became insubordinate and refused to march against those they regarded as brothers.

A report of Lieutenant General de Choisy, commanding the 7th military division at Grenoble, summarized very well the kind of connivance between the revolutionary people and the army:

> This regiment, which has been sound until now, resisting incitements to indiscipline, has been harassed by the clubs wherever it has passed.
>
> Five companies ordered to proceed to Barraux refused to go unless a certain Corporal d'Ambreville, detained for military infractions, was released. Citizens from the club had already demanded his release by petitions of a kind not approved by law.
>
> I went to the soldiers and urged them to remember their respect for the law. They were disposed to obey, and I set them on their march. A crowd of people blocked their passage, crying "Don't go! We will support you!" By these incendiary words they succeeded in raising an insurrection among them. . . . One company broke ranks in disorderly fashion and went to the citadel where the military prison is located, followed by a large crowd of people who set d'Ambreville at liberty.

Yet the final picture must be qualified. There were cases when the troops did not sympathize with the rioters. In December 1790, for example, a detachment of the Languedoc Infantry took action at Gourdon against peasants demonstrating against seigneurial rights.

In an attempt at statistical analysis of units not fraternizing with the people in town or country, or of regiments in which soldiers were most often accused of uncivic language, one is struck by the frequency with which cavalry regiments are mentioned. All reports of the commanders of military divisions note that cavalry was by far the most effective force against insurrections, and that the people so feared it that its mere presence was enough to restrain them or to prevent excesses. Even in 1793 the mere appearance of a cavalry regiment in a town was enough to create panic, so deep in the collective psychology was the idea that a troop of horse was meant to inflict a blind and brutal repression. The cavalry regiments were less susceptible to patriot propaganda, suffering as they did less from the absenteeism of noble officers, less affected by desertion, and continually getting new recruits from their officers' home districts. For this cohesion, which worked to the advantage of officers of the Old Regime, there is also a simpler explanation. Where a regiment of foot soldiers became scattered in controlling an area, a cavalry regiment preserved its battalion formation. Its mobility allowed it to act more quickly from a given center, and its squads could return to the "ghetto" of their unit when their action was completed.

To summarize, an important part of the army, especially in the infantry and artillery, had been won over to the revolutionary spirit. Many were the soldiers who wished to be considered as citizens, and wanted the work of regeneration undertaken by the Assembly to affect the military as well as the civilian society.

What was the response of the Constituent Assembly?

CHAPTER II

• • •

The Military Policy of
the Constituent Assembly:
The Royal Army and
the Bourgeois Army

Many members of the Constituent Assembly, especially those from the Third Estate, wished to see a transformation of the professional army into a national army. But their fear of a more radical revolution held them back from applying this principle, and made them adopt a policy of compromise with the existing command of an army which they hoped to control. The king's flight to Varennes led them to create a bourgeois force alongside the royal army. Hence came the volunteers of 1791, who were drawn from the national guards.

1. PHILOSOPHERS, PEASANTS, AND SOLDIERS

The eighteenth century dreamed of a New City. Would it need men to guard the gates? If so, should war making be a professional occupation or a right and duty of all citizens? Philosophers and publicists at first showed their bourgeois concerns by their fears of the military. In an age that was to be an age of fraternity, with war proscribed, it seemed that armed men would be an anachronism.

They would nevertheless be dangerous. They might contaminate the citizens, because they were perverted by habits of violence (it was said) and would remain, as Marat wrote, the carriers of "the chains of despotism." "From the time of Sulla," said Voltaire, "those who usurped supreme power had permanent hired forces, paid for by the money of citizens, more to keep the citizens subjugated than to subjugate other nations."

In the same vein Mirabeau declared that men at arms were slaves by trade, prejudice, and ignorance. "They are the ones who have done the most to promote despotism and it is by them that despotism sustains itself." Carra, echoing Condorcet, insisted that "standing armies are always dangerous to liberty in time of peace."

Whether peace would ever be established in Europe was doubtful. For all their yearning for universal peace, many bourgeois were well aware that war was not about to disappear from the continent. After the confusion that followed the Seven Years War, a more warlike spirit, or spirit of revenge, gained strength even among some of the bourgeoisie, as among the nobility. An army would therefore be necessary in future years. To prevent its becoming an instrument of despotism, it must become national.

"Whatever his occupation," said Diderot, "the citizen must have two suits of clothes, one for his trade and one as a soldier." Rousseau affirmed in his *Considerations on the Government of Poland* that standing armies were good for only two purposes: either to attack and conquer neighbors, or to enchain and enslave the citizens. As he put it in the *Social contract*:

> Every citizen should be a soldier by duty, none by trade. If a foreign war comes, the citizens march off calmly to combat; none thinks of flight; they do their duty, but without passion for victory. They know better how to die than how to be conquerors.

The idea of a national army was shared by some professional officers. Jacques-Antoine-Hippolyte de Guibert, a *maréchal de camp* in 1786, had published in 1772 an *Essai général de tactique*, which contained a "Preliminary discourse on the present state of policy and military science in Europe." He condemned the armies of his day, composed of mercenaries, vagabonds, and foreigners, who joined the colors because they were restless or in need, and who were kept there only by discipline. He contrasted them with the troops of ancient Rome, in which the soldier was a citizen, and the citizen a soldier. Guibert's solution was to have an armed nation, but if the citizens were to bear arms without pay for the common defense, the people would have to be free to govern itself. The armed nation thus supposed a revolution. Some denied this implication. A militia already existed, and some officers, like the chevalier de Pommelles, studied ways to develop the militia into a system of conscription.

What the country might think of plans for a national army was another question. The country meant the peasants who formed the majority. It was still true in the eighteenth century that "the Frenchman liked powder." He kept a fowling piece hidden in his barn or cottage, although the seigneur forbade it. On the tiniest farms of the frontier provinces it was known that any odd weapon could be used in defense of land and family. Against foreign invaders, since the seventeenth century, it was an accepted duty to strike a few blows against regular soldiers. But this attitude was far from acceptance of the principle of a national army.

Between the peasantry and the bourgeois there was a lack of understanding. For the bourgeois the transformation of the militia into a national army, while involving a brief loss of individual liberty, was the best guarantee for the community as a whole against the "mercenary" menace. As a public service required of all, the national army embodied the principle of equality. For the peasantry, militia and national army were much the same thing, reinforcing inequality in either case. "Conscription" would affect the king's subjects differently because of differences of fortune or occupation. How could there be anything in common between enlistment of the son of an artisan and the son of a peasant? For the latter, it meant one man less at the plow or the hoe, a diminished property, and in the extreme case ruin and destitution.

For the peasant, it was impossible to reform the royal militia. It would always be a tax that took persons rather than money or goods. Here was a reality that all political personages came up against, from the eighteenth century through the Empire, when they tried to make the army more "national."

Reality for the peasant was what he saw and felt when, rising at dawn, he took his way through the fields. Whether in his vineyard, garden, or portion of the open field, it was his beloved soil that the peasant kneaded with practiced fingers; it had been left to him by his ancestors who merged into it by returning to dust when they died. At a time of only trifling technical progress, the worker in the fields knew that the soil was nourished only by the accumulated labors of generations past. If it was still to be productive, the hands of all a man's sons were needed. To remove them was to condemn the land to death; even worse, it would cut the ties that bound the living to the dead and turn men into nomadic inheritors of Cain. For a long time, defense of the *Patrie* meant not only wielding a bayonet but leaning on the handles of a plow.

Opposition to a national army came not only from peasants, but also from military men who had no confidence in the ideas of Guibert. In addresses to the king in 1789 and in those to the minister of war from 1790 to 1792, we can hear regular officers reject a national army as too costly and ineffective in battle. A general knowing the ruses of war, with only 100,000 men, could cut to pieces an army of 300,000 relying only on valor.

"Forget those who know no more about an army than to have three million men," wrote one officer; "let us talk to military men who are good citizens, educated, and devoted to the public good; they will say that there is no better course, if you would continue to have an army worthy of respect, than to preserve the one that exists and keep it constantly active."

What counted for these professionals was to have good leaders, "for the soldier is like a cannon ball; he is only worth what is produced by the powder (the non-coms) and by those who aim the cannon (the officers)."

Officers affirmed also that the army could well become national without having to recruit massively in the social body. By reforms of structure an army could be brought closer to the Nation, escape the traps of despotism, and at the same time retain the character necessary for a force of professionals. These theorists revived the language used a few years earlier by such writers as Servan. Paradoxically, in *Le Soldat-citoyen*, Servan had seen the soldier as primarily a man of peace whose labor earned him a place in the heart of society. Employed at tasks useful to the community, he would belong to the great national family. To escape from the idleness of camps he would live in a kind of military manor, a vast agricultural workshop from which he would go out to clear land and bring new regions under cultivation. The manor would also serve as a home for veterans and a school for army children.

The soldiers could work not only in agriculture but on projects of national interest, such as the opening of roads, digging of canals, and construction of dikes. While thus uniting them with the people, such labor would have a regenerating moral effect on the military, who would learn to see society as composed of "citizens, magistrates, and laws." They would themselves be citizens before being soldiers. As soldiers, they would benefit from the endurance acquired, and the discipline freely accepted, in the course of labors performed for love of country. Military status would regain its dignity as it became more like the status of other Frenchmen, and would be more readily accepted by other citizens in time of war. The idea of the worker-soldier ran through the century and was heard in the Jacobin clubs in the time of the Constituent Assembly. As a Jacobin of Melun wrote, "The soldier will alternate between peaceful functions and drilling in the manual of arms. . . . He should be occupied during part of the year on public works."

Was it then enough simply to reform the royal army, or was it necessary radically to transform it?

2. THE CONSTITUENT ASSEMBLY AND THE ARMY: FROM AFFIRMATION TO VIOLATION OF PRINCIPLE

Debate on reorganization of the army opened in the Assembly in November 1789, that is, at a moment when the deputies were still endangered by counter-revolutionary elements in the army that wanted the king to recover his full powers and the aristocracy to regain its privileges. But the deputies also remembered the peasant revolts of the preceding summer and the rising of popular masses in Paris in July and October.

A double threat, not easy to dispel, thus hung over the projects for reorganization. For military force to be effective it was necessary to have speedy orders, coordinated movement, and unified action. There had to be a single commander. Should it be the king? The constitution designated him as such. But with the king in a position to use armed force to restrict liberty, it might be necessary to nationalize the army by changing the mode of recruitment and instituting conscription. It was so argued by Menou in a speech of December 12.

Creation of a national army might mean escaping from one peril only to fall into another. The Assembly had denounced popular disturbances that endangered the control of property. It had attempted to contain them by partial reforms on the night of the 4th of August. It seemed hardly wise to give arms to the people at the very moment when the national guard, issuing from the bourgeoisie, was attempting to take from them the arms that they already had. Moreover, how could some of these popular elements be required to accept military service as a duty, when they were being defined as "passive citizens" and, as such, made unable to vote or hold political office?

The Assembly therefore rallied to a proposal offered by Bouthellier and somewhat modified by Dubois-Crancé. As on so many other occasions, the Assembly affirmed principles that it then immediately qualified. It declared that all citizens had both rights and duties, and that one of these duties was military service. In practice, it rejected conscription. To replace the militia there would be a force of 100,000 auxiliaries, recruited among the people, but by voluntary enlistment and no longer by lot. Those enlisting would receive 3 *sous* a day in time of peace; in time of war they would be incorporated into existing units of the royal army.

The deputies gave technical reason for this departure from principle. Liancourt in a speech of December 15 observed that war had become a science requiring a long apprenticeship. Others said that to raise a national army was impossible in the absence of adequate statistics on the populations of various regions of France. Argument was piled upon argument: there were such differences in mentality and physique among the French provinces as to make conscription chimerical for the present; men of the south were shorter than other Frenchmen and so less able to handle an army musket; time would be needed before southerners would accept a military service, which people living near the frontiers regarded with less aversion.

So the professional army was kept in being by the Constituent and, after it, by the Legislative Assembly. In both assemblies the deputies wished to transfer control of the army from the executive—that is, the king—to the legislative power. In principle, until August 10, 1792, except for the interlude of June 21, 1791, the king remained the chief of the army and worked through a ministry that carried on the reorganization begun under the Old Regime. In fact, by a decree of February 28, 1790, the Assembly reserved to itself the possibility of encroaching on the executive domain. It provided that, at each session of the legislature, the Assembly should determine the funds needed to maintain the army and assure its pay. The Assembly would also control the number of enlistments.

Terms of enlistment were transformed by decrees of March 7 and 9, 1791. Enlistment was no longer a contract between one man and another; it became a contract between the individual and the State, represented by the municipalities and the directories of the departments. The municipal administration was required to keep itself informed of the operations of recruiters in its area. The recruit had to be brought before the civil administration, which had the power to nullify the enlistment. Enlistment was for eight years, and the recruit had to be between eighteen and forty years old, with good moral character and physical aptitude. Foreigners were disqualified. No body of foreign troops could be admitted to service of the State without consent of the legislature. The former Alsatian regiment received the French regimental uniform as a reward for services rendered. At the time when Bouillé was trying to assist in the king's escape from Paris, the 96th Infantry, then called the Nassau Regiment, had been under his orders, and its men now suffered from the suspicion that these orders aroused. They ripped the buttons off their uniforms and tore off the lapels bearing the emblem of Nassau. They announced that they would not serve in a foreign uniform; they were French and wanted to be considered French in the service. In July 1791 the Assembly decreed that all foreign regiments should form part of the French infantry, wear the same uniform, and be under the same discipline.

Through its military committee the Assembly multiplied its efforts to subject the whole military apparatus to its authority. It did so in practice for a while after the flight of the king. At that time, commissioners representing the military committee were sent to the various armies to assure their fidelity. Barnave, Pétion, and Latour-Maubourg received powers of command. The army was to obey only decrees of the Assembly, and take an oath not to use its arms except in defense of the country and to uphold the constitution.

The better to master the army, the Assembly undertook to eliminate esprit de corps and propagate a national spirit. The customary names of regiments disappeared and were replaced by mere numbers. Companies also were to be known by a number, not by the name of their captain. Regimental flags, symbols of each regiment as a community by itself, had to carry an attached tricolor, to signify that all military men were servants of the Nation.

The Nancy affair impelled the Assembly to take measures to improve the soldier's condition. He was to be better fed, clothed, and cared for. The application of such measures was at first haphazard; many unit commanders pointed out that the rising cost of living affected the military as well as civilians. The mayor of Grenoble wrote to the ministry that the Monsieur and d'Enghien regiments were in a state of complete breakdown, of which agitators were taking advantage.

Before marrying, a soldier continued to need the approval of his unit commander, but the military law saw an important improvement in provision for the soldier's wife. "The widow of a man dying in the public service will be qualified to receive a pension for her support."

The Assembly made the legal status of soldiers and citizens more alike. The rights of an "active" citizen—that is the right to vote—were suspended during the period of military service, but only in the place where the soldier was garrisoned, and the right was not permanently lost. The law of February 18, 1790, specified:

Any military man on active duty preserves his domicile despite absence due to the service, and may exercise the function of an active citizen if he meets the conditions required by decrees of the National Assembly, and if, at the time and place of elections, he is not garrisoned in the canton where his domicile is situated.

To be an active citizen it was necessary to pay a tax equal in amount to three days of common labor, but

any military man who has served sixteen years without interruption and with a clear record shall enjoy the full rights of an active citizen and be dispensed from the legal requirements with respect to property and taxes, except that he may not exercise these rights if in garrison in the canton where his domicile is situated.

As in civil society, crimes and punishments were codified, with guarantees for the accused. In any court martial judging such military offenses as insubordination, treason, desertion, or theft, a war commissioner sat with two auxiliary commissioners. When the charge was heard and an indictment drawn up, the garrison commander assembled a jury of accusation. To be a juror, it was necessary to be twenty-five years old, know how to read and write, have had two years of service, and receive a favorable reference from the company commander. For the jury of judgment, three of its nine members had to be of the same rank as the accused, who had the right to reject jurors. The jury retired after hearing the accusation and the defense. In its deliberations the lowest-ranking member spoke first. For a verdict of guilty seven out of the nine votes were required.

The reform of military justice was considerable but incomplete. Men like Marat and Robespierre observed that officers of the courts martial were agents of the executive power and that, because they remained in control of indictments, they could overlook the misdeeds of royalist satellites while making trouble for the friends of liberty. The penalties most offensive to human dignity were suppressed, but the use of the iron collar, or the tying of the guilty man to a post with a sign fastened to his neck to publicize his offense, remained realities for a long time.

Procedures for the recruitment and promotion of officers were also full of ambiguities. The better to recruit officers on technical grounds, while preserving principles of justice and equality, the National Assembly left the nominations largely in the hands of officers already in place. A decree of September 20, 1790, gave the non-coms one in four vacancies for the rank of sub-lieutenant, to be filled sometimes by seniority and sometimes by selection. In the latter case it was officers of the unit who made the nomination. It was the same for the selection of non-coms; those of this rank drew up lists from which the company commander chose three names to present to the colonel, who made the appointment.

For further promotion, seniority in grade remained the exclusive criterion, except that for the highest ranks, in time of peace, the executive power could fill half the positions. From top to bottom of the hierarchy, the screening of talent and merit was done by aristocrats.

In November 1791 the Legislative Assembly modified these decisions by putting a premium on patriotic loyalty. Half the posts as sub-lieutenant were reserved for non-coms, and the other half for active citizens or their sons who had served in the national guard. This belated measure was not entirely satisfactory to the non-coms. They had been competing for lieutenancies with nobles; now they had to compete with young bourgeois also. Under their pressure, the army became in fact an army of professionals in its officer ranks in 1792 and early 1793, but with many noble survivals still in evidence.

All this made some sans-culottes think of the army as a Bastille still standing in the New City.

3. THE VOLUNTEERS OF 1791

The bourgeoisie began to organize the national guard in 1789, in part to oppose the aristocrats, and in part to present a common front against those who would "share the wealth," that is, those who not only attacked seigneurial dues but would go on to restrict the rights of property. It was among the ordinary people, however, that the idea arose of using this national guard as the source of militia to defend Paris against possible enemies. We find citizens assembling also at Mège and at Clermont-Ferrand, opening registers, and enrolling volunteers in the first half of 1791. Petitions soon accumulated on the desk of the Assembly, all demanding the organization of such a militia at the national level. It was being said everywhere that France was threatenened by a counter-revolutionary army under the prince of Condé. On June 12 the

Assembly voted to prepare a part of the national guard near the French borders for possible military action. Volunteers would engage themselves for combat while not ceasing to belong to the national guard. They would operate along with the regular army for only one campaign. Their discipline would be that of the national guard, less strict than for the army. They would elect their own chiefs. Since their expenses would be considerable, they would receive higher pay than regular soldiers.

The system of recruitment and organization, the procedures of enlistment, and the type of tactical unit chosen, the battalion, all indicated that the Constituent Assembly intended to possess an armed force of its own. Recruitment was by volunteering, and the volunteer had to come from the national guard. In principle, membership in the national guard was only for active citizens, those sufficiently prosperous to pay a tax equal to three days' wages of labor. In reality, in some places, poorer men had been taken in to fill up the ranks. They were often subordinated to the more well-to-do in the guard as in everyday life.

Election seemed the most democratic method for the choice of officers. In practice, with a few exceptions, only "notables" could become battalion commanders. In a given town the vote was seldom secret, and the town authorities, emanating from the local bourgeoisie, controlled it. Sometimes there was only a vote by acclamation to accept the man presented by the town government. Until the end of 1791 the law required that officers elected by the volunteers had to be already officers, or at least former officers, of the national guard. They were thus members of the bourgeoisie, and often the richest. At Lyon it was specified that the higher ranks were reserved for the most well-to-do, who alone had the funds necessary for their equipment.

The tactical unit was the battalion, a small group of 574 men. This offered advantages: the small unit allowed a better financial and administrative management; it enabled the chiefs to know their men better and more quickly; and in a small formation, with cultural, social and spatial "proximity," one obtained better cohesion in combat and more lively movement over the terrain. But cohesion could have pernicious effects if the spirit prevailing in a battalion was contrary to the spirit of the existing regime. In that case, a small unit could be more closely watched by the central or departmental administration, and if necessary more easily dissolved.

In forming a battalion the bourgeois leaders called on religion to get obedience to chiefs whom they had in fact named. When a battalion was constituted, its departure was preceded by a ceremony in the church. The priest blessed its flag, and the volunteers took an oath "to die rather than abandon it." The battalion departed with a chaplain whose duty was not only to offer the comfort of his ministry but also, if necessary, to remind the men of their oath of obedience.

From the election of its officers until its arrival in the theater of operations, the local authorities continued to control the battalion that they had formed, both by correspondence with its officers and by emissaries.

The most prompt in forming battalions were the departments near the frontier where the danger was most pressing, as well as the departments of the Seine, the Seine-et Marne and Rhône-et-Loire where the influence of the patriots of Paris and Lyon was felt. It was also these departments that furnished the largest contingents. They were also more hard pressed by the government than the departments of the interior, some of which indeed, in the Massif Central and the Aquitanian basin, were exempted from the volunteer program. The Meurthe furnished five battalions, whereas the Indre-et-Loire and Vienne furnished only one. On the other hand, some departments where a great effort was made failed to meet expectations, including Finistère and Côtes-du-Nord in Brittany and Haut-Rhin and Bas-Rhin in Alsace. In several of these departments religious troubles impeded the levy. The towns provided more than the rural regions, though still with differences from one department to another. Rural areas in the north and east were better informed than those elsewhere, and more

The departments of France as created in 1790.

(From D.M.G. Sutherland, *France 1789–1815* [New York and Oxford: Oxford University Press, 1986].)

alarmed by the flight of the king, so that they produced volunteers more rapidly and in larger numbers.

The volunteers were young, with 79 percent under twenty-five years of age. Some were even younger than the official minimum of sixteen. Almost 3 percent were adolescents under fifteen. Some of these were boys who had left home seeking adventure, others were abandoned children, accepted in either case to fill the ranks. The youth of the volunteers of 1791 largely explains their average shortness in stature. The troops included many soldiers who had not reached their full growth.

Some women wanted to form battalions of their own. Early in 1792, before the official levy of that year, the Legislative Assembly received the following petition signed by 304 women:

We wish to obtain:

1. Permission to procure pikes, pistols, and sabers, and even muskets for those who have the strength to use them, while submitting to the usual regulations for their control.

2. To assemble on Sundays and holidays in the field of the Federation or other suitable place for training in the use of the said arms.

3. To have former French Guards to command us, while always respecting the ordinances that the wisdom of our mayor may prescribe for the maintenance of order and public peace.

No women's battalions were created, but some patriots enlisted by disguising their sex under men's clothes. The department of the Nièvre recorded a petition received in 1794 from Félicité Duguet:

Citoyenne Félicité Duguet, called Va-de-bon-coeur, a native of Versailles in the department of Seine-et Oise, declares that, the sacred love of country by which she is animated not allowing her to view the dangers that menaced it with indifference, she had disguised her sex and marched voluntarily in defense of the country; that she constantly accompanied the

1st battalion of the Nièvre and shared in its labors and dangers; that she was seriously wounded; that under the law excluding women from the army she could no longer remain with the said battalion and so received a leave with certificates of honorable service; and that she then established her domicile in this department; for which reason she requests the administration to obtain the relief for her that is necessary and legitimately due.

These women volunteers were not numerous, only thirty at most. Famous among them were the Fertig sisters. Daughters of an ex-sergeant of hussars, they went under fire in French Flanders; Dumouriez noticed them and enrolled them in his army.

When the registers and enlistment rolls allow us to judge the social status of the volunteers of 1791, we find that for the most part they come from the world of the workshop and small retail trade. In Paris, for example, in the section of Bonconseil, 90 percent of the volunteers were artisans and shopkeepers, 5 percent were day laborers, and 5 percent bourgeois. In the 1st and 2nd battalions of the Ille-et-Vilaine there was the same large cohort of butchers, bakers, tailors, and weavers, but also a few from white-collar activities, such as lawyers' clerks and students. It was the same in the 2nd and 4th battalions of the Meurthe, where men connected with the law joined with public scribes and dancing masters as well as an important group of artisans, butchers, shoemakers, and wigmakers.

Those in higher positions came from a more elevated background. The most remarkable fact is the presence of nobles in command of almost half the battalions sampled. There were of course men like Charles Oudinot, son of a merchant; he was an ex-soldier who became a merchant brewer, was elected an officer in the national guard and then lieutenant-colonel of the 3rd volunteer battalion of the Meuse. But alongside him were marquises and counts. Jean-Pierre Chazot was a count, who, after having been a volunteer in the Reine-Infanterie in 1753, and then a *ma-*

réchal de camp in 1790, had settled in the Puy-de-Dome to enjoy a well-earned retirement at the age of over fifty; he was elected as battalion commander, and was soon a general. This presence of nobles is not surprising. Their bourgeois neighbors chose them for their military competence, and also in line with the policy of compromise that followed the flight of the king. As Barnave then said, it was a matter of common interest for the Revolution to be halted and for property-owners threatened by the popular move-ment to unite. For, in his words, "Is there now any aristocracy except that of property?"

Most often the nobles who became battalion commanders were of the lesser nobility who now received the rank that their talents had made them hope for, but which the aristocratic reaction had prevented them from attaining. Other battalion commanders who were commoners came mostly from the liberal professions. Com-pany-level officers were mainly of the middle and lesser bourgeoi-sie. In the latter category, which held almost half the officer posts, we find especially those whose occupation made them sensitive to the revolutionary ideology: fully qualified lawyers (39 of the 1,582 officers whose occupation is known), notaries (28) and their clerks (16), attorneys (13) and their clerks (10), but also sim-ple legal counsellors (5), court ushers (12), bailiffs (4), and a gen-eral category of *hommes de loi* or "law people" (36). In the liberal professions, those concerning medicine supplied many captains and lieutenants (25). Surgeons, notably, finding themselves not chosen for their special art, nevertheless enlisted and received the votes of their fellow citizens. Numerous also were office clerks (37), who were often the sons or relatives of notables.

The most compact group among company-level officers was that of students, who numbered 155. The law students were the most numerous. As young bourgeois they escaped most easily from the constraints and compromises of life. Readers of the "phi-losophes," they were impatient with an education that was una-dapted to the needs of the day. With the generosity of youth they were eager to fight in defense of the new order. A scene many times repeated occurred in the colleges at the time of the distribution of prizes, when, at the announcement of a name, he was said to be absent for *défense de la Patrie*.

Artisans elected to be company officers were less numerous than in the line army. Mostly they came from occupations having to do with food and drink: butchers, bakers, and brewers. Next most important were those from the building trades: carpenters, joiners, and painters. Then came those from the clothing trades and the metalworkers, including those who knew how to shoe horses.

Few peasants were elected as captains or lieutenants, only 13 percent and 19 percent respectively, and most of these were former soldiers chosen for their military experience.

Among common soldiers and noncommissioned officers in the volunteers were very few who had been soldiers of the king, yet here, too, there were differences between battalions. Representation in the 1st battalion of the Aube, with 12 percent from the old royal army, clearly was above the average. The officers, on the other hand, often understood the profession of arms. As General Schérer wrote in 1793:

> The first battalions of volunteers were almost all headed by officers who were retired noncommissioned officers, and who, from love of country, hatred of despotism, or perhaps a love of glory, had come excitedly out of retirement and taken again to arms. The brave volunteers who had patriotically rushed to arms at the first cry of *la Patrie en danger!* were first disciplined by these officers and then led by them to face the enemy.

Almost a third of the company-level officers had done some military service before their enrollment in the volunteer battalions. These soldiers of the Old Regime had generally left the army some years before, because of the noble exclusivism that barred the promotion of commoners. Some non-coms left the line army to become officers of volunteers. They did not always stay with the volunteer battalions, but rejoined the regiments in which their rank was now recognized. Volunteer officers who had previously been in the army had on the average fewer years of service than officers of the line. Most came from towns and had a good level of education. They were younger than the line officers, and they showed great tactical agility in the campaigns of the Republic.

The volunteer battalions soon became seasoned troops. Only a minority remained far from the fields of battle, stationed in fortified positions. The generals kept them constantly on the march and learning the trade of war. When war was declared, in April 1792, they were soon put into contact with the enemy and received their baptism of fire without flinching. Too much has been made of the writings of contemporaries, often tendentious, dwelling on their indiscipline and on the panic by which they were sometimes gripped. Not enough has been said of such facts as this: during the rout that resulted in the murder of General Dillon, the first to return to their posts in combat, along with the Esterhazy hussars, were the soldiers of the 2nd battalion of volunteers from Paris.

Line officers themselves testified to the good performance of the volunteers of 1791. A certain Lieutenant Simon wrote in 1792:

> We have here several battalions of volunteers. They are much better instructed and disciplined than our regiments; if they remain for a year they will be excellent troops, and if the Nation understands its own interests it will put them into regiments and keep them as long as it can.

In the school of war the volunteers understood the necessity of a willingly accepted discipline. The following text comes from a group of officers, of both the volunteers and the line army, at the headquarters of the Army of the Center in September 1792. While reflecting a concern for social preservation, it shows also how the volunteer officers meant to hold their men in strict obedience to command:

Citizen-soldiers, destined to serve your country declared to be in danger, the first lesson you must learn is that of discipline.

The word discipline derives from the word disciple, which means someone who observes some law, and which clearly tells us that discipline means nothing else than maintenance of good order and proper regulation, without which any kind of constitution is vicious, especially in parts relating to the military. . . .

Exact observation of discipline requires four absolutely essential things: first, regularity in morals; second, perfect obedience by inferior to superior, relatively to each rank; third, continuing vigilance by chiefs in execution of the law; fourth, total impartiality in the imposition of penalties. . . .

There are some who think that soldiers in a war have more liberty than others to violate the laws of virtue and religion. Such an absurd and impious belief will never strike deep roots in the heart of a true military man. He will always remember that he is a man and soldier, that in his quality as a man he owes all to the Supreme Being of which he is the image, and that as a soldier (that is, a citizen) he is bound to perform his functions with honor, courage, intelligence, and speed. He should have in him more virtues and fewer vices, more courage and fewer weaknesses, than the men whom despots would see killed to satisfy their own jealousy and ambition, and who have nothing left after the war except a life of poverty and habit of enslavement.

To conclude, if esprit de corps sometimes made the regular regiments pick quarrels with the volunteers, the volunteers were not very different from them in age and social background. The war brought them together in 1792.

CHAPTER III

• • •

The War: The Danger of Caesarism
and the Democracy in Arms

The war declared on April 20, 1792, presented in a new form the problem of the army as a force of intervention in political struggles. Contending parties strove to win it to their side. Generals attempted to use it to check the course of a revolution that was now penetrated and radicalized by popular masses allied with the Jacobins.

1. THE DANGER OF CAESARISM AND ITS COLLAPSE

The ranks of the émigrés had been growing since July 1789. They gathered around the king's brother, the comte d'Artois, first at Turin and then at Coblentz. Counter-revolutionary troops formed in the electorate of Trier. French aristocrats urged foreign sovereigns, the Emperor, and the king of Prussia, to take action against a revolution that was subverting the established order of Europe. Did it not proclaim the right of peoples to self-determination? Had not an insurrection in Belgium since 1789 forced the Austrians to evacuate that country? Had there not been troubles in Savoy and Piedmont? The seigneurial rights possessed by German princes in Alsace had been contested. In the papal territories of Avignon and the Comtat Venaissin, the populations called for union with France. The two sovereigns, thus importuned, issued a declaration at Pillnitz on August 21, 1791, in language that was all the more violent since in fact they refused to take any immediate action. But the proclamation was presented as an ultimatum, and the French patriots were alarmed.

When the new Legislative Assembly met, in October 1791, its members on both the right and the left favored war. On the right the Feuillants, after at first preferring peace, rallied to Lafayette. For the marquis war would mean command of an army, with which, hoping also for support from the national guard, he might make an end to the Jacobins and the popular agitation. On the left, the Girondins (who were Jacobins at this time) believed that war would unmask the king and the traitors. In their view, a victorious war would settle the internal problem, consolidate the Revolution, and restore the credit of the paper money, while surrounding France with "liberated" peoples and opening the markets of Europe.

In circles about the king, Barnave and the foreign minister de Lessart advised prudence. They feared that a national upheaval would carry the Revolution farther. But the king and queen opted for war; they expected the war to be disastrous, so that the king could then come forward as arbiter between his people and the enemy and so recover his full powers.

For Robespierre, as for Marat, war would be harmful for the Revolution, since they saw all the generals as counter-revolutionaries who would increase their hold over the army. Whether in victory or in defeat, they would impose a policy favorable to the aristocracy and the king. Nobles remained numerous in the higher commands, despite soldiers' revolts against noble officers and despite the appeals in royalist journals, such as the *Ami du Roi*, urging the nobles to join the emigration. Some 69 percent of the generals were *ci-devants*, and almost half the colonels in the royal army and the volunteers were members of the aristocracy. Officers who were only courtiers had for the most part been weeded out. Those who remained were veteran professionals, who since 1791 had worked to regain control of their units. In this they were assisted early in 1792 by the minister of war, Narbonne, who took a stand against soldiers' petitions and tried to impose a passive obedience.

The king, risking a policy of making matters worse, surrounded himself with a set of Girondin ministers. He appointed Dumouriez to the foreign ministry. Son of a war commissioner, with a career behind him as an officer and a spy in turn, fomenter of troubles in Poland, and commander of the national guard at Cherbourg, Dumouriez was an adventurer who played on all tables. He was seen at the Jacobin club. He haunted the court and gave advice to the king. He pressed for war, trying to dominate the war ministry by taking over its operations. Among the generals, it was Dumouriez whom a man like Marat saw as a potential dictator. But the tribune of people was the only one to denounce him.

On April 20, on proposal by the king, war was declared on "the king of Hungary and Bohemia." The Austrians were soon supported by the Prussians. The French army, commanded by Rochambeau, Luckner, and Lafayette, was defeated and in its headlong retreat sometimes massacred its own chiefs, including General Dillon. The Girondins called for revolutionary measures, one of which was to establish a camp near Paris of 20,000 national Fédérés, to defend the city if there should be some move by the factious generals. The king vetoed the plan and dismissed his Girondin ministers. Revolutionaries began to prepare for an insurrectionary "day."

Lafayette, whom Robespierre had long denounced as likely to attempt a coup d'état, now intervened. On May 18 Lafayette induced Luckner and Rochambeau to join him in a coalition against Dumouriez, in which they would refuse to accept orders on the ground that preparations for war were inadequate and that they alone were qualified to make military decisions. It was not the military arguments that were the most important, for the marquis intended political action against the Jacobins. For that, he needed the army, and he cultivated his popularity with the men. He demanded strict discipline but welcomed subordinate officers to his table. He secretly asked the Austrians for a suspension of hostilities so as to be able, if necessary, to turn his forces against Paris. For the moment, he had his troops draw up petitions urging respect for the constitution. But for the first time in the history of the Revolution a general was trying to attain a political objective by the use of armed force.

On June 16 Lafayette sent a letter to the Assembly, declaring that France was menaced not only from outside but also internally by the Jacobin faction, which must be destroyed. After the insurrection of June 20, when the sans-culottes invaded the Tuileries but failed to get the king to rescind his veto, Lafayette rushed to Paris. He again used addresses from his army and from Luckner's army to denounce the episode of June 20 and demand the arrest of the Jacobins. But addresses and petitions were not enough. Force was necessary, and the marquis did not have it. He returned to the army, but continued to keep in touch with other generals with a view to political intervention.

Then came the uprising of August 10 and the fall of the monarchy, brought about by the sans-culottes and the Fédérés. The Legislative Assembly and the new revolutionary authorities feared the reaction of the army. It was learned that Lafayette was having his troops take an oath of loyalty to the Nation, the Law—and the King. He was said to be about to march against Paris, accompanied by General Dillon of the Army of the North, the brother of the general who had been murdered. The Army of the Rhine, commanded by the nobles Custine and de Broglie, might follow. Luckner also was suspected. The clan of generals seemed about to overturn the Revolution of Equality.

But they did not act.

Their failure has sometimes been explained by the personality of Lafayette: a poor politician, he failed to see that the balance of forces had swung around during the summer of 1792, and that nothing could be accomplished without the physical presence of the army in Paris. Or their failure has been attributed to misunderstandings among the generals: they agreed that some move was called for after August 10, but they were divided by mutual jealousies and none of them was enough of a man of action to deliver a decisive blow.

Historians have emphasized also the promptitude of the Assembly in dispatching commissioners to the armies to inform them of the events of August 10 and win their adherence. As inspectors and judges, in the words of Marcel Reinhard, these commissioners "raised against the generals and civilian officials the absolute and redoubtable power of the national sovereignty." They showed no pity toward officers and officials who deserted their posts. At Sedan, when Lafayette learned that he had been replaced in his command by Dumouriez, he put the commissioners under arrest. He tried to get the army to follow him. It refused by an overwhelming majority, and the marquis had to flee to foreign parts on August 19. At the Army of the Rhine Carnot, Constard, and Prieur de la Côte-d'Or, supported by the troops and the clubs, suspended suspected officers such as de Broglie. The civil power prevailed over the gun. Had it not been so, the Revolution of August 10 might have come to nothing.

But the pusillanimity of the generals and energy of the commissioners only partly explain the attitude of the troops. We must again turn to the army and analyze it from its own registers.

2. The Transformation of the Royal Army in 1792

The years 1790 and 1791 were the years of crisis as the ranks grew thinner. Recruitment was more successful at the end of 1791, when a fear of hunger brought men into the camps. With the declaration of war in 1792 new efforts were made to raise the number of effectives. The patriotic ardor that brought enlistments in the volunteer battalions, when the country was declared in danger, also induced some to respond to the call of the regular recruiting sergeants. Thus in 1792 the enlisted ranks of the royal army were full of young men, most of whom had joined the colors since 1789 and had taken part in the protests and insurrections within the army. About 38 percent of the common soldiers had less than a year of service. Almost all were French (with only 4 percent now foreigners); they came from all parts of France and mostly from rural places. More of them were peasants than in 1789, but village artisans and shopkeepers were the most numerous. As in former times, townspeople were overrepresented, with 31 percent. More than a third of the soldiers had left civilian society at a time when sans-culottes of town and country demanded the right to a liveli-hood and were putting this question, along with equality, on the political agenda for the Nation. Among such men the voice of the clubs and the popular societies was often echoed. In this army of the young (65 percent were under twenty-five) there was no end to disputes with aristocratic chiefs. Early in 1792 some soldiers appeared in Paris, before the Assembly, to denounce the conduct of their officers. When Narbonne had them arrested, the Jacobins were indignant. At Lille, the ministry tried to punish a garrison that complained that the military regulations were too severe.

These men, worked upon by the clubs, were commanded by company officers who had recently been non-coms and hence were commoners. Among them were sons of members of the lib-eral professions, or *rentiers*, or families formerly employed in the royal administration. But a third of these company officers were sons of shopkeepers, journeymen, and even peasants. Their social origin, close to the sans-culottes, helps to explain the rejection of any compromise with aristocratic chiefs who might draw them into a *coup de force* againt the Revolution.

There was also an esprit de corps, encouraged by the aristocrats, which in the end turned against them. Before belonging to the national army a man belonged to his regiment, which, though now designated by a number, proudly remembered its traditions. When the 50th regiment mounted an assault at Jemappes the sol-diers cried, "Forward, fearless Navarre!" and the 17th shouted "Glorious Auvergne forever!" It would be against the honor of a soldier to leave the unit in which he faced the enemy to plunge into civil war.

Beside them were the volunteers of 1791. Though commanded by nobles and moderate bourgeois, they came from the common people, with whom they continued to have close connections. They, too, were thrilled by the calls for Equality. Between "whites" and "blues" there were frequent conflicts. It would be useless to deny them. But there were also factors, as in 1791, that brought together troops that hardly differed in the internal composition of their companies and the kind of lieutenants and captains that they had. Both armies had gradually accepted military discipline if only it allowed for their rights as citizens. Together, they had faced the ordeal of battle; the human groups that made them up were welded together by a common struggle. Attempts were begun in August to put them together in brigades. In the d'Harville division, the 1st and 2nd brigades contained two battalions of volunteers and one battalion of the line. The measures taken in the Year II were thus anticipated, in which the battalions were not merely put side by side but the men themselves were mixed. Thus the 102nd, the 103rd, and 104th infantry regiments were composed of French Guards and national volunteers.

A clear comradeship in arms often grew up between the former army and the volunteers who were Jacobinized in varying degree. For example, at the camp at Tiercelet, on April 3, 1792, there were about 6,000 men, "whites" and volunteers. When the volunteers were short of cartridges the "whites" gave them some, and swore eternal friendship. Such fraternity was felt outside of combat, and sometimes turned against officers in whom a pre-Revolutionary spirit was too obvious. The volunteers, like citizens in the clubs, gave instruction in their rights to the regulars.

The correspondence of the army commissioners throws light on these coalitions between volunteers and regular troops. The commissioner sent to the Army of the Rhine, reporting on courts martial, wrote on July 11, 1792, that volunteers and artillery men were combining to form juries "composed entirely of clubbists and Jacobins."

The line regiments, according to a report from Carnot, were no less patriotic than the volunteers. More than one regiment (for example, the 34th on approaching Châlons-sur-Marne) went under fire singing the *Ça ira*. It was also while chanting this sans-culotte song that the troops held firm at Valmy while cannon balls fell around them. Soldiers from the people and newly promoted officers fought for the new *Patrie*. Kellerman understood this when, at Valmy, he urged on his men by putting his hat with a tricolor plume on the point of his sword and crying *Vive la Nation!*—a cry echoed by his whole army.

It is still true that both armies were worked upon not only by Jacobins but by Feuillants, Fayettists, and royalists who favored an absolute monarchy. There were still signs of counter-revolutionary influence. But what basically dissuaded the factious generals from taking action against the Revolution of August 10 (who can doubt it?) was "the great stirring of valorous poverty" (in Jaurès's words) that rose in 1792 in defense of Equality.

3. The Volunteers of 1792: The Sans-culotte Army

One man was called Pierre-François Gerbaud. He was eighteen years old in 1791 when the first battalions of volunteers were formed. His father was a lawyer, a leading citizen and local official of Chénérailles, and later a magistrate at Guéret. Gerbaud was elected quartermaster, in charge of lodgings and accounts.

Another was named Fricasse. He was nineteen years old in 1792 when the country was declared in danger. Like his father, Fricasse was a gardener. He enlisted and became a soldier of the Republic.

One was an educated bourgeois, the other a rural sans-culotte. They symbolized the two formations of volunteers. Those of 1791 constituted an army recruited from the people but officered by bourgeois and in some cases even by nobles. They were the army of the first stage of the bourgeois Revolution. The volunteers of 1792 also came from the ranks of the people, but their organization and command were much less controlled by the bourgeoisie, at least at first. They may be called the army of the sans-culottes. Along with them various free legions and free companies were also raised.

On July 11, 1792, the Assembly published a declaration of emergency:

> Citizens, the country is in danger! Let those who want the honor of being first to march in defense of all they hold dear remember that they are French and free. Let their fellow citizens at home maintain the security of persons and property. Let the magistrates of the people be vigilant. Let all await the signal of the law with the calm courage that is the sign of true strength. Then the country will be saved.

The next day a law ordered a first levy of 50,000 men for the line army and the creation of forty-two new battalions of volunteers, or 33,600 men to be furnished by the departments.

On July 22, in Paris, as a cannon fired each hour at the Pont-Neuf, the legions of the Paris national guard assembled at the Place de Grève beginning at six o'clock in the morning. At eight the Place de Grève began gradually to empty, and units of the guard paraded through the streets bearing banners on which was written *Citoyens, la Patrie est en danger!* At every open square platforms were erected, or tables set up on two drums, with tricolor oriflammes flapping in the breeze. The enlistments began instantly. In a week there were 15,000 volunteers in the capital.

As before, the frontier departments were the first to respond and provided the largest contingents. This time there was less hesitation in the Bas-Rhin and the Haut-Rhin. The record for enlistments was set by the Haute-Saône with eight battalions in four days.

There was less enthusiasm elsewhere. The departments next to the Pyrenees and those of the West and Center acted more slowly and provided smaller contingents. It was not so much a lack of patriotism as poverty and the land that held even the patriot back.

The municipality of Esternay in the district of Sézanne wrote in September that "such requisitions become burdensome. . . . they interfere with work in the fields." At Montgenot in the Marne the municipality explained why no one came forward voluntarily: it was because the wine harvest was about to begin, and the commune had already provided five volunteers and four men for the regular army. In the Ariège the commune of Bastide-de-Congouse, with five hundred inhabitants, protested that it had already furnished twenty-one young men, and that all families would suffer from the departure of sons who provided bread for their mothers and fathers. In the department of the Marne local administrators intervened in favor of a widow whose son had been designated to depart:

> We the undersigned municipal officers of Marsangis certify that Nicholas Rondeau, chosen by lot to go in defense of the country during the visit of the commissioner appointed for this purpose . . . , is absolutely necessary to his mother, widowed since May 18; that he is the only person in her house able to work her land; that if he is required to depart she will be obliged to employ others, and so would find herself in difficulties in view of the scarcity of laborers and the exorbitant wages that they demand, because this woman can manage her affairs successfully only by strict economy and the labor of her son.

In departments where volunteers were insufficient men were chosen either by lot or by election. Sometimes the more well-to-do thus rid themselves of more revolutionary elements in the commune.

The poverty was real, and it made it hard for a man to leave when he knew that his family would be in want and that prices were continually rising. Although there were popular demands for price controls, the Assembly rejected controls, and in September took only half measures to provision the markets. It was widely thought that the more wealthy should be the first to go and that, if they would not go, they should contribute to relief of the family of the sans-culotte volunteer. In the Bouches-du-Rhône, on July 28, a bounty of 50 livres was offered for enlistment. In the Maine-et-Loire the recruiters paid 12 livres. At Saint-Georges-sur-Loire 73 livres, 10 *sous*, were paid for nine volunteers. The bounty varied from one department to an other, or within the same department: at Morannes 11 livres were paid for a volunteer, while at Soucelles in the same department of Maine-et-Loire only 3 livres, 10 *sous*, were enough.

To induce enlistments some municipalities organized festivals. At Avallon, for example, after placarding the town with notices that "the ferocious Austrians after slaughtering your fathers and ravaging your properties" would march "over their bleeding bodies to reach you yourselves," the constituted authorities and the popular society met together under the tree of Liberty. The Brunswick Manifesto was read aloud, threatening the complete destruction of Paris if the royal family should be touched. The manifesto was then burned before the eyes of the assembled people, with singing of the Marseillaise and exhortations to the young men to do their duty. At Remiremont in the Vosges, on July 25, 1792, the local authorities called the people together at the foot of the altar of Liberty, and the mayor made a speech:

> It is not today a matter of conquering, but of preserving. Preserving what? Brave youth, it is to preserve the finest privilege of which the human race can boast! The first to enroll under the flag of the French people will be a privileged soul who has deserved well of his country.

No sooner had these words been spoken, so we read in the record of these deliberations, than François André Cuisnier rushed forward to the altar. He was the first to sign. He had been a captain; he became a simple musketeer, and was proud of it. A crowd of other signers followed. In a town of not over 4,500 persons 65 citizens enrolled.

In the end many volunteers poured in, including numerous

peasants. One reason is that the government announced certain decisions that, besides granting the vote to all, had the effect of enlarging the scope of *la Patrie*. Peasants received assurances of access to property. The principle of division of common fields, and of sale of émigré estates in small lots, was affirmed on August 14. The peasant who had been struggling against feudalism also learned at this time that, henceforth, it would be more difficult for the seigneur to claim indemnity for the loss of seigneurial rights; he would have to prove in court that the rights he claimed had not been usurped. But the proofs of such rights had largely gone up in smoke in 1789.

Rural people thus responded to the call of *la Patrie en danger*. A sampling in the army registers shows that 69 percent of the volunteers of 1792 came from the countryside, as opposed to only 15 percent of the volunteers of 1791. Among these rural people were many peasant proprietors. In the department of the Manche, out of 1,628 volunteers whose occupation is stated in the Archives de la Guerre, there were 1,111 peasants (68 percent) and 386 artisans (23 percent). The hired men and day laborers among the peasants formed only 18 percent of the whole. The same social profile appears for the levy in the Yonne, the Basses-Pyrénées, the Haute-Garonne, and the Cantal. Yet urban recruitment remained strong in proportion to urban population, with small towns yielding more than the larger agglomerations, always with the exception of Paris. In the towns also it was the more humble social categories that filled up the contingents. These poorer men were more often fathers of families than in 1791. Of 147 citizen soldiers on the first list established in the Bouches-de-Rhône who were still in the army in 1795, there were 75 family heads. Some of them, fearing that their wives would not be able to feed their children, took them with them on joining the army. In the Yonne, a citizen Terrasson departed with his five children. In the 3rd battalion of the Maine-et-Loire a hairdresser of Saumur, Etienne Laillet, enlisted along with his wife. Some of these women bore children in the camps, and the child's name would then be entered in the troop register.

The volunteers of 1792 were on the whole younger than those of 1791. A sample shows that three-quarters were twenty-five or younger, and between 10 and 15 percent less than eighteen. But there were also men of mature age, so that the top of the age pyramid was more spread out for the volunteers of 1792 than for those of 1791. Men of thirty-six or older made up 3.8 percent in 1791, and reached 6.7 percent in 1792.

The effects of the sources of recruitment and age distribution of the volunteers of 1792 were evident in their physical characteristics as a group. The volunteers of 1792 were shorter. Those less than 1.67 meters in height were 52 percent in 1791, 64 percent in 1792. Those with a height of 1.62 meters or less formed 12.5 percent of the volunteers of 1791, but one-third of those of 1792.[1] More detailed indications on physical traits were given by the commissioners who organized the levies. Thus in the Manche they found that 154 individuals had to be removed from the battalions as physically unqualified or because of uncompleted growth. A special commission sent to the camp at Châlons reported to the Legislative Assembly: "We are relieving you in advance of children, old men, and men with physical deficiencies who rely on their ardor rather than their strength, but would only hamper your operations and consume the provisions." At first glance the officers of 1792 would seem to resemble those of 1791. They were young; 60 percent of the captains were less than thirty-four. As in 1791, one-third of the officers had had some military experience. Many came from bourgeois homes: 43 percent of the captains and lieutenants, 32.8 percent of the sub-lieutenants.

We see differences on going into details. Of the battalion commanders of 1792, fewer had had military experience than in 1791. Captains and lieutenants had had only from one to six years of

---

[1] The equivalent values for 1.67 and 1.62 meters are, respectively, about 5 feet 6 inches and 5 feet 4 inches in Anglo-American measurement.

professional soldiering. Where the volunteer officers of 1791 had often reached the rank of sergeant before leaving the regular service, those of 1792 had sometimes left it only with the rank of corporal, and more often had been simple privates.

Differences in social origin may also be detected. There were no more nobles among the volunteers of 1792. As for the bourgeoisie, more officers had been law clerks, students, or lesser legal practitioners. There were fewer lawyers, physicians, and merchants as officers, but more who had been office workers or other commercial employees. Peasants in command of companies were more numerous in the 1792 battalions than in those of 1791, accounting for from 13 to 15 percent of the captains and lieutenants.

The officers of 1792 were men of goodwill, brave, but with less education. With fewer talents,[2] and with less social or economic background than those of 1791, they were less able to resist influence by their men. The officers of 1791 were notables in the habit of getting themselves obeyed, and did not depend on promotion for a significant improvement in their condition. Those of 1792 came more often from the common people, and the army for them could be an avenue of social advancement. To rise in a military career, they needed the votes of their soldiers. To get them, they were more lax in applying discipline, which in any case the volunteers of 1792 were likely to regard as a means of subjection invented by aristocrats.

The indiscipline of the volunteers of 1792 may also be explained on technical grounds. They were organized by companies. It was not as in 1791, when a battalion was formed from the very beginning under the eyes of the local authorities. It often happened that a company was no sooner created than it immediately departed. Other companies joined it on the march or on the field of battle.

---

[2] The French *talent* often refers to an acquired skill or qualification, obtained by education or experience, rather than to an aptitude or potential that precedes education or experience, as so often in English. It is sometimes best translated as "ability." In either case "talent" is understood as preferable to favoritism, family connection, social position, purchase, or mere seniority as a basis of appointment.

Only then was the battalion formed. Newcomers sometimes challenged the authority of chiefs they had not elected. Group homogeneity, and hence the capacity to accept rules for life in common, suffered also from the coming together of companies whose men originated in cantons or even in departments that were distant from one another. Finally, and it is worth repeating, these men had been levied at a time when, more than in 1791, the notion of regarding another man, whatever his rank, as one's equal in rights had come to be a habit. Many of these citizen-soldiers, especially the Parisians, devised and implemented a direct democracy in their camps as in their hometowns. Leaders were seen as mandatories whose orders were to be examined and contested, if necessary, and who had to be kept under control or even dismissed.

Ardent and generous, this "stirring of valorous poverty" produced a horde that was sometimes troublesome for the generals. Listening to their complaints, we may forget what a psychological shock these volunteers delivered to the enemy. They were, as a contemporary put it, "a mass in action." Their presence on the great roads and in the by-ways, in towns and villages, in fields and woods, gives an impression of a general swarming that can be felt at a distance of two centuries by anyone who looks into the manuscripts that speak of them. They were a France unanimously rising against "tyrants." They knew why they were fighting, and were ready to make the ultimate sacrifice. Their officers taught and repeated the meaning of the war. Let us hear one of them, Joseph Serre:

> The tyrants want to restore royal authority, the rights and privileges of nobility, a religion that they do not yet understand, the old judicial system, the intendants and the subdelegates. . . .
>
> Will you cower again under the rod of despotism? Or tremble before the threats of some petty tyrant, be again a slave to a haughty lord, an object of scorn to an insolent rich man, a dupe of priests and monks, a beast of burden to an

indolent noble, the prey of a greedy magistrate or starving lawyer? Do you want the *banalités*, the *cens*, the *corvées*, and the *lods*?[3] Choose then between equality and nobility, between justices of the peace and parlements, between family tribunals and lawyers, between directories and subdelegates. Choose, in a word, between civic crowns and the baubles of pride and ambition; and never forget that you are about to decide the great question of Europe enslaved or of Europe free.

Europe enslaved or Europe free? This was in fact the moment when certain political leaders, notably the Girondins, thought of transforming the defensive war into a war of conquest. It was for this reason that the legions were created in 1792.

4. THE LEGIONS AND THE FÉDÉRÉS

The legions were created for two reasons: to provide an instrument of war that the army lacked; and to use political militants to propagate the revolutionary ideas and win the support of foreign populations among whom the kings recruited their mercenaries.

In designing them as a tool for combat the military committee of the Legislative Assembly was inspired by lessons from the wars of the eighteenth century. From about 1740 a need had been seen for light troops, combining infantry and cavalry, to act as scouts, assure the security and provisioning of encampments, and wear out the enemy by skirmishes and alarms that would demoralize and weaken him. These light troops, recommended by the Maréchal de Saxe and created from 1740 to 1761, were severely criticized by some able strategists such as Guibert. These autonomous and often large detachments worked against the "war of mass" as

---

[3] French words for dues and obligations owed to the seigneur or lord of the manor. The "justices of the peace" were the lowest courts set up in the Revolutionary judicial system. The "directories" were governing bodies of the new *départements*, here contrasted with the *sub-délégués* or assistants to the *intendant* under the Old Regime.

he envisaged it, a war in which the army should be engaged as a whole simultaneously in a single block. He denounced such troops as animated by a particular spirit, attempting "to keep themselves intact, independent, cooperating only in their own interests, and indifferent to successes and failures that were not their own." The seven legions existing in 1776 were suppressed by the comte de Saint-Germain.

As war became imminent, projects for organization of light troops, and more especially legions, were taken up by the military committee and by the Assembly in discussion of its report. The "technicians" were opposed by Lazare Carnot. He accused the spokesmen of the committee of wishing to imitate the foreign armies, which he said offered no model "suited to our character or our topographical situation." He objected to the creation of units which, in the effort to combine what was hard to amalgamate, namely infantry and cavalry, would be veritable tactical monsters. His attention fell also on questions of politics and morale. He warned the Assembly against the natural propensity of legion commanders not strictly to obey the orders of the general:

> To put the army under the orders of a general, and at the same time to entrust to particular chiefs some sections of this army, sections that may be large enough to thwart it by false moves, is to put the fate of the country in a plurality of hands, any one of which might bring ruin, and whose interests, jealousies, and ambitions might only too often go along with disloyal intentions.

The Assembly decided against Carnot, and on April 24 declared the raising of six legions. Never applied, this decree was reshaped by a law of May 31. This law authorized the levy of fifty-four free companies and three legions to be organized in the principal field armies by their commanding generals. Recruitment was voluntary, but the officers as much as possible had to be experienced army men, and discipline was as in the royal army. Chiefs were named at the discretion of the generals of the several armies, on condition that at least half of those selected should have had experience in command.

While the law required that officers must give proof of talents, it also insisted that both officers and men should show evidence of civic reliability. Whenever the French might enter enemy territory, these light troops would come into first contact with the local populations, to whom they would bring the message of liberty. Coming in close to the adversary, they would try to subvert the soldiers and tyrants by talking to them or distributing tracts.

This political aspect of the light troops was even more marked in the legions formed by foreign patriots who had taken refuge in France. These legions composed of foreigners were different from those just described. Their formation and organization was set by a "capitulation," a legislative act for each legion specifying most notably its conditions of enlistment. On the initiative of the committees of political refugees the Assembly approved the levy of Batavian, Germanic, and Allobrogian legions.[4] The colonels and principal officers of these legions were members of their committees or named by them. Thus, Dambach and Van Heyden of the Germanic committee went ahead, with Clootz, to supply officers for the Germanic legion, after verification by the ministry of war.

Not all these foreign legions were raised on the initiative of political refugees. Some owed their existence to French politicians or the favors of generals. Hence there were two Belgian legions—the Legion of United Belgians and Liégeois, from which Dumouriez hoped for support for his projects, and the Liége Legion that was under the protection of the minister Lebrun, and so had Girondin connections. The Montagnards distrusted these legions for the use that the Girondins might possibly make of them. The sans-cu-

---

[4] Batavian meant Dutch; Germanic referred to the many states of the Holy Roman Empire; Allobrogian meant French-speaking Savoyards and Swiss. In the next paragraph note that "Belgian" was then only a word referring to the Austrian Netherlands and the bishopric of Liége, which was a separate territory within the Empire. Most of these regions had seen indigenous revolutionary or quasi-revolutionary disturbances in preceding years.

lottes denounced them for escaping from the common lot of the armies, and for having privileges and special features that recalled unpleasant memories of the Old Regime. They became more and more disturbed by the presence of politically suspicious foreign elements, not only in the foreign legions but in those that were French. Had not the decree of May 31 called for the incorporation of the former Saxon Hussars and cavalrymen of the Royal German of sinister memory? And the Swiss, whose regiments were dissolved after August 10, were put into newly formed legions, notably the one bearing the name of Luckner.

A curious case was the existence for a few months of an "American Legion," composed of free blacks living in France but originating in the French Caribbean islands. On September 7, 1792, a delegation of *hommes de couleur* submitted a petition to the expiring Legislative Assembly, declaring that although they differed from other Frenchmen in "external signs" they shared the same ardor for rushing to the defense of the country, and requesting permission to form a military unit of their own. The Assembly complied, and authorized the formation of a cavalry unit of 724 men, to be called the *Légion des Américains et du Midi*. One of its lieutenant-colonels was Alexandre Dumas, father of the novelist of that name. He had been born in 1762 in Saint-Domingue (the later Haiti) of a French father and a black mother, sent to France for an education, and joined the royal army in 1786. He became a general in 1793, and after service on various fronts was a division commander under Bonaparte in Italy and Egypt from 1796 to 1799. The *Légion des Américains* was incorporated into the 13th regiment of *chasseurs* in March 1793.

It seemed that legions organized by the generals, the foreign committees, and even by private persons might become dangerous refuges for enemies of liberty. The sections of Paris expressed such fears. By a law of September 9 the Assembly, to prevent certain levies of light infantry from becoming a mask for public enemies, ordered that citizens wishing to organize such units must post, for three days, a statement showing their names, services, titles of citizenship, and their plans. Citizens wishing to enroll in such units were also to produce certificates of good civic behavior and evidence of "active personal service in the national guard." But despite the distrust that they aroused the legions were not dissolved, and some new ones were even created by agents of the executive power. Such was the mountain legion or "Miquelets" formed of smugglers' guides, whose detailed knowledge of the mountain passes in the Pyrenees was of great service to the army in its operations against Spain.

Eight French and seven foreign legions existed in February 1793. A sampling of personnel files shows that the officers, whose average age exceeded thirty-five, were older than officers of the volunteers and predominantly urban in origin; many had careers as professional soldiers. These mature men, mostly bourgeois, were in command of very young soldiers (with average age of twenty-three), mostly rural or from very small villages and towns. Agricultural workers, servants, or day laborers, they were of the same popular classes as the volunteers of 1792.

Battalions of men called Fédérés existed along with these special troops until September 1792. They were a revolutionary force mobilized for intervention in the interior rather than for service at the frontiers. The preamble to the decree of June 8, 1792, makes this clear:

> Whereas it is urgent that troops of the line now in the capital be sent to the frontiers; and whereas it is important to take all hope from public enemies who conspire inside the country; and whereas it is advantageous to tighten the bonds of fraternity that unite the national guards of the other departments with that of Paris. . . . The Assembly decrees:
>
> Article 1. The armed force already authorized will be augmented by 20,000 men.
>
> Article 2. This augmentation will take place in the departments, and all cantons in the kingdom may participate.

Article 3. The 20,000 men of the augmentation will meet in Paris for celebration of the coming July 14.

When the king refused to approve this decree, his veto was a cause of the revolutionary "day" of June 20. The Fédérés were nevertheless levied and streamed into the capital. They played a decisive role in the uprising of August 10 that resulted in the deposition of the king. The Fédérés from Marseille are the only ones to have caught the attention of historians, because they brought with them the song ever since called the Marseillaise. But the Fédérés from Finistère in Brittany kept up a correspondence with the administration of their department, in which they explained how on their way to fight the invaders they were welcomed by the Jacobins and sans-culottes of Paris, who strengthened their democratic feelings. They decided, against opposition by their leaders, to remain in Paris and combat the counter-Revolution. On August 10 they proved to be such resolute fighters that one of the sections of Paris (the Gobelins) changed its name to Finistère in their honor. These Fédérés were men of humble station but not such paupers, jailbirds, and criminal repeaters as the royalists claimed. While the Marseillais and Bretons returned home, other Fédérés went on to the camp at Soissons and remained in the army, where they reinforced the democratic current. With the volunteers, in this period of high prices, they helped the poor to enforce controls in the markets on the price of basic foods.

To sum up, by the beginning of 1793, to support the Republic One and Indivisible, there were diverse armies in which the men were separated by differences in pay, discipline, and rules of promotion. In some of them, those in command were still marked by the spirit of the defunct regime, and they might have an influence on their men. For both military and political reasons, it was necessary to unify these armies and make the democratic ideal more strongly felt.

CHAPTER IV

• • •

Reorganizing and Democratizing the Army (September 1792 to Summer 1793)

The nation in arms saved itself by the battle of Valmy. It also founded the Republic. "From that day and at that place," as Goethe later put it, "a new era of world history can be dated." The French victory transformed the war, which now passed from the defensive to the offensive. The ex-marquis de Custine crossed the Rhine, taking Speyer on September 30, then Worms and Mainz, and finally Frankfurt. Nice was occupied and Savoy penetrated on September 29. In Belgium Dumouriez's victory at Jemappes opened the way for him to its great cities, Mons, Brussels, and Antwerp. England was alarmed; it began to move from its neutrality in the face of the territorial and revolutionary expansion of France, and now that France appeared as an economic competitor in countries providing customers for London. The execution of the king on January 21, 1793, was an act of defiance to Europe.

The sovereigns might well fear the spread of revolutionary agitation in their own countries. In February a coalition against France began to form. Gathering around England, it included Holland, Austria, Prussia, Spain, Portugal, Piedmont-Sardinia, and the kingdom of Naples, with the lesser German states coming in later and, at least formally, Russia. France was engaged in a difficult war that seemed likely to be a long one. To conduct it, it was imperative to organize all the forces that had surged up spontaneously. But to the technical necessity of military organization were added political implications that further divided the bourgeois leaders now in power.

The group called the Gironde was dominant in the Convention. It had wanted the war. It was supported by political exiles such as Clavière, who came from Geneva, and Anarcharsis Cloots, from one of the Rhenish territories of Prussia. Such men pressed for a war of expansion and annexation, seeing the Rhine as the natural boundary of the Gauls. But the Gironde resisted the social consequences of the war. To maintain and enlarge the army, it was necessary to recognize the people's right to existence and equality of "enjoyments" for which demands were now heard. Price controls were needed to assure a minimal subsistence for all. The bourgeois Girondins lived in fear of militants who called for a division of land and economic controls. Their political adversaries, the Montagnards, coming gradually to understand the economic and social consequences of the war, looked for support among the sans-culottes. Against them the Girondins were ready to mobilize the volunteer battalions of the sympathetic departments. They resisted a military reorganization in which they might lose the possible future support of the royal army. To remain in power and overcome the Montagnards, the Girondins were disposed to make use of certain victorious generals.

1. Unifying the Separate Armies: Technical Needs and Political Goals

To unify the armies meant meeting the elementary needs of a state at war: to know the number and distribution of soldiers in each field army, so as to assure a better supply of weapons, ammunition, provisions, and equipment, and also to fill up the shortages in numbers that might make operational orders impossible to execute. The Republic possessed armies, but it had a poor knowledge of them.

The line regiments were cut up into battalions, companies, and squads scattered along the whole front and thus separated by several leagues. In such conditions it was hard for a quartermaster to know the internal movements of his unit. As for the volunteer battalions, their administration was often nonexistent. Resisting assimilation into the regular army, the volunteers objected to keeping records. Moreover, in their ranks men of ability were often in short supply. An organization of all units into brigades would make it possible to redistribute the "paper shufflers" of whom the regular army had a good number, and who would give the "blues" the indispensable habits of management. Brigading would produce an accurate account of the available forces.

Reports received by the war ministry, from December 1792 to March 1793, clearly revealed the ignorance of the government as to the number of its soldiers. But clearly there was a crisis of numbers in the opening months of 1793. The campaign in the Argonne and in Belgium had been costly in men, and with the winter the roads were crowded with volunteers who, seeing their enlistment for the campaign now ended, were returning to their homes. The extent of the losses is uncertain. In his report on organization of the army Dubois-Crancé described the situation at the end of 1792. There then existed 98 regiments of line infantry which, with the light infantry, should have contained 133,000 men. There were also 35,000 in the cavalry and 10,000 in the artillery. The 517 battalions of volunteers supposedly provided 289,114 men (the volunteers of 1791 having exceeded 100,000). The number of men under the colors was estimated at between 400,000 and 460,000. Estimates for the first quarter of 1793 reduced this figure to 351,000, with the numbers in the coastal army and the eastern fortresses unknown. What was certain was the lack of men in readiness to face the enemy. A new levy was necessary, by which men could be incorporated into existing units as needed. But how could this be done without resistance by the new recruits, unless the pay, discipline, and system of promotion was made the same for all? Without a unification of the armies the new men would demand admission to the volunteer battalions, where the pay and discipline were better.

A final technical need was to put companies and battalions into a larger framework. With the formation of brigades, and after the rules for promotion had been made uniform, there could be an end to the disparities in rank and authority that were harmful to the armies at the moment of combat. Some battalions, which had sustained losses through desertion and death, continued to provide all officers from their own ranks. In others, notably those in the regular regiments, there was a scarcity of both officers and non-coms. The ministry was slow in filling vacancies, or men suited for command were too few. There was a continual coming and going of officers between the volunteers and the former royal army.

To bring up the strength of battalions, combine them in larger units, and produce the kind of tactical units required by the war— such were the technical needs. Beyond them were the political struggles for control of the army. Democratization was promised by the commission sent by the executive power to the Army of the North, when it exhorted the troops on August 19, 1792: "Stand fast for the sacred cause that you defend and for the new blessings you will receive from the Nation, when it extinguishes the last traces of aristocratic distinctions that still survive the Revolution in the army of Liberty and Equality."

The new war minister, Pache, set about fulfilling this promise. Succeeding Servan in the ministry on October 6, 1792, Pache had been a principal subordinate in the Girondin ministry under Roland. With him, the Girondins thought themselves well installed in the war ministry. They were soon undeceived, as Pache soon demonstrated a cold and total independence from the Brissotins. His choice of his staff made it plain that his preferences went to the Montagnards. A *maréchal de camp*, Meusnier, a convinced Jacobin, became his closest adviser. The topographic engineer Hassenfratz, a militant sans-culotte, and Vandermonde of the Academy of Sciences made their scientific knowledge available and provided a link with the popular movement. Pache chose as his first secretary Xavier Audouin, former vicar of the church of Saint-Thomas-d'Aquin, and more recently a committeeman of the Paris section Fontaine-de-Grenelle and member of the insurrectional committee of the Paris commune in August 1792. Audouin brought in Vincent, one of the young leaders of the Cordeliers club. To read Hébert and Marat and be a patriot "of August and September" were the criteria of choice for the minister's administrative personnel. This political color of the central service portended a purge of the generals, a political control over the appointment of officers, and a diffusion among the troops of Montagnard and sans-culotte tracts demanding a unification of the army. There was an even stronger political reason for unification. The spirit of the volunteers, and especially of the volunteers of 1792, would thereby pass into the old army, which was still suspected of following its aristocratic generals blindly. Since the defection of Lafayette, the distrust of what was called the "generalate" had become much greater. It was feared that the war, as predicted by Robespierre in 1792, might end up in Caesarism.

The generals were therefore closely watched by the Montagnards and sans-culottes. As early as September 19, Montesquiou, commander-in-chief of the Army of the Alps, was subjected to denunciations that produced a confrontation between Montagnards and Girondins. At the same time General Moreton was accused of incompetence. General Lenou was suspended, and General Duboux, another *ci-devant*, was called upon to justify himself before the Convention, which also debated the case of General Dillon, suspected for the tone of his correspondence with the enemy. The public safety being in question, any general might be removed. The Republic must "show itself terrible" to the generals; it must not wait for time of peace to send them back, as it were, to the plow. The new regime intended to apply the rule of strict subordination of the military to the civil power. But the Girondins meant to use a general to overcome their opponents. This general was Dumouriez.

Dumouriez was compromised in an ugly affair. At Vouziers two battalions of Paris sans-culottes, those of the sections Mauconseil and République, had massacred some enemy deserters suspected of being émigrés. General Chazot had imposed penalties, which Dumouriez had approved. The affair made a great noise; the Paris sections supported the volunteers, and Marat defended them against what he called the abuse of power by the generals. Dumouriez was able to pacify the sections by flattering them. The matter rested there.

In December 1792 the conflict reopened between the Montagnards, the war minister Pache, and the general. Since his victory in Belgium Dumouriez was conducting a personal policy. Seeking support of the local bourgeoisie against those he called extremists, he promised the Belgians their independence and respect for law and property. The Convention preferred to export the Revolution to Belgium, ordering suppression of the existing authorities, abolition of feudalism, expulsion of the nobility, and transformation of the country into a satellite. Dumouriez refused to carry out these measures. Another cause of conflict came from the directory of purchases in the war ministry, a new organ of centralization for military requirements, organized by Pache. This directory gave the minister a better hold over the army. Dumouriez denounced it, saying that it caused such confusion as to deprive his army of what it needed. Dumouriez especially objected to Ronsin, whom he called a bungler. Even so, the Montagnards put up no continuing struggle against the general. Robespierre declared on December 12: "Although Custine and Dumouriez are denounced, they are not traitors. They are seeking glory. Dumouriez despises Brissot and his faction."

In their struggle against the Montagnards, the Girondins hoped that, before calling on Dumouriez, they might make use of some troops under their influence, the Fédérés. Some of these from Marseilles who remained in Paris had turned violently against

Marat. They accused him of denouncing as counter-revolutionaries the dragoons housed at the Ecole Militaire, whom they regarded as brothers in arms. On October 31, 1792, the dragoons and the Marseillais had marched through the street where the Cordeliers club was meeting, and had shouted, "Marat to the guillotine!" On November 3 some six hundred dragoons, again accompanied by the Marseillais, had paraded through Paris from the rue de Varenne to the Boulevard du Temple, crying for "the heads of Marat, Robespierre, Danton, and all those who defend them. Long live Roland! No trial of the king!" On the next day the Fédérés appeared in the Convention with more complaints against the Montagnards. When Letourneur, speaking for the minister Pache, proposed sending the Fédérés to the army, he was vehemently opposed by Buzot.

It was not only among the Fédérés that the Gironde carried on such manipulations. The volunteer battalions were subjected to their propaganda. Even later, after the insurrection of June 2, 1793, which produced the expulsion of Girondins from the Convention, some of these battalions, such as the one from Ille-et-Vilaine in Brittany, came to the defense of the expelled members by attacking the "Maratist anarchy" in addresses to the Convention.

To prevent fusion of the armies was to curry favor with the old royal army. Many of its officers feared that their careers would be jeopardized by a brigading with the volunteers, in which advancement in rank would depend on election. To block plans for unification, they had to get control of the ministry, and they succeeded. They obtained the dismissal of Pache and appointment of one of their friends, Beurnonville, as his successor. The battle over unification began. This was in February 1793.

2. The Political Battle over Unification

Troops might be incorporated, amalgamated, or brigaded. Incorporation meant dissolution of the volunteer battalions and use of their members to fill up the battalions and companies of the old army. Robespierre and his friends rejected any such project. Amalgamation meant to merge the two armies by creating altogether new units in which the more numerous volunteers would submerge the "whites." But such an operation required time, and time was lacking. There remained the process of brigading. This meant to juxtapose one battalion of the line army with two battalions of volunteers to create what was called a demi-brigade. This was the project favored by the Montagnards and presented by Dubois-Crancé in the Convention.

By this plan, as the forming of brigades went forward, the distinction between the two armies would be suppressed. The uniform would be identical, and in the national colors. The pay scale would be the same for all, and would vary with rank, with the highest pay for each rank taken as a base. In the appointment and promotion of officers the plan gave an advantage to men of the line army. At first this was not evident either to those concerned or to the members of the Convention, so that to rally the line officers Dubois-Crancé felt obliged to send them a special message explaining this favor. The proposal provided that appointment to all grades, except those of brigade commander and corporal, should take place in one of two ways: one-third by seniority of service within the demi-brigade as a whole, and two-thirds by election within the battalion in which the vacancy was to be filled. The merit and talent of the older military men would thus in large part be rewarded.

As for merit, the seniority to be considered was not seniority in the existing grade, but the total duration of service since the date of enlistment as a simple private. Thus, as between two sergeants who had received their grade as noncommissioned officer on the same date, one originating in the volunteers and the other in the line army, preference would go to the one with the longest experience in the army. Justice would thus be done to the non-noble career soldier who had suffered from the old nobiliary exclusionism. On the other hand, there was reason to fear an aging of the command structure, and the discontent of those who, having reached their grade under the Old Regime, might see some of their subordinates with longer service be preferred for future advancement. The law might even seem to confine in their existing grades the nobles who were still in the service, as well as "officers of fortune" who were thought by some to be "gangrened" by an aristocratic spirit.

As for talent, the danger was that the good technical man might be overlooked in elections, and the demagogue allowed a rapid climb up the ladder of the military hierarchy. This was to forget what army men knew from experience—that a soldier who in the barracks might prefer an officer who could not exert his authority would soon see on the battlefield the resulting disadvantage for his own survival. In fact the troops came to appreciate the man who could lead them calmly and prudently under fire.

In any case, the Dubois-Crancé project provided for measures of selection to keep out the unfit. For one thing, candidates for election had to show credentials; they could be taken only from the grade immediately below the grade to be provided for. In addition, the system of promotion depended on co-optation as well as on votes. The troops presented three candidates among whom officers of the grade to be provided for made the choice. In most of the demi-brigades to be formed, this screening meant that the existing captains, who were mostly professional soldiers, would control the appointment of new captains to command companies.

Robespierre was alone in denouncing the contradiction at the heart of the law. He concluded his speech as follows:

> I have only one reproach to make to the War Committee, and that is their not giving enough extent to the principle of election. . . . They have directly violated it in proposing that those in the grade below that of the vacancy do not appoint directly, but only present three names to a superior who chooses one of the three. It is a kind of incomplete election mixing two opposite systems, choice by the superior and

choice by the subordinate. Either one or the other must be adopted.

What was to be feared was that the existing officers, mostly fashioned by the military spirit, would follow the tendency of any social organization based on co-optation and dominated by a majority, and reinforce the homogeneity and cohesion of their own group, by preferring their old companions in arms rather than the younger talents as revealed in the war.

Thus, except for the grade of corporal, dependent on vote of the company, and of colonel, dependent first on seniority of service and then on seniority in grade, the recruitment and promotion of officers and NCOs passed into the hands of officers already in place. The state, meaning the ministry held by a Girondin, lost control. Was not such a situation ominous for the future? Facing a dilemma that other revolutionaries would face after him—whether to prefer the competent professional even though politically suspect, or to favor the inexpert patriot, Dubois-Crancé chose the former. He did so because matters of promotion were only part of a larger whole. This whole consisted in the brigading and unification of the army and the democratization of military society. The proposed law brought soldiers together in a bond of equality and united them in a sentiment of fraternity; it attached them to the new *patrie* by a promise that poor men, at the peace, and with aid from the state, would accede to property. To republicanize the army and make its chiefs respect the civil power, it was essential that the process of brigade formation should go forward.

The project was denatured by the suspension of this essential measure. The Girondins, except for Lamarque, rejected it, while the Montagnards, except for Garnier de Saintes, gave it their support. Opponents found the project too extreme in identifying military with civilian society, and saw a corruption of discipline as a consequence of the new procedures for designation of chiefs. They called brigading a "utopia." To bring together all these battalions into demi-brigades would disorganize the army. Troops at the front would be distracted by the operation needed to bring about the new formations.

The final decision on the Dubois-Crancé project, reached in February 1793, was the worst possible. Nationalization provided for the same pay, discipline, and procedures for promotion in all battalions. But brigading, the essential element from both the political and the technical point of view (the demi-brigade was an indispensable tactical unit), was put off until the end of the campaign.

3. THE LEVY OF 300,000

On February 24 the Convention decreed a levy of 300,000 men to bring the effectives in the army up to strength. It thus seemed to introduce the principle of conscription, since all men of ages from eighteen to forty, unmarried or widowers without children, were put in a state of permanent requisition. But the principle was violated in the application. There was a difference between the departments in the numbers to be raised; those that had so far furnished fewer recruits than others in proportion to population, like the Vendée, now had to furnish more. Voluntary enlistment was also maintained. In cases where volunteers would not produce the numbers set for a commune, "the citizens will be obliged," as the decree expressed it, "to complete the number immediately, and for this purpose will adopt the method that they find most convenient, by a majority of votes." The decree also authorized replacements (that is, substitutes) for the men designated.

Both the decree and the circumstances explain why the levy went badly. Among the circumstances, the execution of the king had divided the country and frightened moderates who no longer wished to defend an increasingly radical Republic. The king's death had also made the religious tensions worse, for many of the French feared that religion would go the way of the king. Refractory priests preached this message. The struggle between Girondins and Montagnards was upsetting to some parts of public opinion and weakened the revolutionary current. The defeat of the French at Neerwinden on March 18, and the ensuing defection of Dumouriez, seemed to some to sound the knell of the Republic. For the lukewarm the cause was desperate. So why go?

The decree fell short of imposing obligatory military service upon all. The individual was affected only within his own commune. Not every local community had to fill a comparable quota. Protests poured in. The municipalities of Senarpont, Bernapré, Chilly, and Sailly in the Somme, for example, protested against the number assigned to them by the central administration. They claimed to have already furnished more men than they were given credit for. There were also complaints in the Dordogne: the figures for men already furnished as given by the administration were said to be false; the department now owed not 6,345 men but 5,887. Some other communities, while admitting their previous deficiencies, declared themselves unable to make up their "arrears" so abruptly. The sudden removal of an important part of the active population would be ruinous to work in the fields. The time for spring plowing was at hand. For many peasants this was all the more important because the crisis in food supply gave them incentive for more intensive cultivation, by the sowing of "round grains"—that is, peas and the various kinds of beans. The hands of all agricultural workers were needed, as well as those of artisans who repaired the farm implements.

The method of selection was left to the discretion of local governing officials, who were greatly embarrassed. Most of them had no desire to impose a method, and preferred to have the decision made democratically by an assembly of the inhabitants. But who should attend such an assembly, all men of whatever age or only those directly affected by the decree?

Solutions varied from one commune to another. Everywhere there was hesitation between election and drawing by lot. Where election was used, it was sometimes employed as a means of getting rid of the most patriotic elements. In the district of Roanne, at Saint-Just la Pendue, the sixteen patriots present in the assembly were all elected. At Duerne the constitutional curé was the first to be designated by the vote. At Durette the mayor and the *procureur*, known for their Jacobinism, and despite their age (forty-five and fifty-one respectively) were both chosen. At Faverolles, in the Indre, a clique formed to send off thirteen patriots, who were elected by acclamation.

It was not only counter-revolutionaries that might thus use election for their own purposes. Some municipalities used it, inversely, to remove persons suspected of royalism. Even later, in the summer of 1793, this strategem was used when a decree ordered a supplementary levy of 30,000 cavalry. The Marquis de Longueil wrote in his journal:

> The municipalities had the right of designation. The one at Saulzet made use of it to designate me for the levy. I rushed to my mother to ask her advice, and we decided that to escape the death that threatened us I must not hesitate to take refuge in the armies of the Republic. But we also resolved to spoil the triumph of the people of Saulzet, and the only way to do it was to go and enlist in the town of Grannat.

To avoid being elected some aristocrats who had preserved an influence in their community persuaded the mayors to do what was being done elsewhere: choose volunteers by lot. But drawing lots recalled the time of the kings. The peasants thought it restored the old militia.

The use of replacements allowed those who were designated to escape from serving. The poor were outraged, believing that no one could afford a replacement except the rich. A vast traffic developed between town and country. Carnot denounced it:

> Some men have the habit of selling themselves like cattle. They make a trade of deserting five or six times from successive battalions, and able-bodied men designated to serve get themselves replaced by the lame, the dissolute and the vicious.

Some agricultural communities sent emissaries to neighboring towns to buy replacements at 600 livres each; and these, who were often poor artisans, then in turn bought "volunteers" for 300.

Some communes opened subscriptions to raise money for replacements. The rich were asked to pay more than the poor. In the words of the local authorities at Péronne:

> Is it not a sacred duty to safeguard the holy laws of Equality? [Is it not disgraceful] that the indifferent rich man should slyly watch the patriot exhaust his strength and fortune while he himself contributes nothing from his effort or his fortune to the defense of *la Patrie*? These thoughts have induced the commune to order an addition of 6,405 livres to the sum of local expenses, to be paid only by citizens whose property tax exceeds 10 livres.

Replacements sometimes made up a third or a quarter of the contingent raised in a department. Such was the case of the district of Le Puy and the department of the Haute-Loire. But when it is possible to combine the figures for several departments, the proportion falls to 11 percent.

As the agitation mounted, the Convention decided to send out two of its members invested with extensive powers. Some local administrations then developed a method of recruitment without the disadvantages of the lottery or of election. The department of the Hérault ordered a direct and personal requisition. A committee named by commissioners from the Convention designated the citizens most likely to be useful to the Republic by their courage, character, and physical qualifications. The revolutionary authorities took the matter in hand. Gradually other departments or communes followed the example set by the Hérault. Paris raised 12,000 for service in the Vendée.

In some places the levy produced revolts. In the Indre-et-Loire, the Vienne, the Haute-Loire, and the Aveyron, force had to be used against the protesters. Often there were aristocrats in the background. The most serious troubles broke out in the West. In the Ille-et-Vilaine peasants assembled to cries of *Vive le Roi!* In the Morbihan, the villages of La Roche-Bernard and Rochefort were in the hands of insurgents, and Vannes was surrounded. At Cholet the peasants refused to take any part in the levy. Everywhere they raised scythes and pitchforks against the armed force sent against them. The war of the Vendée was beginning.

Everywhere the levy of 300,000 proceeded slowly. Sometimes battalions were still being formed after the *levée en masse* of the following summer. Some departments acted more rapidly, such as the Meurthe, which promptly furnished its contingent of 3,000 men. It was the same in the Doubs and the Haute-Saône. But a report of May 17 to the ministry of war showed only 96,895 who had actually departed, with 37,515 ready to depart, in the departments still under control of the Revolutionary authorities. In the northern departments there was a deficit of 28 percent, which reached 74 percent in the Alps and 79 percent in the Pyrenees. The most optimistic evaluations found only 150,000 men raised by the beginning of the summer. One battalion commander wrote:

> Most of the men of the 300,000 suffer from incurable maladies: some are imbeciles, others are one-eyed, hunchbacked, or lame. Some are too old, others too young or not strong enough to support the fatigues of war. Others are so short that their muskets are taller than they are.

An analysis of some contingents, such as those from Le Puy, the Haute-Loire, the Yonne, the Vienne, and the Charentes, shows that some communes sent a large minority of very young or overage men. Yet one study of the registers shows that 66 percent were from eighteen to twenty-five years old, the ages later called up by the Levy in Mass. But the same percentages were of short stature, less than 1.67 meters.[1]

The drop in the social level is what strikes the inquirer most

[1] In Anglo-American measurement, 5 feet 6 inches.

forcefully. In the volunteers of 1792 we still find lawyers, teachers, students, and employees of the state administration. In 1793 these occupations are represented only by exception. The great majority of the newly enrolled was composed of farm laborers and workers in the most ordinary trades. In the district of Poitiers 63 percent were peasants, and half of these were described as servants or day workers. In the Manche 68 percent were in these categories. In the Seine-et-Oise, in a contingent of 1,923 men, 1,268 or 65 percent were peasants, and more than half were servants or agricultural employees—carters, threshers, cowherds, shepherds, or mule drivers.

The towns furnished large contingents of men in humble occupations—ropemakers, cobblers, and makers of wooden shoes. In the first company of Narbonne, a quarter of the "volunteers" were wage workers.

The levy of 300,000, slowed down by the federalist revolt, went on after the Paris insurrection of June 1793, so that the Montagnards might well fear movements in the army in support of the expelled Girondins. There was not much ground for such fears. Testimonials of loyalty to the Convention flowed in. For example, the volunteers of the section Panthéon français (in Paris) wrote to express their opposition to the Girondin maneuvers. The 2nd battalion of the Loiret expressed its indignation at federalist activities at Orléans. Soldiers in the Army of the Rhine—for example, those of the 3rd battalion of the Saône-et-Loire—wrote home to their department administrators to reaffirm their zeal against troublemakers, or more precisely, those at Lyon. And what of the former royal army? Dumouriez, in defecting, was able to take with him only five hundred infantrymen, about the same number of cavalry, his headquarters staff, and eleven generals.

After April 9 certain members of the Convention were stationed on mission to the armies. Many of them were Montagnards, in a good position to rally the troops. With them the civil power affirmed its hold over the army. These envoys on mission drew a lesson from what they saw about them in the rural areas—that if one wished to raise new contingents for the Republic from the rural people, new measures were necessary, especially for the poorest of the peasantry. This meant an effective division of common lands into small parcels, and a definitive aboliton of feudalism. These things were done in July 1793. The Conventionnels understood also that, if victory was to be achieved, there must be an obligatory military service for all, and an end to a system of volunteering that produced inequalities. They saw also the consequences of a defective organization. There were suspected nobles, but there were also non-noble officers who had obtained their commands by intrigue, by the passing generosity of a few bottles of wine, or by exhibiting more or less crude tastes and emotions like those of their troops. And finally, the fear of Caesarism persisted. To oppose it, the spirit of the Revolution had to pervade an army augmented by mass recruiting.

This national and revolutionary army arose in the crisis of the summer of 1793.

• • •

PART TWO

The Sans-culottes, the Revolutionary Government, and the Transformation of the Army (Summer 1793 to Summer 1794)

Valmy and Jemappes were victories for the Republic, but then came Neerwinden, a defeat. After a brief success the Revolution was again in danger. The Austrians retook Mainz and occupied Valenciennes. Le Quesnoy and Landrecies were the last fortified places protecting Paris; if they fell the future of the Republic would be gravely threatened. The Piedmontese were attacking in the Alps and the Spanish stood at the gates of Perpignan. Within France the Girondin rebels in Normandy and Brittany might unite with insurgents in the Vendée. Bordeaux, Marseille, and Lyon rose up against the Convention. Toulon and Corsica were in the hands of the British.

If there had been victory for democracy in 1792, was it not because the people had risen to reinforce the troops by mass action? If there were now reverses, was it not that the fighting mass in town and country had been allowed to languish? Was it not also that the generals, no longer closely watched by the armed people, had yielded to their natural inclinations to treason? The Paris sansculottes answered "Yes." They had driven out the Gironde in three days of insurrection, May 31 to June 2, 1793. Of the Montagnards that they brought into power, they now demanded Terror—political, social, and military terror, for the three were interconnected.

Political terror meant the pursuit of suspects—not only aristocrats but their lukewarm allies who would end the fighting by compromise with the enemy. Social terror meant pursuit of the aristocracy of wealth, the monopolists and the speculators. A tiny commune in the Somme wrote to the Convention in September 1793 that the "people,"

> that is, the unfortunate class in the Republic, must be invested with an authority that both honors them and lets them watch over the maneuvers of these new rich, who would end up by making us slaves indifferent to the public need. . . . Then the rich man would humble his pride before the poor man. . . . Then, with peace restored in all hearts, and the people gaining new confidence, they would arm themselves with a new strength in defense of the country and the Republic, which could count instantly on two million citizens ready to march at the first signal against enemies without and evil-wishers within.

By forced contributions from the rich, and by price controls, the poor man would be able to leave for the army assured of subsistence for his dependents.

Military terror meant that the people should again rise in mass, take their destiny in their own hands, be in the army and be in control of it. But both in civilian life and in the army there was opposition to this double call for a mass rising and a purge of the officers. In the sections of Paris and in the departments, some of the lesser bourgeoisie, urban and rural, denounced the idea as ruinous to the economic life of the whole country.

The Montagnards hesitated. Robespierre and his friends were afraid of cutting themselves off from the bourgeoisie by precipitous action. They were ready neither for a mass rising nor for the economic planning that the situation required and the sans-culottes cried out for. From an equality of rights the sans-culottes had moved on to a new demand for an equality of enjoyments. They wanted access for all to small-property ownership, with the State intervening against the concentration of land in the hands of a few. They thought that *la Patrie* owed this much to her children.

Politically, the sans-culottes were partisans of direct democracy. Universal suffrage once exercised, and the Convention assembled, they had no intention of leaving all power in the hands of those who governed. They meant to attend meetings of their sections and popular societies to discuss the laws and to control the action of deputies that they regarded as their mandatories and, if necessary, dismiss them.

This attitude had its consequences in their way of seeing the army. For them the army was democracy in arms. It should be composed of sans-culottes, with patriot officers and no more nobles or suspects in positions of command. Soldiers, like all citizens, should have the right to assemble, read the patriotic press, control the action of their leaders, create a new hierarchy, and spread revolutionary war everywhere, a war of extermination of adversaries. For this sans-culotte spirit to impregnate the troops, the army must be unified by "amalgamation."

The Committee of Public Safety, of which Robespierre became a member in July 1793, was not hostile to all demands of the sans-culottes. It became converted, temporarily, to the idea of a controlled economy to save the army as well as the Revolution itself. It accepted the necessity, for a certain length of time, of excluding noble and suspected officers. It agreed to the amalgamation. But the Committee opposed direct democracy in either civilian society or the army. It held that the war required subordination of all persons to a centralized government that could take necessary decisions in secret. The army should not be a forum for discussion, but a docile instrument in the hands of the government. The Committee feared also a manipulation of the sans-culottes by *en-*

ragés such as Jacques Roux, Leclerc, and Varlet who had arisen to contest its power.

The Committee of Public Safety therefore played a subtle game. Relying on the sans-culotte movement, which grew in strength during the summer of 1793, the Committee used it to consolidate its authority and overcome the moderate element in the Convention. But the Committee was determined not to be overwhelmed by the sans-culottes.

The Jacobins accepted the mass rising, but transformed it in August into an organized requisition. The popular movement in Paris continued. An insurrection on September 4 and 5 called for adoption of terrorist measures. The Jacobins took the side of the insurrectionists. One result was the creation of a "revolutionary army" of sans-culottes who scoured the countryside in search of provisions for both country and town. A national scale of maximum prices was instituted for grain and flour, and then for other necessities and for wages. A law of suspects was enacted.

Thus outflanking the *enragés*, the Committee of Public Safety canalized the popular movement and extended its control over the Paris sections. It worked for a strict subordination of the army to itself. Hébert and the ultra revolutionaries, who claimed to be spokesmen for the sans-culottes, stirred up opposition to the Committee during the winter and spring of 1794. They were unsuccessful. The Committee, after a decree of 14 Frimaire Year II (December 4, 1793), held the levers of command as an agency of the Convention. Playing on the opposition between Dantonists or Indulgents on the one hand and ultra revolutionaries on the other, the Committee destroyed them both. Under surveillance by the "representatives on mission" (who were members of the Convention), the army became an effective instrument of war, and at the same time a school of Jacobinism.

There were thus two periods in the formation of a national and revolutionary army. During the summer and autumn of 1793 the "revolutionizing" of the army was the great aim of the sans-culottes. Their efforts often coincided with those of the Jacobins, who, however, rejected the idea of a "deliberative" army whose chiefs would not receive orders exclusively from the government. From the autumn of 1793 to the summer of 1794 the army was subjected to the Jacobins. The requisition, or Levy in Mass, went on through both periods; beginning in late August, it continued throughout the year 1794, and was the joint accomplishment of the sans-culottes and the Jacobins.

CHAPTER V

• • •

The *Levée en Masse* and
Its Incorporation (August 1793)

1. THE IDEA OF THE *LEVÉE EN MASSE* AND ITS APPLICATION

"All the Frenchmen must rise and march together!"[1] In July the idea of a mass rising surged through patriotic circles in Paris and the provinces. Journalists close to the sans-culottes such as Aristide Valcour, *énragés* like Jacques Roux, Hébert in his *Père Duchesne*, all cried repeatedly that all able-bodied men should rush forward wherever there was danger.

In the threatened regions all men were called to arms. Patriots at Lille concerted with those of neighboring departments to bring on a rising to fall "in mass, like the Gauls, on the hordes of brigands" and exterminate them. At Bapaume in the Pas-de-Calais the district authorities ordered the municipalities "to have all men able to bear arms hold themselves ready to march on the first summons." After the assassination of Marat, the demand for a mass rising echoed more loudly in the towns and in the army. A grenadier named Pocral of the 9th battalion of the Seine-Inférieure wrote on July 24: "There should be a departure in mass in all of France to avenge Marat." On August 6 the representatives on mission Lacoste and Guyardin ordered the department of the Vosges

---

[1] The sense requires that *levée* be sometimes translated as a "rising" and sometimes as a "raising" or "levy" of troops; in general, the term "Levy in Mass" will be used, though admittedly awkward in English.

to requisition all unmarried men and widowers without children from sixteen to forty years old. On the 18th the district of Sarrebourg invited its communes to be "in readiness" for the first signal; all citizens were to depart with weapons and six days of provisions.

The signal was sometimes given. Thus a lieutenant Niellon announced in a letter written from the Army of the Rhine: "We are getting men in great numbers, all the departments are sending them, and from the 25,000 or 30,000 that we were our army may have 130,000 today, most of them indeed without much experience, but generally burning with a desire to hit the enemy with cold steel."

The representatives Ruamps and Milhaud reported that the tocsin had sounded in the district of Wissenbourg, where the citizens had armed themselves with pikes, scythes, and guns to pour "in mass" on the enemy. On August 27 they noted the ardor of these patriots: "One man alone killed seventeen Austrians, another one nine; women threw themselves into the mêlée with muskets." A soldier of the 1st battalion of the Doubs wrote on August 29: "Peasants flung themselves on the enemy like madmen; they hamstrung the cavalry horses so that horses and riders fell like hailstones." In September 1,200 men from Laon set off on their own initiative to stop the enemy at Guise.

When delegates from all the primary assemblies in France gathered in Paris for acceptance of the new constitution, they pressed the Convention to authorize a mass rising. Taken up by deputies of the Paris sections on August 16, the idea at first had a strong political content. There was to be an "insurrection" of the people swarming out in the van of the army. In such extreme peril the people resumed their sovereignty, and hence the arms that were its symbol. The people would dictate the mode of combat: unceasing attack and total destruction of the foe.

The term *mass* implied not only numbers but community of thought among the men who were to go. "This terrible mass," once rolling in action, would consist of "all sans-culottes of the

Republic"; it would fan out in "republican columns to cover the soil of liberty." The term *rising* was a reminder of the colossal figure that symbolized France in popular prints, who with quick, powerful movements liberated himself from the chains of slavery and hurled his captors away. As a defensive reflex, a will to revenge and destruction, the rising was a spasmodic effort requiring citizens to forget all else except to save the Republic. It would be an effort of short duration. "A week of enthusiasm could do more than seven years of combat," said Sébastien Lacroix. The representatives also promised hesitant peasants that the rising would not last long: it would only be a "helping hand" to the army.

Responsible leaders denounced the utopianism in such a "tumultuous" movement. The legal officer of the department of the Manche observed: "Why call up a multitude of men hastily assembled and wholly unskilled in the use of arms? Would it not be better to have a well-trained and disciplined army?" In Paris Chaumette asked how one could arm, equip and feed such a large number when necessities were in short supply for the existing troops. How could the country live if those most suited for industry and agriculture were under the colors? For Robespierre the mass rising was a project for disorganization and so inspired by the counterrevolution. What was needed, he thought, were patriotic soldiers and virtuous generals.

The project was saved with the assistance of Danton, when he proposed that the number of men to march should be in relation to the available amount of arms and bread. On August 23 the Convention accordingly decreed:

> From this moment and until all enemies are driven from the territory of the Republic all French persons are placed in permanent requisition for the service of the armies. The young men will go to battle; married men will forge arms and transport provisions; women will make tents and clothing and serve in the hospitals; children will shred old linen; old men will have themselves carried to public places to arouse the

courage of warriors and preach hatred of kings and unity of the Republic.

Thus the Levy in Mass became a requisition, which made soldiers only of unmarried men and widowers without children; the soldiers would range in age from eighteen to twenty-five. As an integral part of the Terror, the requisition would be, for many of the French who were simply waiting to see what happened, the moment of decisive political choice.

To find arms, clothing and equipment, foresee the places of encampment, provide for subsistence, and arrange with the generals for assignment of contingents to the various armies and forts was henceforth the main occupation of all agents of government stationed anywhere near the armies. Below the representatives on mission it was first of all the departmental directories that had to watch over the execution of the law. These bodies, often composed of only moderate patriots, tried to unload the responsibility on the military authorities. They had to be reminded that the battalions of draftees[2] were not "military" until they were organized and had been reviewed by the war commissioners.

The levies went ahead rapidly. Thus at Poitiers on September 7 the local authorities issued a proclamation to the people. The call to arms was heard in the streets on the morning of the 9th, inviting the citizens to assemble in their sections. There a committee appointed by the municipality drew up the list of draftees and proceeded to consider exceptions. On the next day, to the sound of the tocsin, the draftees assembled in the public square. A provisional leader was chosen, and the men were made ready for the road. A military committee began to requisition muskets and clothing, and to place orders with artisans.

At Châtellerault, a courier arrived with orders for the requisition on September 8 at five o'clock in the afternoon. For two

---

[2] The requisitioned men were called *requis* at the time, and the term is used by the author in distinction from *conscrits*. There were no "conscripts" until the conscription law of 1798, and *requis* is translated here and elsewhere as "draftee."

hours members of the district directory, aided by volunteers, made copies of letters to be sent to surrounding municipalities. At seven o'clock a deputation from the Friends of Liberty arrived to offer their services in any work necessary for the requisition. A committee on defense and security was formed, made up of judges and local officials. On the next day sextons of the local churches, helped by volunteers, sounded the tocsin for citizens to meet beneath the tree of Liberty. On the 10th the first contingents of peasants from the surrounding countryside arrived.

Levy agents, named by the departmental directories and the representatives on mission, were the true mainsprings of the requisition. Receiving 300 livres for expenses, these agents were sometimes notables such as justices of the peace in the Loiret or a constitutional bishop who traveled through rural parts of the Berry. Most often they were ordinary artisans or ex-soldiers. In the Charente-Inférieure the principal agent was a man named Fischer, a former battalion commander of the 77th Infantry, and an ardent Jacobin. At Bourg-en-Bresse, Bon l'Aîné, and Gervais, former soldiers were chosen as secondary agents. They visited the local municipalities, assembled the young men, and consulted the baptismal records to learn the age of those designated to depart. Some went to the Catholic Mass, sure to find there the largest number of such men liable to the draft.

Review councils operated at the canton and district level. An inspector measured the recruits, a surgeon examined them, and a local official quickly settled with the surgeon the cases of those to be discharged. The law made no mention of required height, but the authorities excluded those who were too short. The height of the men taken varied between departments, but in general was about 4 feet 8 inches (1.51 meters).[3] The review councils had to be vigilant, for some draftees pretended to physical disabilities. In the Rhône, for example, draftees resorted to village magicians, like a certain Mignard, who used drugs to transform bodily parts to

[3] In Anglo-American measurement, 5 feet.

make them seem "broken or worn out." The councils were subjected to many pressures, as at Pionsat, in the Puy-de-Dôme,
where the Jeuge brothers owed their discharge to intervention by
their father, a local official. In the same department, at La Cellette,
two young relatives of the levy agent were excused. Threats came
from the Convention; malingerers were to be imprisoned until the
peace. In some places the popular societies purged the councils or,
as in the Gard, replaced them with committees made up of the
fathers of soldiers.

The law authorized no replacements, but some districts accepted them. At Montdidier on October 21, Louis Demancourt,
aged fifty, appeared at the council proposing to serve as a replacement for his son, who he said was not well. The draftees, wanting
to have an experienced man among them, supported his request,
which the council granted. At Auxy-la-Réunion, Gaspard Wallard
was replaced by his brother Jules, aged twenty-six. At Amiens,
Jean-Baptiste Bullot, more than twenty-five years old, replaced his
younger brother. In the Marne, Pierre Le Plaige remained at home
with his father, who worked sixty acres, while his younger
brother, of less than the legal age, departed.

In principle all men from eighteen to twenty-five were requisitioned, but the law carried with it a list showing the minimum
number of battalions expected from each department. Department administrators therefore felt justified in discharging draftees
as soon as this number was attained. Other mistakes were made
with the age classes. One representative of the people called up all
bachelors and widowers without children between eighteen and
fifty. Sometimes the popular societies wanted to requisition all unmarried citizens from sixteen to forty. Some representatives, including Tallien, Ysabeau, and Baudot, thinking that the levy
should fall less heavily on poor farm workers than on the rich,
stipulated that for the "rich" the age limit should be extended to
thirty-five.

Between the time of the levy of 300,000 and the decree of August 23, some representatives and generals had ordered requisi-

tions that caused confusion for the authorities at the time of the Levy in Mass. In the Marne, for example, an order of the representatives, dating from before August 23, had called up all men from eighteen to forty years old. The representatives held to their decision. In the Lot, on October 19, widowers without children were drafted up to age thirty-five. In the Gard, an order of August 31, signed by the department authorities, took bachelors and widowers without children from sixteen to forty years old, "in view of the urgent needs of the Republic." The presence of men not of the required age can be explained also by volunteering. Poverty, impulse, and also patriotism pushed some men into joining. Pierre Herbulot, a cloth cutter, aged thirty-three, presented himself on October 30 at Saint-Denis, in the Seine; he had no work or means of subsistence, and wished to enlist. A volunteer from the Ariège later wrote to his parents, in 1794, asking them to excuse him for having "acted thoughtlessly." In the Saône-et-Loire a young boy asked to enlist because he was a patriot and wanted to fight along with his older brother already in the Army of the Alps.

The law exempted married men. A veritable rush to marriage followed in some regions. In the Landes the department authorities announced that citizens marrying after publication of the law in their district towns were and remained liable to the levy. Despite the law, some men who were long married or were widowers with children were included. One man, who married a pregnant woman after publication of the law, applying for exemption, asked whether it was "not legal status but paternity that makes a marriage?" When the question was put to Carnot he answered in the affirmative, and men in his position were exempted. Others, fathers of several children, had been recruited by various generals shortly before the law of August 23. They protested, but were required to remain in the army, "because in an emergency all should serve." At Albi, on September 30, when the number of draftees was insufficient, sixteen married men and fathers were taken to fill the contingent.

Some draftees were indignant that fathers should be excused.

They thought it a favor accorded to the rich youth who could found a family at an earlier age. At Chateaulin in the Finistère, the district officials declared that "married men are subject to the requisition; if they are let alone for the time being, they will have their turn when the need of the country requires it."

The law allowed no exemptions except for age, infirmity, or family situation. But other exceptions were sometimes requested. In the Seine and the Pas-de-Calais, there were families that asked for exemption for young men who had always been regarded as "saints"; one was even said to have risen from the dead. In some cases exemptions seemed unavoidable. Local officials could with difficulty be replaced. Arms makers were necessary. The Committee of Public Safety decided that arms makers, ironworkers, and men employed by the army should be exempt. There were resulting abuses. In the district of Brest there were 2,496 draftees, but only 400 were actually inducted, because 500 were sailors, 1,248 employed in construction works for the Republic, and the rest unqualified.

Well-to-do persons tried every means to get their employees and workers exempted. At Caen, in April 1794, the levy agent wrote that his office was overwhelmed by requests for exemptions from the rich farmers. At Hardinghem in the Pas-de-Calais, a district administrator whose father owned a coal mine managed to circumvent the representatives of the people and obtain exemption for his father's workers. The father profited by paying lower wages to exempted men. Another way of escaping service was to find employment in the military transports, from which desertion was easy. Or one could take a job with an army paymaster. One of them, Cillart, had eight clerks of whom six were draftees. And there was always the search for the "republican saltpeter" needed for gunpowder. Many general adjutants denounced young men who said they were so occupied, but who in fact remained peacefully at home.

Sporadic exemptions were authorized by representatives of the people and even by generals. At Caen the bakers were excused. At

Lorient actors obtained a dispensation in November because "the theater, which has always by rights been a school of morals, is now the only school of patriotism, because a national education is not yet established." At Neville, in the Loiret, many individuals called themselves millers, an exempted occupation. Local goverments requested exemption for notaries, because the notary was the only man who held the key to the different regulations that kept pouring out. Even some generals protected young men from the requisition by taking them as domestic servants. Such exemptions irritated the draftees, who said that it was always the rich who benefited.

If some tried to escape the requisition others—specifically, nobles and refractory priests—used it as a refuge. Foreigners were suspect, especially those from countries with which France was at war. They enlisted to avoid possible imprisonment. Thus we find a Dutchman and four Austrians on the enlistment roll at Orléans.

With the contingents formed, the question was where to send them. The law prescribed that three-quarters should go to garrison towns, and the remaining one-quarter be used to fill vacancies in the battalions. But the orders were confused. The district of Vesoul, for example, received word from both the Army of the West and the Army of the Rhine, both of which said they expected draftees from that district. The confusion was long lasting; as late as August 1794 the district of Aurillac was instructed to send its contingent in three different directions. The intervention of engineering officers upset some plans when they took masons, stonecutters, and carpenters as they needed them.

Plans prepared by the agents could also be changed by the wishes of draftees. The law allowed those offering to equip themselves with a horse at their own expense to serve in the cavalry. Battalions of dragoons were thus constituted, such as the Volunteers of the Tarn. The popular societies saw here another way for the rich to postpone their departure, and claimed that such mounted units were composed only of sons of merchants and government employees. The law also gave the draftee a choice of going into the navy or coastal batteries, for which the agent was to draw up special lists. The agents reported a sudden taste for this kind of service, which they said was used to escape the requisition. Men sent to the coast guard could return home after purchasing replacements.

Most often the draftees remained without moving for weeks and months, sometimes in their own district town. To keep them from a "pernicious idleness," they were set to learning how to use their weapons. Camps were organized to "lick the recruits into shape." According to the Jacobins of Niort: "We all know how to load, aim, and fire a musket, but that is of no use unless our movements are regular and uniform; if you move too much you will cause trouble for your neighbors, and if you don't move promptly your defense will be too weak." Generals were sometimes asked to send noncommissioned officers to instruct the draftees. In other places the local governments hired ex-soldiers for this purpose, paying them 100 to 150 livres a month. They drilled the draftees twice a day; for the rest of the time the draftees did guard duty or busied themselves on works of public utility.

2. THE RESISTANCE TO THE *LEVÉE EN MASSE*

While the sans-culottes of Paris and frontier towns and villages responded with enthusiasm to the call of the Convention, there arose, in rural parts of the interior, a resistance that showed itself in draft evasion. The authorities attributed it to the same causes as in March 1793: the counter-revolution was corrupting the peasants. "Muscadins" from the towns, they said, went about telling the villagers that the whole republican regime was delivered over to anarchy but would soon be overturned by foreign troops, so that order would be restored. Representatives on mission also blamed refractory priests for using their pastoral office to dissuade fathers and mothers from letting their children go. In one canton in the Rhône, according to the representatives, a group of draftees, worked on by refractory priests, had cried, "No religion, no soldiers!" They called themselves "forest boys" and defenders of the Catholic faith. Bands of them cut across the surrounding country.

But counter-revolutionaries developed their activities only where circumstances favored them, and local officials again told the representatives that peasant hostility came from their fear that the land would die. "What would become of me and my animals," asked one peasant in the Puy-de-Dôme, "if I am left all alone? Even if you leave me the oldest and the youngest of my servants I will have to sell my livestock at any price I can get, and leave my crops to rot in the fields." It was hard to be swayed by the heated urgings of a representative of the Revolutionary Government who said "there is no more time for talk, we must act, the people have risen in mass regardless of fields and meadows for *la Patrie!*" But what would become of the vines if they were not pruned, or the soil if it was not turned? The representatives, pressed by the demands of the generals for reinforcements, first refused to listen to the peasants and then stigmatized their attitude. The Revolution, they said, had enriched the peasants not only by suppressing the tithes and feudal dues but also by the rise in prices. In return, they should now aid the Republic. But the peasants could not be treated as a single block. There was a difference between the well-off farmer and the poor man who worked on shares. The sons of the latter protested that their father had no other help; if they left him his fields would have to be abandoned. "Isn't it enough to serve the country by supplying our brothers in arms with something to eat?"

The village municipalities supported these objections. In the Saône-et-Loire, for example, they declared that work in the fields had deteriorated "since a year ago when the young men went off to rescue the country. It seems that the war will not end soon. We hear always of victory but we are losing a lot of people, which causes great consternation for families with only the old and the infirm to cultivate the fields."

District agents made the same appeals. They asked that the Levy in Mass be rescinded as disastrous to the countryside, and argued that if the law were strictly enforced thousands of workers, indispensable to their families and for rural labor, would fill up the prisons. An agent in the Marne wrote, "Every day I hear these heart-rending pleas for exemption from fathers and mothers whose livelihood depends on their children; and their number is greater than is imagined."

There were indeed not enough men. It was not only the Levy in Mass that took them. To the Levy in Mass were added various other levies that went on from March to September and beyond. Thus in the Dordogne the levy of 300,000, begun in April, continued into the autumn. The representatives on mission in the southern departments, on August 13, ordered a levy of 12,000 selected men which was carried out in October. A levy of volunteer cavalry went on from April 1793 until March 1794. In the Haut-Rhin, at Morsvillars, men were still drawing lots in the summer of 1793 for a levy ordered in the preceding spring. In the Haute-Loire, the levy of 30,000 cavalry, decreed in July, did not begin until September and lasted for a year. In several departments the exceptional levy for the war in the Vendée was still in progress in October 1793. In June men were levied in the Haute-Vienne to block a counter-revolutionary coup; the resulting battalion was still recruiting in September, and so competing with the levy of 300,000 and the raising of 30,000 cavalry.

Thus, by the autumn of 1793 a man who worked a few acres saw the disappearance not only of his younger son who had just turned eighteen, but also of an older son who had been taken by some exceptional levy ordered two or three months before. For the poor peasant the burden was unbearable. He thought it contrary to "sacred equality." The Levy in Mass was an important catalyst in arousing the poor against the rich.

It is well known that from 1789 to 1793 the peasantry remained united in opposition to the feudal dues. Antagonisms within the rural communities appeared when the confiscated properties were sold and the communal lands were divided. Solidarity was also compromised by the food shortages of the summer of 1792, and when the poor tried to block the free movement of grains. In 1793 the feudal and seigneurial dues were definitively abolished when indemnification was no longer required. A tie that had held together the poorer and the wealthier peasants was broken. The poor complained that abolition benefited their well-to-do neighbors more than the little man who had only a tiny parcel of land. If the poor peasant tried to rent a piece of land, he faced rising rents, and accused the owner of including in the lease the amount of the tithe formerly paid to the curé. Moreover, in some regions the concentration of farms in a few hands continued, so that less land was available for those of small means. The protests of the latter were supported by the sans-culottes, who had come to believe that high prices were due to the way in which land ownership was distributed.

In the autumn and winter of 1793, when officials called up the sons of poor peasants, they were told that they should first call the sons of the rich, "who have always been reluctant to defend their property themselves." Men who possessed nothing refused to go, "on the pretext," as one official reported, "that they had no property and no interest in defending the property of others." In the Sarthe, the poor were heard to say that they alone were supporting the Republic and were the only ones forced into the army because they had no money to buy exemptions. One such, named Janois, at Mamers in October, declared that he would not go "unless all the rich young men also marched in defense of the Republic." His comrades applauded, so that the village officials for a while were afraid of sedition. In the Rhône, when the representative Girard, on his own authority, decided that men with appropriate skills could remain at home working for the gunsmiths, there was a general hue and cry. The order would favor the rich, "who, with their money, would protect their sons by placing them in the workshops." The local officials supported the petitions of their fellow citizens in this matter.

In the towns as in the open country the poor insisted that local officials should put themselves at the head of departing contingents. Thus, at Châtellerault, despite "their desire to remain at their posts," the district administrators "yielded to the wishes of the people." One of them, Martineau, wrote on September 11, that "on the angry demand of rural citizens who would not decide to go before seeing us go first, and to avoid a frightful disorder, I am going immediately although the law requires me to stay at my post." At Rambervillers, in the Vosges, citizen Baudot was accused of inciting the draftees not to comply with the requisition until officials and administrators of the nationalized properties were enrolled.

The antagonism between rich and poor was redoubled by a conflict between town and country in some departments, as in the Ain, where the farmers complained that

> draftees in the country are doing necessary work, while those in the towns have nothing to do and live with their parents, for example those who have no job or skill, or the sons of bourgeois who have studied in school, are well fed and well maintained and are just looking for daily amusements. These are the ones you ought to requisition to save the country.

Hostility to the levy grew as the time of waiting for departure lengthened. The draftees pointed out the contradiction between promises that the levy would be of short duration and the prolonged inactivity in which they now found themselves. Time was needed to arm and clothe so many men. Some draftees learned that they would depart without military insignia. So there was another ground for protest: if they were captured, would they not be treated as mere partisans or irregulars?

Arms were lacking. Peasants concealed their firearms, which, when discovered, were hard for the gunsmith to transform into weapons of war capable of holding a bayonet. It was unusual to see, as at Calais, the draftees depart "armed with good muskets to bash the faces of aristocrats all over the world." On September 30, for 2,600 men in the three battalions of Saint-Quentin, assembled at Guise, there were only 600 muskets and no cartridges. On October 17 the 2nd battalion of the district of Vervins left for camp at La Bohérie; not 1 man had a musket. At Sainte-Menehoud there was an average of 20 muskets for 100 men. At La Rochelle, on November 11, of 1,722 men only 714 were armed. In the Calvados half the arms given to the draftees were unusable.

Rather than keep the draftees in their home localities, where their presence only contributed to the rise in prices, despite the legal maximum, the authorities often preferred to send them off armed with pikes, or sometimes even with pitchforks or scythes. Some draftees, as at Montdidier, objected to going without muskets. If they were sent anyway, the generals refused to receive them, saying that they had no idea what to do with unarmed men. So they dispersed, to enlarge the bands of draft evaders that began to be noticed from one end of France to the other.

Evaders remained most often at home, protected by their parents and neighbors. When enforcement officers sought them out, they gathered into bands. Hiding in forests and mountains, their numbers were increased by deserters. The generals reported to the ministry that their armies were melting away because the volunteers of 1792, and even those raised by the levy of 300,000, regarded their enlistment as expiring with the approach of winter. Some men went into the hospitals, where they managed to obtain certificates of leave to escape their pursuers. When exposed, they pretended to be rejoining their units but in fact wandered as nomads and so mingled with the evaders.

In some places evasion developed into open revolts, which were only transitory with rare exceptions, and failed to grow into persistent "little Vendées." Disturbances caused by the requisition began first in the west, where they added to the ranks of the numbers of the Chouans.[4] Such troubles were reported by the representative with the Army of the Côtes-de-Cherbourg, and on November

---

[4] *Chouans* and *chouannerie* refer to the insurgency against the republican government that went on for several years in Brittany.

18 a riot broke out at Lesnevan in the Finistère, where the patriot mayor was wounded and the army sent two hundred men to restore calm. In the autumn insurrections were reported in the Tarn, where draft resisters pillaged the homes of patriots and uprooted the trees of Liberty. It required two hundred national guards and seventeen gendarmes to regain control. In the Vosges, at Rambervillers, at a ceremony held for the departure of the draftees, a member of the local municipality provoked a rebellion in the company in which he had been inducted. Local officials and national guards had to intervene when a contingent rebelled at Limoges. It was also in the winter of 1793 that half a battalion of draftees in the Ariège revolted and assaulted the gendarmes. Draftees at Angers rebelled in February 1794. Troubles arose from the Levy in Mass in the summer of 1794 in the Corrèze, where bands of draft evaders held control of the rural areas.

3. MEASURES TO SUPPRESS DRAFT EVASION

In its struggle against evasion the government employed a mixed policy of coercion, civic education and social measures. All these had been demanded by the sans-culottes and the Jacobins, and the popular societies assisted the representatives on mission in their implementation.

Coercion was first exercised through the local authorities, which were urged to enforce the law strictly, post lists of evaders on the doors of municipal offices, and then hunt them out. For sans-culottes and Jacobins, a republican could be recognized by his force of character, and a royalist by cowardice; the evader, being a coward, was a counter-revolutionary. Militants in the Ariège demanded on September 5 that evaders and their parents should be responsible with their property for treasonous behavior. Two weeks later the property of refractory draftees was already being confiscated in the Jura. On 1 Nivôse Year II (December 21, 1793) the Convention decided to impose the death penalty for talk against the requisition. Local communities were held collectively responsible for concealing evaders. They were forced to provide relief for needy parents of soldiers. The mayors were also threatened; those in the Pas-de-Calais were warned that they bore the first responsibility for evasion. "You are an exception in the Republic," wrote the representatives on mission. "Your battalions must be complete. If the law is not executed within a week you will be responsible to the Republic in whose name we now address you."

Then came the *garnissaires*, soldiers who installed themselves and obtained bed and board in the families of evaders. They appeared in the Hérault, the Morbihan, the Tarn, and the Lot. Sometimes all inhabitants of the commune were obliged to provide money also. Forming mobile columns, and joined by members of the national guard who were the fathers of soldiers, they scoured the country to ferret out the fugitives. Soldiers on leave, like the battalion commander Lhullier, lent aid to these expeditions. Whole battalions, like the 4th of the Aube, alerted by the sans-culottes and Jacobins, announced that they were coming some day to demand a reckoning not only from hoarders who starved their families but from sluggards who refused the draft. Meanwhile, they said, they would appeal to their brothers in the "revolutionary army." These "revolutionary armies" were paramilitary formations of armed sans-culottes, created in the autumn of 1793 to counteract hoarding, supply the army and pursue suspects; they also assisted the popular societies in tracking down evaders and deserters.

Along with coercive measures, the popular societies used psychological action. The peasants had to be told the meaning of the war again and again. For this purpose letters from patriotic soldiers were read aloud and commented on. Here is an example, written by an officer:

> Let the father whose love for his son has overcome for a moment his manly vigor and republican courage yet press him to his heart, and say: Go and fulfill your task, and remember

that this paternal embrace will be the last if you leave the army before tyranny recognizes your independence and mine. Let him say also, pointing to his house and field: Here is your property, remember that you go to defend it, and never forget that a good man owes himself to his country.

Sans-culottes and Jacobins composed letters addressed to their fellow citizens and posted them on walls. Three themes were intermingled.

The first theme was the national army in which everyone served. Old injustices were recalled—the favoritism involved in drawing lots for the former militia, the arbitrary decisions made by sub-delegates, the money that had allowed the rich to stay out of the lottery. The new equality in the service was stressed. It was noted "that plowmen are soldiers and soldiers do not disdain the honor of the plow. The soldier's trade was once thought dishonoring; now it is an honorable profession." Equality in recruitment and equality in the command structure: All citizens could henceforth reach the highest grades by merit and talent. Officers and men were all commoners and regarded each other as brothers. Equality finally in mode of discipline and the course of daily life: "The Republic esteems brave sans-culottes and provides food and clothing for your children."

The second theme was protection of the gains of the Revolution. Among them the one most often repeated was the "Sacred Equality" that reigned in society as in the army. There were no more nobles "who used to despise you, crush you, take shots at you as if you were rabbits even when you did no wrong." No more nobles "who thought themselves made of a different clay than you, and did you nothing but harm." No more priests and their allies "who filched your purse for masses and prayers that had no effect either for good or for bad." No more king, "a miserable personage that you never saw and who grew fat on your sweat and your substance. He never loved you, for there is love only between equals, not for slaves." No more tax officers, lawyers, parlements, and law courts. "These rogues" are now in league with "the Austrians, Hanoverians, and English coming to murder you."

The third theme was the liberation of the land. It was relieved forever from the burden on it of feudalism, seigneurial rights, and the tithe.

But all these benefits of the Revolution were endangered by the vast conspiracy of aristocrats and their foreign satellites. If the Levy in Mass was unsuccessful, these enemies would prevail and would, without doubt, spare no one. We find the following on a poster displayed in four widely separated departments: "They will take off your sons, your daughters, your wives, and your possessions." They were "cannibals who cut off the hands that planted the tree of Liberty." "They cut off the breasts of mothers nursing their infants. They tear out the entrails of pregnant women and slit the throats of old men." Ruin followed wherever they passed.

The conclusion of this poster was an appeal for unity: Other Frenchmen were already in arms fighting for all; those remaining must rush instantly to join them, and demonstrate fraternity in a war that was indispensable for survival of the whole nation.

The assembly of the draftees for departure was the occasion for a civic festival, well organized to touch popular feeling and promote a collective psychology. Early in the morning the draftees were invited into the "communal hall." The town or village officers welcomed them as drums and fifes played the Marseillaise, and the refrain was sung by the audience. Other patriotic war songs were sung while the whole gathering left the hall. A procession formed, to be the living symbol of close union between the people and the army, and so act out the clauses of the decree of August 23. At the head of the parade came a detachment of soldiers from the former royal army. Next came the national guard, preceding a banner carried by delegates from the primary assemblies. A second part of the parade was made up of old men, surrounding the draftees; on the preceding night the old men had heard read to them the decree of August 23, with comments, and they knew that they were to preach hatred of kings and unity of the Republic. They were followed at a distance by members of the popular societies and by girls wearing tricolor sashes. Fathers of families closed the procession, surrounded by men from the armed forces.

To the sound of a cannon, all paraded through the streets to the public square. There, around the tree of Liberty, the commissioner in charge of the Levy had the draftees draw up in their companies. Their elected leaders were publicly recognized. Then the legal papers confirming feudal rights were brought up and burned while the crowd sang patriotic songs. With silence restored, the flag advanced. In its folds could be seen the inscription: "The French people rising against tyrants." A municipal officer touched the flag with the tables of the Constitution, as if to purify and sacralize it. Then the representative of the people, or in his absence the district president, delivered a speech that usually ended somewhat as follows:

Citizens, the administration entrusts you with this standard of Liberty, which declares the French rising against tyrants. Hold firm; your glory and the country's salvation depend on it. Imitate your brothers in arms now crowning themselves with laurels, and be resolved to fight to the death the brigands who befoul our territory.

Draftees and spectators all raised their hands to heaven and cried, "We swear it! We will defend our flag until death and not see our homes again until we have cleansed the French territory from barbarians." Cries of *Vive la République* and *Vive la Montagne* mingled with the sound of artillery salvos. All joined in singing the hymn of liberty, and the civil authorities, followed by the draftees, passed beneath the folds of the flag. Fraternal dancing with the farandole and the carmagnole brought an end to this civic communion.

During such ceremonies the Jacobins described the nation as a free and fraternal community of equals who helped one another. In the fall and winter of 1793 the patriotic version of the Last

Supper did not yet exist. The reality was the land, in one place cultivated by numerous hired workers, in another lying fallow; or reality was in one place the well-provided table, in another the poor man's board where bread was too often lacking. The popular masses contrasted their day-to-day existence with the speeches of the Jacobin authorities. They forced the Montagnard bourgeois to translate his words into actions.

The months of the requisition were a time when local administrations, under pressure from soldiers and their families, took social measures that anticipated what the Revolutionary Government would enact later, in February 1794.

The first decree granting aid to soldiers' families dated from November 26, 1792. Two million livres had then been put at the disposal of the minister for distribution to fathers, mothers, wives and children who had no resource except the work of citizen-soldiers, volunteers of all ranks, in the service of the Republic. Payment was to be made every three months from the date of the minister's signature. The yearly aid was 40 livres for children under eight years old, 25 for those between eight and twelve. Fathers and mothers aged sixty received 40 livres, or 60 if they were aged seventy or more. Not until June 4, 1793, were war widows' pensions set at half the husband's salary if he died while in the service, or half his pension after death at any time if he had more than thirty years service, but in no case could the pension exceed 1,000 livres or fall below 150 (decree of July 29, 1793). Needy brothers and sisters of volunteers dying in the service could also receive aid after May 4, 1793. But there were many delays, so that administrators on July 18, 1793, obtained the power to finance aid of this kind by drawing on tax receipts at the department level.

Aid to families was in fact often slow to arrive. A lieutenant in the 4th battalion of the Aube wrote home in May 1793 to the administrators of his department:

It is with sadness that I see every day brave defenders of the country who are with me here come and show me letters from their wives saying that they could not find bread for themselves and their children. They say they have applied to you, the administrators, both to have bread and to receive the benefits allowed by law to the brave wives of defenders of the country. You have rejected their requests. I remember that just before we departed you told us: "Go and crush these rebels, and we will be fathers to your children."

Certificates from the battalions concerning a relative had to be presented to the authorities, but many families were unable to establish contact with the battalions. The draftees knew this, and were concerned about their mothers and fathers.

The local administrators did whatever they could think of to show goodwill to the draftees. They drew on funds accumulated from management of common lands, they levied contributions on the rich, they dipped into the fund marked "income from émigré property," they opened subscriptions. Helped by the popular societies, they persuaded well-to-do inhabitants to assist the families of draftees and other soldiers as befitted their position. They went so far as to sell the pews of churches to help poor draftees of the communes.

There remained always the care of the land. Local government and popular societies promised that other citizens would assist the fathers of agricultural workers taken in the requisition. Administrators and sans-culottes pleaded with the government for relaxation in enforcement. In anticipation of later official decisions, draftees in some cases were allowed to postpone joining their battalion until the seasonal labors of cultivation had been accomplished. Facing such a multiplication of provisional leaves, the Committee of Public Safety, on January 25, 1794, authorized the temporary withdrawal from military induction of volunteers of the first requisition who were indispensable in agriculture. But this ruling was so abused that it was withdrawn on the following March 3.

It was well understood in the popular societies that a factor in draft evasion was the long waiting period in the home communities. To speed their departure it was necessary to provide them with arms and clothing, for which the popular societies took action with varying success. Here, too, their efforts when combined with those of the government tended to show the draftees the fraternity and unity of the Republic. There were to be no front and rear areas, but a whole people rising in their own defense.

4. THE *LEVÉE EN MASSE* ON THE WAY TO THE BATTLEFIELD

The contingents, once formed, were in charge not only of their own officers but of men called "conductors." These were appointed by the district administrators, who usually chose one of themselves. The conductors, usually ex-soldiers, were paid 20 *sous* a day. Some of them were Jacobins who offered to serve as guides for the draftees, handle the expenses along the way, and keep up patriotic enthusiasm. Some conductors were such ardent revolutionaries that on approaching the combat zone they abandoned the draftees and went off to join in the fighting. Such a one was Barbé, conductor of draftees on the way to the Army of the Pyrenees, who joined a company of *chasseurs* despite the protests of his contingent, who feared being left alone. Wounded and brought to the hospital, he continued to uphold the morale of the men around him.

Though selected with care, some conductors were rascals hoping to enrich themselves at the expense of the Republic. They stole the draftees' pay or the rations issued at stopping places, and by collusion with district agents obtained papers allowing them to return home. Sometimes municipal officers, informed of such malfeasance, took to the road themselves to fill the deserted posts.

"To relieve the boredom of a long journey, distract inexperienced men away from home for the first time, and dispel the gloomy thoughts generated by their prejudices," the conductors sometimes hired traveling musicians who played bagpipes and oboes. It was a precaution most often used by conductors of contingents originating in the west. They knew, as one from Quimperlé in Brittany put it, that "such instruments, placed on ships, could overcome the homesickness and apathy that might be deadly. By dances in the evening they forget the fatigue of the road and think themselves close to the fields where they were born."

The distance between daily halts varied with the topography and the season, but usually did not exceed thirty kilometers. The men rested one day in two weeks, because they were often barefoot and there were numerous stragglers. To prevent desertion a few gendarmes went alongside, and sometimes brought back a man in chains. Some draftees made the journey alone. One wrote to his parents to tell of his adventure:

I had good weather from Orléans to Etampes, but from Etampes until today it has rained with no sign of ending. It cost me 30 *sous* a day from Orléans to Etampes, 50 from Etampes to Paris, and 30 from Paris to Maubeuge, for a total of 27 livres, 5 *sous* from Orléans to Maubeuge. From Orléans to Maubeuge it is about ninety leagues. I asked to be admitted to a hospice at Soissons, but was refused, though I was very tired from walking. It is hard to get any rest. I have had no trouble with anyone, since I go alone.

As a means of getting them away from their familiar surroundings as soon as possible, even contingents whose home was near the combat zone were sometimes made to march for hundreds of kilometers. The journey might take several weeks. An Arras battalion, departing in November, arrived in January. Draftees from Bellac in the Haute-Vienne were put on the road on May 7, 1794, and reached Colmar on June 1.

Couriers went ahead to make arrangements for lodging. Most often the conductors preferred to keep the draftees in groups for more effective supervision. They requested the municipal authorities to place beds or straw mattresses in churches or convents. "We need a building easily guarded," said one conductor, "because at first these country people think only of deserting." The draftees felt that they were in a prison, and sometimes revolted in attempting to escape.

When unable to find a place large enough to receive a contingent of more than a thousand men, the local authorities distributed the draftees among the inhabitants, and the popular societies took it upon themselves to choose the richest. The latter, concerned for their daughters and their property, rid themselves of their undesirable "guests" by paying for beds at the nearest inn. The arrival of a contingent in a town was always followed by a steep rise in prices. In the inns, a civilian traveler had to pay up to 25 *sous* for a night's accommodation.

Certain large villages, at the intersection of several roads, complained of having to support charges that others escaped. At Sivry-sur-Meuse, a place of 800 or 900 inhabitants, 3,583 were housed from June 1793 to March 1794. Over half of these passed through in the four months from November 7 to March 3. The popular society of Villeneuve-sur-Vannes, in the Haute-Saône, wrote to the Jacobins of Paris to complain: From January 1 to September 1 the villagers had received troops seventy-two times! During the passage of the garrison retreating from Mainz they had lodged as many as 30 or 40 soldiers per house. They felt anxiety at every arrival of draftees, for there was a shortage of everything—wood, candles, fruits, vegetables, beds, and sheets. It is easy to understand with what sighs of relief a commune saw the departure of a turbulent youth that gave rise to scuffles and brawls.

The long marches hardened the draftees for war. They forgot the pains of the day in the pleasures of the stopping-places and the wonders of what was newly seen. The draftees from Puy-de-Dôme, on reaching Nice, discovered the sea. They noted the customs of the people, and were amazed at the differences of outlook and variety of revolutionary attitudes. "Here," wrote one of them, "they still say the Mass and do not tear down crosses," but in another place we camped "in a church where religious services are no longer conducted." Days of scant rations were punctuated by brief episodes of feasting, and there was astonishment at seeing towns where restrictions were unknown and merchant ships arrived with heavy loads, bringing that "wheat from Turkey that makes such delicious bread!"

Men for whom the farthest village hedgerow had enclosed their world now discovered their country. They were thus made more ready to unite with other Frenchmen in the bosom of regiments and demi-brigades.

5. SOCIAL ANALYSIS OF THE DRAFTEES

How many of these young draftees actually departed? And how many arrived in the camps? The Convention expected 537 battalions of 900 men, or 483,000. Barère announced in the Convention on August 17 that the Levy would produce 400,000 but the government hoped that certain populous departments would furnish more than 1,000 men per battalion, so that there might be as many as 537,000 new recruits. To read the reports of representatives on mission and the announcements of the Committee of Public Safety, we might think that this figure was attained. Perrin, for example, representative of the people with the Army of the Ardennes, reported on September 22 that the requisition in the Marne was entirely successful. The authorities of the Yonne, on the same date, reported the levy of 10,000 *défenseurs de la Patrie*. In the Lot the requisitions proceeded "marvelously well," and they were said to encounter no opposition in the Lot-et-Garonne. It was reported in October that the Haute-Garonne, the Gers, and the Landes were ready to provide 15 battalions of 100 men per company. In the Haute-Vienne and the Corrèze the levy was actively carried out. Dubois-Crancé declared, on October 3, that in the Center and the Southeast, "the levy of young men is producing prodigious numbers." Laplanche, in the Cher, concluded his report with these words: "You may give your orders, citizen colleagues. The Levy in Mass is ready."

Hearing these triumphal affirmations, the researcher goes in quest of figures. At the War Archives he finds the forms that the districts were supposed to send in—they are blank. At the National Archives he pores over the correspondence of the representatives on mission, and he finds only a few figures submitted by a few levy agents. When departmental archives are consulted, they yield a meager harvest. The researcher learns to have his doubts. The levy agents say that their figures are often only approximations. Sometimes the agent could keep no regular account because he was under pressure to send away the draftees in small groups. Sometimes the agent's papers have disappeared in a fire, or they reveal serious lacunae. When we find an account, it may contain arithmetical errors. For example, the agent in the Sézanne district of the Marne counted 420 men too many. Catching his mistake, he excuses himself: "You will realize that in the perpetual hubbub in which I find myself it is impossible to verify everything exactly."

A second difficulty is that the figures received by the authorities were those established at the time of departure of the draftees. But what is important, for judging the war effort really made by the departments, is the number who in fact became soldiers of the Republic. Desertion along the way or at the moment of incorporation was considerable. Some historians, like Boissonnade in writing the history of the "volunteers" of the Charente, have made no allowance for this fact. He avers that the Charente raised 15,000 draftees in the Year II. But these battalions, when sent to the Vendée, lost more than a third of their effectives by desertion.

The correspondence of the representatives on mission—not what they wrote to the Committee of Public Safety, but what they wrote to the departmental authorities—includes their letters to the levy agents and to the generals. They call desertion "a drain that has no end." The representatives on mission to the Army of the Rhine wrote in September 1793 of "considerable desertion in the battalions of draftees." Several representatives concluded by admitting that their first reports had been too optimistic, and that desertion had reduced the newly levied battalions by half. Goupilleau complained that "of 25,000 expected draftees we hardly have 2,000." The departmental officials of the Somme observed that "most of the men of the first requisition have returned home." In the Aisne, Finistère, Gard, Oise, and Tarn, the agents estimated the deserters in the hundreds. In the Haute-Loire 500 draftees departed on May 13, 1794, but only 353 arrived at the army. The district of Saint-Cêré sent off 658 men in May 1794, and a quarter of them deserted. The 6th battalion of the Ariège lost a whole company of 100 men on one evening in December 1793. A quarter of the draftees of Châteauneuf in the Maine-et-Loire took flight in March 1793. The extreme case was that of the 3rd battalion of Béthune, which on arriving at the front was composed of 5 draftees; its commander, in desperation, had to return its flag.

When incorporated into the battalions of the regular regiments or of the volunteers, the draftees still continued to desert. The battalion from Ruffec slipped from 2,304 men to 94. Draftees who did not attempt desertion asked to be admitted to the hospital. Or they refused to give their name and domicile at the time of incorporation, objected to serving in the front line, and insisted on being assigned to military works in the rear area.

Although figures supplied by the departments are fragmentary and doubtful, making it impossible to construct an exact map of the requisition, it might be thought possible to derive a sum total of the requisition from reports of the military commanders to the Committee of Public Safety. But here, too, the researcher must be skeptical. The generals subtly modified or sometimes even falsified their report. For some, to inflate the numbers was a way of obtaining more supplies or funds. For others, to understate them gave a basis for asking for reinforcements, or for excusing a lack of success after the event.

Even if these reports are used, there is a problem in understanding the language of the army staffs. Many historians, enamored of statistics, unwittingly deceive their readers. They in fact do not know the meaning of the word *effective* that they read in the documents. By this term, the military designated all men paid and maintained at the expense of the state. They included, along with men present under arms, those who were in hospitals, those facing courts martial, those in military detention, prisoners of war, deserters, and men in convalescent depots who were in many cases permanently lost to the army. To judge the importance of these "non-valids" it is enough to quote Napoleon Bonaparte on the Army of Italy: "Effective strength on the books of the war ministry was 106,000 men, but 36,000 were dead, deserters, or prisoners of war, and we had long been expecting a revision to efface them from the records."

The Convention used the figures supplied to it to inflame the imagination of the revolutionaries, and to frighten the enemy by the prodigious mass that it would have to overcome. Thus arose what has been called "the myth of the million."

In reality, the strength of the army, estimated at nearly 500,000 by Saint-Just in July 1793, was not doubled by the requisition. The Levy in Mass brought about 300,000 soldiers into the camps. This estimate is reached after examination of the troop-control registers. Two-thirds of the draftees arrived from September 1793 to January 1794. Beginning in the summer of 1794 the contingents became less numerous, thanks in part to the political crisis, and in part to the needs of the harvest, when draftees were kept at home by more or less disguised agreement with the local authorities.

Although some men were furnished by all the departments, real enthusiasm and goodwill were found most often in the departments surrounding Paris, in those near the frontiers, and in those verging on the west that were hostile to the *chouannerie*.

The correspondence of the levy agents reveals, and the statistics confirm, that the draftees were not all of the legal age. About 87 percent were indeed between eighteen and twenty-five, but more than 2 percent were young adolescents or even boys, more than 10 percent were over twenty-five, and of these about 1 percent were thirty-six or older. Yet the requisition did rejuvenate the existing armies, and it provided the generals with fighting men capable of physical prowess. They remained on the whole of short stature; in the battle infantry 65 percent were of a height of 1.67 meters or less, with one-quarter less than 1.62.[5]

We have only fragmentary information on the social origin of the draftees. In some departments "sacred equality" was respected, without regard to rich or poor, and with the blood of the indigent considered as pure as that of his more well-to-do neighbor. The townsman and the countryman were to go under fire together. Statistical study shows that 16 percent of the draftees came from towns, corresponding to the percentage of the French population then considered urban. The decree of August 23, authorizing the Levy in Mass, modified the social composition of the demi-brigades in process of formation. The more comfortable class appears again in the camps. Thus, in the battalion of the district of Bar-sur-Seine, several merchants, a teacher, and a cleric mingled with vine growers, artisans, and ordinary laborers. In the district of Caen 10 percent of the draftees came from commercial houses or notaries' offices. In the district of Lisieux 12 percent were connected with the business bourgeoisie. In the district of Orléans 7 percent of those that we can analyze belonged to commercial circles in the city and its suburbs. In the 15th battalion of Paris a professor of mathematics and an architect were fusiliers or plain infantry soldiers, a lawyer was a corporal, and they served with shopowners under the orders of a merchant who was the battalion commander. They went under fire alongside a cabinetmaker, a dancer, and a man employed in the shop where the paper money was printed. The presence of the bourgeoisie, both of trade and of the liberal professions, may be noted also among the draftees from Riom, Cany (Seine-Inférieure), Abbeville, Péronne, and Avignon.

But there are some indications that the bourgeoisie furnished fewer than it could have. In Paris the 15th battalion was largely recruited in the Section de l'Indivisibilité, the former Place Royale (now the Place des Vosges). We know that the bourgeoisie comprised 30.9 percent of this section, and its domestic servants 36.8

---

[5] Or 5 feet 6 inches and 5 feet 4 inches in Anglo-American measurement.

percent. But the percentage of both bourgeoisie and their servants among the draftees is much less. Artisans and day workers, who formed respectively 11.6 and 14.6 percent of the population, produced twice this percentage for the battalion.

But the army of the Year II, in which members of all social classes marched side by side, was nevertheless an army with a strong peasant coloration, and in this it contrasted strongly with the army of 1791. The agricultural population dominated numerically in the army, as in civil society. There were exceptions, reflecting different kinds of rural labor. Thus, in the Somme, the requisition fell less heavily on the farms than on the cottage industry that had grown up around the larger towns. Among artisans, men in occupations hitherto hardly represented in the army were now compelled to serve. In the coal regions of the Nord ordinary mine workers, and the carpenters and carters in the underground galleries, were brought up from the pits and assembled in a battalion of draftees. Private concerns were to cede to the general interest, and each man in the army had his duty of fraternity to perform.

This was the lesson taught by the patriots, but the pockets of resistance that they met with in the Levy gave evidence, for them, of the need for an assiduous pedagogy of *civisme*. The spirit of the Revolution must be made to pervade the troops.

But who would educate the army—the sans-culottes or the government? At first, from September to the winter of 1793, it was the sans-culottes who exerted the strongest impact.

CHAPTER VI

• • •

The Sans-culottes and the Army
(Summer to Autumn 1793)

By their action the sans-culottes had obtained the first prerequisite
of an army for victory—large numbers. Still lacking in their eyes
were other requirements for a decisive success. The army must be
made to understand, and to adopt, the aspirations and political
tendencies of the sans-culottes. It must be "sans-culottized"; this
meant a purging of its command and an "amalgamation" to allow
a better diffusion of popular ideas through wide circulation of the
revolutionary press in the camps. In the summer of 1793 the sans-
culotte movement began to penetrate the army, lending it strong
moral and material support.

1. THE SPREAD OF SANS-CULOTTE IDEAS IN THE ARMY

Sans-culottes and Jacobins both kept close watch over the troops.
Without the certificates of reliable citizenship that they delivered,
it was impossible to obtain confirmation of rank or appointment
to an army staff. Thus, General Ferino was denounced not only as
a foreigner but also "because he had no certificate of good citizenship." The sans-culottes, like the Jacobins, welcomed the units
passing through their town and tried to win them over. They
formed committees of correspondence to keep in touch with
"their brothers in the armies." Those of Paris maintained ties with

the volunteers and draftees of the capital. They even went further; in June 1793, when a company raised in the Paris section called the Gardes françaises was stationed at Tours, the section maintained two commissioners at Tours to work with its officers. On September 4, at the headquarters of the Army of the Côtes-de-La-Rochelle, the chief of staff issued a pass to François Lemaitre, a commissioner of the section of the Gardes françaises, to allow him to go wherever he wished.

Provincial sans-culottes did the same. Those of La Réunion in the Lot-et-Garonne, of Ganges in the Hérault, and of Foix in the Ariège dispatched letters and emissaries to the battalions that they had raised and sent to the Army of the Eastern Pyrenees. The war minister, Bouchotte, whose connection with the sans-culottes will shortly be seen, urged the generals to conduct their men to club meetings. Soldiers appearing in the assemblies often acted as convinced sans-culottes, determined to purge them of their moderate elements. In the Hautes-Pyrénées, soldier sans-culottes were ahead of their civilian brothers in driving "moderates" out of the departmental administration. "For too long," they said, these officials "have allowed refractory priests to enjoy protection and light the torch of fanaticism even on the altar of Liberty." They demanded and obtained house searches and even proceeded themselves to arrest suspects. At Tours, in August, some soldiers excited by the sans-culotte spirit caused a disturbance in the rue de la Loi by plundering a literary club suspected of federalism. At La Brugière the commander of the second battalion of the Tarn was heard to declare, in true sans-culotte fashion: "Let the poor man find help and consolation among us, and the rich man abjure his self-interest and feel sentiments of goodwill."

Clubs were organized even inside the battalions, as in the 2nd battalion of the Dordogne. Troops of the Army of the Pyrenees, encamped at Ascain, decided in September 1793 to create a patriotic society to work with the society at Bayonne. Representatives with the Army of Italy wrote: "A club has formed in which all the soldiers take part. It follows good principles, so that the army is beginning to recover from the federalist errors into which Biron, Brunet, and others had plunged it."

The Montagnards attempted very soon, well before the autumn of 1793, to control these clubs by having them affiliate with the Jacobins of Paris. Cases in point were the club of the 68th regiment and the clubs of the former Berry and Beauce regiments.

The second avenue by which sans-culottes reached the army was by way of the ministry of war. The minister, Bouchotte, after every popular rising, sent addresses to the army explaining and justifying the revolutionary demands. He exalted the insurrection of May 31 to June 2 in which the sans-culottes drove the Girondins from the Convention. He reported to the troops on the popular demonstrations of September that led to the organization of the Terror. The task he assigned himself was "to identify the fighting men with the nation as soon as possible." He distributed the new constitution to the soldiers, instituted *fêtes révolutionnaires* in the armies, showed his willingness to support the purge of officers as desired by the sans-culottes, and worked to develop new hierarchic arrangements in the army "so that the soldiers would no longer make sport of the generals." And he sent out copies of the patriot press, especially Hébert's *Père Duchesne*.

It remains questionable whether Bouchotte consciously embraced the program of the ultrarevolutionaries. His secretary, Vincent, was indeed an extremist against whom the Committee of Public Safety had to take action. Vincent filled the bureaus of the ministry with his creatures, and used agents of the executive council to tighten his grip on the army. These agents most especially scrutinized the spirit and principles of the military chiefs. For such a delicate mission, as one of them wrote, one must be careful to observe everything personally: "It is by seeing everything with your own eyes, sharing in the labors of our brave brothers in arms, showing yourself everywhere at their head, that you encourage the troops and keep watch over the generals and their staffs." Vincent's agents were thus in competition with the representatives on mission.

Bouchotte himself, according to his historian, General Herlaut, was not an ultra. He used Vincent and then Hébert in his conflict with the Dantonists, but abandoned them when he saw them publicly opposed by the Committee of Public Safety. The danger was that the army might escape control by the government. The Committee reacted in April 1794 by suppressing the war ministry, and replacing it, as it did the other ministries, by an executive commission under its orders.

The press was a vehicle for sans-culotte thinking, and especially for the most advanced wing of the popular movement, for which Hébert claimed to be the mouthpiece. The war ministry paid him 118,000 livres for delivery of a total of over a million copies of his *Père Duchesne*. By reading this journal the soldier absorbed the slogans of the *exagérés*: a purge of all administrative bodies and revolutionary committees, pursuit and intensification of the Terror, vigilance over the authorities and even over the Revolutionary Government whose social policy was thought too moderate. When the political assemblies of the sans-culottes came under control by the government, the *Père Duchesne* remained, for the army, an organ of transmission for the extreme sans-culotte aspirations until March 1794, when Hébert was arrested.

Hébert was not the only ultrarevolutionary journalist to be read in the republican armies. Armand Guffroy, a member of the Committee of General Security, advanced the same opinions in his journal, *Le Rougyff*,[1] which the war ministry distributed in great abundance.

Yet it is not to be supposed that the whole army was "sans-culottized" by these journals. Other journals, originating with the government, were in a position to combat them. But above all, despite the large totals that were furnished, only a few copies

---

[1] An anagram of the journalist's name.

reached the troops. Commanders often intercepted them and refused to distribute them. A certain cannoneer, named Brazenil, of the 5th battalion of the Yonne, wrote: "I don't say that the defenders of the Republic don't have the satisfaction of reading these bulletins and journals. I attack no one. But it may be that the chiefs give them out regularly to one company to be passed on to others, and that they remain often with the first."

Songs were no doubt the best means of transmitting sans-culotte aspirations to the army. The soldiers of the Revolution, like all soldiers, liked to sing. They sang to relieve the fatigue of long marches, to taunt the enemy, and to banish fear at the moment of attack. Gouvion de Saint-Cyr reported that in the Army of the Rhine, as an assault began, the band first played a jolly air to draw the enemy's advance and then the Marseillaise when the signal was given for the counterattack. General Dumerbion recalled in his correspondence that in July 1794 the Army of Italy attacked with guns still slung in their shoulderbelts but singing the Carmagnole; the enemy supposedly took flight in terror at this kind of combat.

Songs were more accessible than the press to men who were often illiterate, and they were easily memorized. By affecting the heart rather than the reason they would, as one pamphleteer put it, "unite the citizens of the Empire in one feeling and make them agree on the best way to express their enthusiasm." But songs had to be "revolutionized." Until now they had only been intended "to vaunt the joys of the table or the love of luxury and pleasure"; they had been written "for persons of high society and hence showed contempt for the people; or if someone composed a song for the people it seemed intended, by its triviality of thought and vulgarity of language, to keep the people in a state of degradation." Things would be different under the reign of Liberty: songs would combine purity of style with elevation of thought by expressing the great themes of the Revolution. Skillfully composed, they would become "an elementary course in politics and war, in which our defenders would learn the rights and duties of citizens and soldiers."

The songs composed for soldiers were produced on orders from Bouchotte, in whose accounts we find a sum of 80,000 livres paid to citizen Théodore Rousseau, a member of the Committee on Public Instruction of the National Convention. Rousseau wrote songs also for Chaumette, an official of the Commune of Paris after the uprising of the 10th of August. The collection prepared for Chaumette contained seventeen songs. They were printed in September 1793, and a copy was to be presented to each "volunteer" on his departure for the army. "We are French, and we know the value of a stanza," said Chaumette. One song in the collection, a patriotic hymn, was distributed in multiple copies to the Army of the Eastern Pyrenees. Other songs were written by sans-culotte soldiers. They can still be found here and there in the files of the War Archives and the National Archives—for example, a patriotic hymn by a hussar named Leguay and a patriotic chant by a Captain Baudet of the 1st battalion of the Aisne. When the journals and pamphlets of the advanced sans-culottes had disappeared from the camps, who could blot out the memory of songs that had been well learned?

These songs borrowed their music from the best-known civic chants or the airs that were then in vogue. In a third of the cases they used the music of the Marseillaise and often plagiarized the words. There was also much borrowing from the Carmagnole and the Salut de l'Empire. Among popular tunes, those most often serving for military singing were "C'est ce que nous console" and "Lisette est faite pour Colin." Verses of six or eight syllables were grouped in eight to twelve stanzas. The theme most often sounded was that of the model sans-culotte. Citizen and soldier, he sacrificed all for his country; whatever happened, he gave proof of courage and abnegation. His valor contrasted with the cowardice of enemy soldiers, as mocked by the poet:[2]

---

[2] Because the effect of rhymed verses cannot be reproduced in translation, the French originals are given in Appendix II.

> A soldier of Liberty,
> Exalted by her,
> Is worth all alone more than a hundred slaves.

This was a favorite theme found in many letters by volunteers, as when the commander of the 2nd battalion of the Tarn wrote to a friend that one Frenchman was worth ten Germans, Prussians, or Spaniards.

A song by a brave patriot corporal taunted a poltroonish aristocrat in its refrain:

> To combat as to a ball
> I rush, as to a carnival.

Or the refrain by Théodore Rousseau in his "Pot-pourri on Cadet Mirabeau":

> The curled moustaches of aristocrats
> Are just right
> For scaring children.

Or the *Journal de Paris* on September 20:

> Of these warriors dear to France . . .
> Do you see the standards float?
> To the altar of our country
> Their steps are drawn by love.
> All to their beloved mother
> Will be devoted unto death.

Aristocrats were cowards who had been able to rule only by dreadful crimes, according to an "Invitation to patriots to rush to the Vendée." They "thirsted for blood with the most infamous vices," in a song on the "old-time government." Their soldiers? In a song sarcastically called "The Heroes of Coblentz," their soldiers were "slaves, helots, dwarfs, braggarts, empty scarecrows." But a song called "The departure of sans-culottes for our armies" was reassuring: "These midgets, these gluttons, these man-eaters" had

in truth little taste for fighting. The sans-culottes would exterminate them, for

> On the salvation of our country
> Depends that of the Universe.

But other peoples must lend aid:

> Enemies of tyranny,
> Rise up and take to arms.
> From all downtrodden Europe
> March with us into battle.

And a "Hymn to Republicans":

> Let the world have for its sovereign
> Only a people of sans-culottes.

The liberation of peoples should be under the aegis of Equality,
for

> Liberty is but a trap
> So long as the word "privilege"
> Offends Sacred Equality.

Equality was aimed against the aristocracy of birth and against the
aristocracy of wealth. The principle of social classification should
be not blood or fortune but merit and talent, as acquired by education, which the sans-culotte claimed as a right, in "Principles of
a true republican":

> By his talents, by what he knows
> Not what he has,
> Each mortal should advance himself.

In a stanza by Citizen Dorli of the Montagne section in Paris the
sans-culotte is hungry and the hoarder is denounced:

> The greedy and the selfish
> Take refuge in the dark.

> We will penetrate the lair
> Where these traitors lie hidden,
> Attached to their treasures,
> And rending their mother's breast.

There should be an equality of citizens, "sowing everywhere fruits and flowers," as in "Homage to a good patriot." Good citizens should aid and assist the indigent, as in "The duties of the good citizen."

Among these themes common to the whole *sans-culotterie* we find others more radical. Away with Christianity! Only the cult of Reason should triumph, according to a "Hymn to Liberty":

> The old blindfold of ignorance
> Is torn off by Reason.

Or in a stanza by Citizen Dorli:

> Stop, you vain deceitful oracles
> That subjected us to your laws.
> Reason has regained its rights.

And in "The vow of all peoples wishing to be free," Reason

> Overthrows the altars
> Of profane lies,
> And everywhere breaks
> The chains of error,
> And everywhere pulverizes
> Our bloody oppressors.

Religion was not only a political chain invented to govern men; it was also a source of enrichment for some but damaging to the people. This social aspect of dechristianization was noticeable in Théodore Rousseau's "Idea of the rage of hypocritical, rebellious priests." No more God and no more saints!

The days themselves were revolutionized. When soldiers had not yet heard of the revolutionary calendar, adopted in October

1793, sans-culotte war commissioners proposed simple and easy means of teaching the new calendar to all.

With the saints proscribed, and even before the revolutionary calendar, militants in the army exchanged their Catholic given names for revolutionary ones, and incited their fellows to do the same. In some companies the morning roll call became a veritable political incantation. The sergeant no longer called out the names of Fanfan-la-Tulipe or Bois-sans-soif (see page 361 below), but a list of Liberties, Equalities, and Fraternities, along with Terrors, Mountains, Brutuses, Marats, and Pères Duchesne.

The cult of Reason, preached by radical sans-culottes, made headway in the army. Hardy, an agent of the executive council with the Army of the Eastern Pyrenees, gave an account of it to Bouchotte. He described a ceremony presided over by Virtue, Union, and Fraternity. He told of soldiers surrounding a bust of Marat and singing revolutionary hymns, with their general acting as conductor. When the Temple of Reason was inaugurated at Perpignan in March 1794, General Dugommier and his staff joined with the constituted authorities. They marched to the temple together to the sound of cannon, preceded by two hundred girls in white robes with tricolor sashes at the waist. On the esplanade where the *Autel de la Patrie* was located, decorated with portraits of the martyrs of Liberty—Le Pelletier, Marat, and Chalier—the higher officers put a torch to pictures of the saints, male and female, of the Catholic religion.

Identical ceremonies were reported from the Army of the Sambre-et-Meuse. In the Army of the Rhine, in October 1793, sans-culotte militants found their way into the army units "to struggle against the rich, against traitors in collusion with foreigners, and against moderates who would help in the conspiracy to put the people to sleep," but also to propagate the cult of Reason in the ranks.

We have only a few indications of how the troops reacted to these propagandists, but all we have are unfavorable to the cult preached by Chaumette, Fouché, and Hébert. Atheism shocked the soldiers, who in the great majority were believers. In the hundreds of letters from "volunteers" that survive, the invocations of God to protect patriots are very frequent. Their faith could be sustained, in some cases, by the presence of priests, who, beginning as chaplains, were transformed into officers or NCOs at the instigation of the men.

The sans-culotte propaganda was too often blocked or forbidden by career officers, especially by officers who were nobles. So a popular war cry, heard well before August 10, 1792, became louder in the summer of 1793: "No more nobles at the head of our armies!"

2. THE PURGING OF THE COMMAND STRUCTURE

The theme of the noble officer suspected of treason was often repeated by those to whom the sans-culottes listened.[3] Marat said on January 27 that there could be no victory for liberty so long as a true sans-culotte was not at the head of the army. On March 8 Hébert demanded the cashiering of all intriguers in positions of command. The treason of Dumouriez, on April 3, involving his attempt to turn his army against Paris, induced the government to take steps against nobles. They were excluded, on April 5, from the organization of a force of 40,000 men to cover the navigable rivers in the neighborhood of Paris. Bouchotte, before the insurrection of May 31, proposed the suspension of noble or suspected officers. But these were half-measures meant to calm public opinion.

The revolutionary uprising of May 31 to June 2 gave new life to the issue. The Paris sections called more loudly for a "purification." "We demand," said an address to the Convention presented

---

[3] Nobility had been legally abolished in 1790, after which a person who had enjoyed this status was sometimes still called a noble, sometimes a former noble (*ci-devant noble*), or sometimes simply a *ci-devant*: The term *ci-devant*, a normal adverb, was popularized during the Revolution as an adjective and noun, often extended to mean anyone attached to the pre-Revolutionary or *ancien* regime.

by the Commune of Paris, "the dismissal of all nobles occupying high rank in the armies of the Republic." During the night of June 2–3, pressed by Chaumette, the general council of the Department of Paris decreed that "no former noble or refractory priest shall discharge the functions of an officer or public official." At the Jacobins, Billaud-Varenne, known for his ties with the sans-culottes, demanded on June 9 "that the Convention order the cashiering of officers of high rank who belong to the nobility, and also the dismissal of all civilian and military officers appointed by Dumouriez and Beurnonville."

On June 13 Bouchotte was replaced in the ministry (temporarily) by the *ci-devant* or ex-noble General Beauharnais. The friends of Bouchotte agitated against Beauharnais. Acting through the Cordeliers club, they got the Paris sections to petition for the removal of noble officers. On June 23 the Jacobins adhered to this call for a purge. Meanwhile the Convention, on report from the Committee of Public Safety, had chosen general-staff officers for the eleven armies of the Republic. In doing so, it had conducted an inquiry, and notes on the generals existed in the war ministry. A cry went up that these notes should be used. Hébert exclaimed on July 24, "Out with the nobles; they are killing us!" On July 28 the surrender of the French forces at Mainz was announced. Who was to blame? It must have been Custine, for not having come to the support of the garrison soon enough. This *ci-devant* must be arrested!

The Custine affair is one of those that contribute to an understanding of the struggle during the Revolution to control generals who became too independent—a struggle carried on first by the sans-culottes and later by the Montagnards of the Committee of Public Safety. As a noble he had had an amazing career. He was first present at a military operation at the age of seven. At twenty-one he was a colonel of dragoons, with a regiment created for him, the Custine Dragoons. To improve himself in the military art he took service in Germany and Austria. He became an enthusiastic admirer of Frederick the Great and his reforms. He then served in the French expedition to America under Rochambeau. When the Revolution began, Custine thought himself the best strategist of the day, who if war should come would have a chance to display his talents. He thus accepted the Revolution, and was a deputy of the nobility at the Estates General. With this record, he was chosen, after the flight of the king, as a commissioner to the armies to assure their loyalty to the Revolution. In 1792, serving under Biron, he took possession of Speier and Worms and campaigned along the Rhine. Without orders, he moved on to Frankfurt and succeeded in occupying it. He was named commander-in-chief of the Army of the Moselle, and then of the Army of the North in May 1793.

He showed an unsullied patriotism. When the Austrian General Wurmser summoned General Gilot, commanding at Landau, to surrender the town, Custine wrote on April 4: "the proposal of General Wurmser is the height of effrontery. Dumouriez has been a traitor to liberty, but twenty-four million men take orders from no one."

But his relations with his officers and men shocked the sans-culottes. He imposed a "Prussian" discipline, had two soldiers shot for pillaging, and two others also shot, chosen at random in a unit that had behaved badly. In the Army of the North he forbade officers to grant leaves on pain of death. A disciplinary code existed, but he paid no attention to it. He abused his generals, including Houchard, and drove some of his subordinates to suicide by the violence of his language. Beurnonville, who was briefly the war minister and was an army general, was described by Custine as incompetent and pretentious—on the very day when the unfortunate minister was captured by the Austrians in connection with the defection of Dumouriez. As for Bouchotte, Custine said that there was no one more stupid or less capable of being a war minister. The Convention? "When I don't like a decree of the Convention I throw it in the fire." He had said that the country could be saved only by a dictator, and that this dictator should be a general.

He rejected oversight by the commissioners sent by the executive council, thought their observations ridiculous, and opposed their political influence in the army. When they circulated patriot writings, he forbade them to be read. The career officers stood behind him. They had accepted regeneration of their units in 1790 and 1791 when it helped them to replace aristocrats whose places they envied. Now that they were in command, they were determined to prevent their battalions from turning into political clubs in which their own powers would be questioned. They were also troubled by new rules of promotion, which they feared might work against them. They were therefore inclined to support their general on matters of discipline, and against "sans-culottization."

On the level of strategy, Custine differed with the commissioners of the executive council.[4] These two, Celliez and Varin, discussed and criticized everything: the location of the headquarters, the use of cavalry and artillery, and the general's plan of campaign. The general thought it astute to obtain the support of commissioners of the Convention against those of the executive council. The latter were arrested by the commissioners of the Convention, who however were disavowed. Increasingly, both the sections and the Jacobins complained of the "despotism" of Custine. The Favart affair was the pretext for his fall.

On April 11, by mistake, two generals had been appointed to command at Lille, Favart and La Marlière. La Marlière was suspected of moderatism by a friend of Robespierre, Captain Calendini. The commissioners of the executive council favored Favart. Custine held out for La Marlière. On July 24 Robespierre denounced La Marlière, who was hailed before the Revolutionary Tribunal and guillotined. Custine was recalled to Paris. He was

---

[4] The executive council, carried over with modifications from the defunct constitution of 1789–1791, existed until its abolition in April 1794. It was composed of six ministers including the minister of war. Its agents naturally sometimes clashed with commissioners of the Convention and with the representatives on mission who were members of the Convention. In April 1794 the several ministries (and hence the executive council) were replaced by "executive commissions" under the Committee of Public Safety.

reproached for his inertia, for disarming Lille, for his rigorous discipline, for his authoritarian conduct, for his support of La Marlière, and for his opposition to the commissioners of the executive council.

After Mainz capitulated on July 22, a letter signed by Custine was produced, ordering the defenders to surrender. The letter was a forgery. But the patriotic press unleashed itself against Custine. The ensuing trial was less a trial of a traitorous general than of the whole "generalate," as the Jacobins said, for its opposition to the Revolution. Custine was accused of not letting the Revolution influence his army and especially his officers. He had to die, that the army might appear as the armed might of the revolutionary people and government. Custine went to the guillotine. To "patriotize" the army and "purify" its officer corps remained the slogans of the sans-culottes. But the men in the government became alarmed: to go too fast in a purge, to replace the suspected expert with an incapable patriot, might disorganize the army. In any case, as Bouchotte himself recognized, there were noble officers who had sincerely joined the ranks of the Revolution. But the sans-culottes renewed their pressure against moderates in the Convention. Claire Lacombe, the famous woman *Enragée*, addressed the Convention defiantly:

> Do you want us to believe that you are harboring no defenders of nobles among you? Then get them out of all the places they occupy. Don't tell us that that would disorganize the army by depriving it of experienced leaders. The more able they are, the more dangerous they are.

On April 26 the Commune of Paris invited Bouchotte to undertake "further purifications." During the uprising of September 5 deputies of the Paris sections joined with the Jacobins in demanding banishment from the armies of "the insolent caste who are always enemies of equality." Barère, in reply, read a report of the Committee of Public Safety that gave satisfaction to the sans-culottes. On September 16 the Committee ordered the removal of all former nobles from employment in the armies of the Republic, and instructed the war minister to prepare a list for each army of the officers to be cashiered. The sans-culottes thus triumphed, but so did the Committee of Public Safety by fending off the attacks against it. This was evident on September 25 with the dismissal of Houchard and appointment of a whole new batch of generals.

Houchard was an "officer of fortune" who had risen in rank under the Old Regime. He welcomed a revolution that gave him the hope for rapid further advancement. He fought valiantly and became a general. In May 1793 he was made commander of the Army of the Rhine when Custine left it, and then of the Army of the North. He was a brave man without much military talent. Sensing his own limitations, he depended willingly on his subordinates. Even before the order of September 16, some capable noble but suspected officers had been removed form the general staffs. Houchard objected to these measures, which, he said, reduced his own staff to "extreme disruption," to the point that he could obtain "no exact knowledge of his army or the strength of his forces." When the armies of the Coalition attacked and the British marched on Dunkirk the counteroffensive was discussed by the representatives on mission and approved by Carnot; the French should concentrate their attack on the British and then turn against the Austrians and Dutch, who had failed to lend the British their support. This plan failed, but in revised form it led to the victory at Hondschoote by which the situation was restored. The victory at Hondschoote seemed to confirm the views of the sans-culottes. A general who came from the people, a sans-culotte general (he had worn the cap of liberty), was worth all the aristocratic generals put together.

But Houchard met not with praise but with accusations. Instead of pursuing and cutting off the enemy, he had let him escape. On September 20 Houchard was relieved and replaced by Jourdan. At the same time the Committee submitted to the Convention for its approval the names of Ferrand to command the Army of the Rhine in place of Landremont, who was dismissed; and of

Moreau to command the Army of the Moselle in place of Schauenbourg, also dismissed. Some in the Convention protested, declaring that one should not remove capable generals while knowing nothing of their successors, and that to destroy the enemy one must entrust the armies to men with military experience. The policy of the purge was thus brought again into question. But in fact behind these protests lay an attack on the Committee of Public Safety. Robespierre was not deceived. He supported Bouchotte's nominations, arguing again that perfidious generals must be dismissed and replaced without delay. As for Houchard, he was hardly a traitor, but Robespierre and the Committee abandoned him. It was noted that he had been an aide-de-camp to Custine and had engaged in correspondence with the enemy. So Houchard met his doom to save the Committee of Public Safety. If operations had not been wholly successful, it was allegedly not the fault of the Committee, on which Carnot sat as well as Robespierre, but of a commander not qualified to carry on the revolutionary warfare desired by the people. The purge could therefore continue. A warning was at the same time issued to the generals—whether nobles or commoners they must submit to the civil power and obey its orders, or else risk losing their heads. Sans-culotte pressure in the army commands worked to the advantage of the Committee of Public Safety, at this moment when it was bringing other committees under its domination.

While imposing the purge, the sans-culottes also desired new hierarchic arrangements in the army. Some even wished a rotation of chiefs so that command would be only temporary. All wanted to proscribe the polite *vous* and require use of the familiar *tu*. They wanted no formulas of deference that smacked of the Old Regime. The soldier should conclude a letter to his superior, or even to the minister of war, with *Salut et fraternité*, "your equal in rights." Whether in camp or outside it, the officer must remain a citizen who regarded his subordinates as citizens also. He should read the patriot press both for himself and for his men. He should be seen in the clubs with the red cap of liberty on his head, discussing matters with the enlisted men as equals.

Many career officers resisted such practices, and hoped earnestly for a restoration of traditional discipline.

3. TOWARD A UNIFIED ARMY

By May and June of 1793 the need for "amalgamation," discussed but not acted upon in February, was becoming urgent. Although the old royal army had come to accept the volunteers of 1791, it still kept its distance from the later levies, which it accused of bringing disorder into combined operations. Soldiers of the old units viewed all who wore the blue uniform with the same contempt. Animosity was made worse by adversity. For any defeat it was the "blues" that were blamed, not the "whites." The attitude of career officers influenced that of the men in whom they were endeavoring to instill an esprit de corps. Officers and enlisted men refused to give up their old uniforms for the blue of the volunteer. It was reported from the frontiers that new uniforms were still being made every day from white cloth. White was the sign of the regular soldier, who, it was said, was ashamed to become the equal of the volunteers. Two representatives reported on April 14: "In general the line officers are not well disposed toward us. One of their main ways of seducing their men is to inspire indifference or contempt for the national uniform." The commissioners Celliez and Varin found in June that "this insistence on preserving distinctions is annoying to the volunteers, and all agree that the line troops can never be counted on so long as they form a separate body."

Brawls broke out between the former royal regiments and the volunteer battalions. The commissioner Barbier, for example, wrote in August that he had barely managed to prevent a bloody quarrel between the old soldiers and the new. At Versailles in August there was a fight with drawn swords between soldiers of the two "armies." In November, in a camp where "blues" and "whites" were united, a captain of volunteers, in his rounds of military police, came upon some regulars who were insulting his own men. He was insulted himself by one of the regulars: "You cheap 15-*sous* soldier, I'll spit on you and chew up your epaulettes!" The others raised their guns, took aim, and forced him to flee. In the Army of the Pyrenees a great disorder was caused in October "by the misunderstanding and schism" between the two kinds of troops.

There were other disputes also. Sometimes members of the legions or free companies picked a quarrel with the volunteers. In April 1793 a sergeant-major conducting a group of volunteers from Vierzon met some soldiers of the Germanic Legion on the road. They taunted his little contingent, shouting "*à bas la République, vive le Roi!*" and "we'll take our Ration but not the Nation! What are you up to, comrades? Going to plant cabbages?" Sans-culottes demanded the dissolution of such units, or at least their amalgamation with volunteers who might turn them into patriots. Sans-culottes and Jacobins were at one also in affirming that amalgamation would foil treasonous generals who tried to use the disorganization of the army to further their machinations.

Technical as well as political reasons for amalgamation, as already pointed out by Dubois-Crancé, now became very evident. In the absence of a quartermaster who knew his business, the accounts of the volunteer battalions were in serious disarray. Dubois-Crancé reported later, in 1795, that at the time of formation of the demi-brigades there were almost no registers, records, or accounts, except for evidence of huge receipts and huge deficits. Another technical reason, stressed more by the representatives on mission than by the sans-culottes, was that amalgamation would allow the line soldiers to teach the trade of arms, if not to the volunteers of 1791 who had seen something of war, at least to those of 1793.

A decree of June 10, 1793, authorized the generals to effect amalgamation, but only where they judged it necessary. Not until August 12 was a method of implementation made public. The new instructions prescribed a different mode of procedure from that of the preceding February. There was to be no more juxtaposition of units but a true integration of contingents of varying origin. Men would be taken as individuals from the three battalions to be unified or homogenized, and reassigned so that each battalion would be made up of companies containing forty volunteers and twenty soldiers of the regular army.

From June 1793 to January 1794 twenty demi-brigades were created. Seven of them were in the armies of the North and of the Moselle, and eight in those of the Alps and of Italy. The Army of the Pyrenees, with few line regiments, had only four demi-brigades, and the Army of the West only one. Integration of the army was thus far from complete. It was the generals who organized these demi-brigades, and the control exercised by sans-culotte commissions was almost nonexistent. The representatives on mission played a role only later. The generals, being professional officers, favored the old soldiers of the king in promotions. They did not always conform strictly to the law of August 12. While ten demi-brigades saw a true internal fusion within the smallest combat unit, others only juxtaposed the existing companies or battalions. There were even fictitious demi-brigades, such as the 27th in the Army of the North and the 17th in the Army of the West. In the 23rd and 100th demi-brigades there was no amalgamation of volunteers and line soldiers but only an incorporation of draftees into the regiments. The 6th demi-brigade in the Army of the Pyrenees was composed only of volunteers.

The desire of sans-culottes and Jacobins for a unified army was thus not satisfied at the end of 1793. But the Jacobins, the representatives on mission, and the Committee of Public Safety understood the danger in leaving the management of these new units in the hands of the generals, and drew the appropriate lessons beginning in Janaury 1794. They knew also that before proceeding further with amalgamation, through formation of demi-brigades, it would be necessary to replace the losses within the battalions by incorporating the draftees of the Year II.

4. THE SANS-CULOTTES AND REVOLUTIONARY WARFARE

The manner of waging war underwent a change during the months from late 1792 into the beginning of 1793. War was no longer simply the armed confrontation of two belligerents. It was also psychological. Rousseau's "people" discovered that to make war on a sovereign meant first of all "attacking the public consensus and all that depends on it, for the essence of the state consists only in that." If the subjects of the allied kings broke the social compact the war would stop, and the monarchical states would be "killed off, as Jean-Jacques said, without one man dying." French soldiers in 1792 attempted persuasion of their enemies. Von Massenbach tells in his memoirs how "the French attacked not with sword and gun but with far more dangerous weapons." They sent German-speaking Alsatians and Lorrainers to parlay with the Prussian outposts, assuring them that the French were the brothers of oppressed peoples. They scattered big bundles of printed matter that explained, in language understandable to common soldiers, the principles of liberty and equality and why the Austro-Prussian alliance was unnatural. Loaves of bread concealing such imprints were thrown to the front-line enemy troops, promising money and security to deserters. The Republic offered "to all soldiers in hostile armies the happy opportunity of living in France as free men." There were few acceptances of these invitations. It was even reported that some deserters were assumed by some of the French to be spies, and so put to death.

With the defeat of 1793 the sans-culotte soldier lost his belief in the virtues of propagandizing the enemy. Because the enemy troops remained the slaves of despots, they deserved no pity. The Revolution was to be the merciless clash of a patriot people with aristocracy and its henchmen. Within France the sans-culotte demanded Terror against nobles and their allies; on the battlefield the enemy should be not merely contained or defeated, but annihilated. He must be convinced by the bayonet:

> Let's fight our enemies hand to hand. We'll throw them to the ground and bring over the Austrian and Prussian sans-culottes to our side, either because they want to save their lives or because they realize that their leaders want to clamp on them the same chains they meant to clamp on us.

The war should thus become a terrorist war; to exterminate the adversary would bring peace the sooner. The draftees under the requisition would then return home more quickly, as they had been promised when told they needed only to offer a "helping hand."

Examples can be gleaned here and there to show that the sans-culotte demands were acted upon, not systematically, but by some individuals. A Captain Dunesme, of the 6th battalion of Orléans, records in the register kept by his unit that two prisoners were taken in a battle near Liège and "immediately sacrificed to the shades of our unfortunate brothers who also had been killed without pity." The theme of the French soldiers martyred by the enemy ran through the camps, and was taken up in popular literature and in songs and engravings sold for a few *sous* as far as the smallest villages. Brothers' blood called for vengeance.

The new warfare was to use mass tactics and inspire terror by fierce attack with the bayonet. Cold steel, and more precisely the pike, gave a reminder of the great revolutionary days on which the people liberated themselves. During the summer of 1793, while the sans-culottes clamored for the Levy in Mass and the government took steps to increase war production, the pike made a reappearance as the ultimate recourse against tyrants. From the sans-culottes the idea passed to the Jacobins. On September 21 the deputy Lejeune declared that the pike could be very useful, that this terrible weapon had been too long neglected, that the aristocrats had intentionally discredited it, and that it was with pikes in hand that the French people had regenerated themselves. Some generals saw tactical advantages in the combined use of pikemen and musketeers: two ranks of men with muskets would be so strengthened by a rampart of pikes as to be unafraid of a cavalry squadron. But along with these zealots of the pike there were doubters. An engineer, Claude Nicolas Closquenet, advised the Committee of Public Safety, on August 31, 1793 (in somewhat confused language), that it would be better

> to give the pikes to women, or our brave sans-culottes with guns on their shoulders could break the pikestaffs on the backs of the faint-hearted who to sacrifice them more surely would see them armed only with a broom handle better suited than a gun barrel to go on these rascals' shoulders.

The army absorbed this myth of cold steel, if not of the pike at least of the bayonet. General Meunier, in charge of a training camp for young recruits, gave evidence of it by calling one of his reports to the war ministry "The Bayonet and the Republic." For him, as for Generals Dejardins and Houchard, cold steel should be often employed as a means of quick success and of sparing casualties. To eulogize cold steel was to be revolutionary; to doubt its effectiveness was to give proof of aristocratism. Collot d'Herbois, repeating what he had said in 1792, and what had then been greeted with murmurs of objection, cried out in the Convention on September 6, 1793:

> What delays our production of arms is dragging along with the routine of manufactures. . . . Isn't it the bayonet, cold steel, that makes the French superior to the slaves of tyrants? While waiting for the production of guns you will cool off this impulsive and holy enthusiasm that is carrying 300,000 men to our frontiers. Let us arm our soldiers with pikes, and remember the words of a Spartan woman to her son. He said to her, "My sword is a bit short." "My son," replied his republican mother, "you will take one more step forward." We,

too, will take one more step forward and knock down the enemies of Liberty all the better.

Responsible political leaders, like Carnot, who had little in common with the sans-culottes, were also converted to this idea of a mass attack with fixed bayonets.

In summary, by the autumn of 1793 the popular movement had pushed the Convention into taking the measures of internal policy necessitated by the national defense. The sans-culottes had pressed for democratizing the army and changing its methods of combat. Some of their aspirations had been favored by the Jacobins, but neither the Jacobins nor the Committee of Public Safety meant to let the army escape from control. The strength they gained against moderates in the Convention, thanks to the popular movement, allowed them now to realize their objectives.

CHAPTER VII

The Revolutionary Government and the Army (Autumn 1793 to 9 Thermidor, Year II): Unity and Subordination

The term Revolutionary Government was used at the time to mean the governing apparatus of France from the late summer of 1793, when the hastily produced democratic constitution was suspended, until the fall of Robespierre and reduction of the powers of the Committee of Public Safety at the end of July 1794. It was authorized by the Convention in a decree of October 10, 1793: "The provisional government of France is revolutionary until the peace." It coincides roughly with the Year II and the Terror.

The Committee of Public Safety had begun to exercise military authority even before Robespierre joined it on July 27, 1793. The first Committee (April 10 to July 10) had included Danton, who had set up a military cabinet composed of military men and technical experts to advise him. In June it had been decided that the minister of war should consult with the Committee of Public Safety, which was now charged by the Convention with the supervision of military operations. The minister thereafter submitted a daily report to the Committee.

The second or "great" Committee of Public Safety (July 1793

to July 1794) soon enlarged its role from mere supervision to the actual determination of military action. The personnel of its war section became more numerous, with bureaus filled with dozens of civil servants more able to answer questions and effectively duplicating the ministry of war. The topographic office attached to the Committee of Public Safety became a veritable general staff.

But the Committee remained a target for the attacks of ultrarevolutionaries. As late as October the journalist Guffroy, of the *Rougyff*, denounced Carnot among others as a protector of aristocrats. The radical press campaign was supported by Vincent and Celliez. But through the intervention of Robespierre and Billaud-Varenne the affair came to nothing.

It was only with the decree of 14 Frimaire Year II (December 4, 1793) that the Committee of Public Safety, as an agency subordinate to the Convention, could become the center of initiative in military as well as in civilian matters. All constituted bodies and public functionaries came under its direct inspection. Generals owed it absolute obedience. "In a free state the military power is the one most in need of control. It is a passive lever to be moved by the national will." The minister of war was required henceforth to send all administrative documents in his possession to the Committee. He was to provide it every day with a summary of the correspondence he had received. He must report immediately all actions that he took. Vincent still attempted to resist. He was arrested, then released; but his numerous friends in the ministry remained obstructive. Only with the execution of Hébert and the ultrarevolutionaries in March 1794, and the transformation of the war ministry into a simple executive commission, could the Committee get the "military lever" fully into its hands.

The role of Carnot in the Committee was considerable. The "organizer of victory" made the army into an effective instrument of war, but at the same time he worked to turn it into a traditional army cut off from political factions, and even took psychological measures to prepare it for the fall of Robespierre. But Carnot was not the only member of the Committee concerned with military questions. Prieur of the Côte-d'Or, for example, had charge of supplies. And the activities of Saint-Just must be emphasized; as the son of an army man himself, he showed real competence in military affairs when sent on mission to the armies; and he strove especially, like other Jacobin representatives on mission, to make the army, once it was unified and more reliably commanded, into a school of Jacobinism.

1. UNIFYING THE ARMY: INCORPORATION, BRIGADE FORMING, AND AMALGAMATION

Like the volunteer battalions of 1792, the battalions of draftees showed themselves to be undisciplined and timid under fire. General Elie wrote on October 15, 1793: "Soldiers of the mass levy are frightened by the *chasseurs* on their flanks, whom they mistake for the enemy. They fire on their own skirmishers, and then flee." He said also that he expected little good from inexperienced troops who had never been under fire, and "who are perhaps animated more by the memory of what attaches them to life than by an impulse to live free or die." Other complaints came from municipalities traversed by battalions of draftees: the young recruits provoked disorder, and it would be better if they were merged into the older units. Finally, there was a political ground for concern: it had been observed that certain counter-revolutionary elements, notably federalists, had sometimes slipped into the higher ranks of these battalions.

Saint-Just, during his mission to Alsace, on 1 Brumaire (October 22) authorized General Sautter to incorporate into the battalions under his command "the number of men of the first requisition necessary for completing the battalions." Hentz and Bô acted similarly at the Army of the Ardennes.

Carnot agreed with Saint-Just, judging that the rapid organization and integration of new recruits was urgent if the full value of the Levy in Mass was to be obtained. The Committee of Public Safety, on 2 Frimaire (November 22, 1793), secured a decree of the Convention for the principle of incorporation. The draftees would first be assigned to the existing demi-brigades to bring their effective strength to about 3,200 men. Other draftees would then be assigned to other battalions, beginning with those of the oldest date of formation.

Many battalions objected. They mixed sociological, political, and military arguments in their protests. "We would prefer to serve together," wrote the battalion commander Couture, a Jacobin from Amiens, "because when men know and like each other the reverses are less discouraging and the successes more a source of pride." When a battalion was a projection from its community of origin, the sans-culotte and Jacobin militants could feel more at home, and carry on the education of their brothers. "Our battalion is a traveling club," protested the 16th battalion of the Haute-Saône. "We teach one another our duties, and we trust our leaders; they are both patriotic and well instructed."

In any case, how could one live with men whose language and customs one did not share? Thus some draftees from the Haute-Garonne asked permission to leave the Moselle battalion to which they had been assigned, and be transferred to the Tarn battalion where the customs were more like their own. "The interests of the Republic will be served with more zeal," they affirmed, "by citizens who fight alongside their relatives and friends."

Sometimes a parochial spirit revealed itself. If the draftees won some success, who would get the credit? Merged into another battalion, "they will be sunk in oblivion under a name not their own." As citizen soldiers, they said, they should preserve the right to choose their own "administrators." But how could they do so, in good conscience, if they were ignorant of the qualifications of those proposed to them? Moreover, according to the 11th battalion of the Meurthe, by remaining united under their elected leaders they would move forward "with more energy and confidence, with the character and attitude that distinguish zealous defenders of their country from mercenary phalanxes."

Municipalities from which the draftees came intervened in their favor. Cases are known from the Corrèze and the Haute-Vienne. If their petitions went unanswered there was the possibility of rebellion, manifesting itself at first in massive desertion.

> We are informed [wrote the administration of Arras on December 10] that a great number of volunteers of the new levy, on learning of the decree of the 2nd of this month ordering their incorporation into older units, are quitting the army and returning to their home towns or villages.

Officers of the draftees, fearing the loss of their rank, pressed their men to refuse incorporation. One company of a battalion of draftees from Beauvais, on the road to Reims, stopped abruptly at Gros-Chêne. It refused to be dissolved. The authorities intervened with force and, to set an example, condemned the company to be shot. Municipal agents of Crépy took the case to Collot d'Herbois. The lives of the men were saved. But the company was imprisoned for six weeks in the church at Dammartin, and thereafter was known in the army by a disgusting nickname.

The government issued threats. Any military man using language that might excite trouble or obstruct execution of the law on incorporation would be brought before a criminal court, and if judged guilty of conspiracy would be liable to the death penalty. At the same time the government called on the Jacobins of the provinces to preach the necessity of incorporation to their brothers in arms. Some clubs complied.

In the midst of these difficulties the incorporation still went on. But it proceeded slowly, and was not completed by the spring and summer of 1794 when the draftees first came into combat. A survey of thirty-three regiments reveals that incorporation brought together men of widely distant places of origin. Lorrainers and Alsatians mixed with men from the West, the Seine-et-Oise, the Center, and the Midi. Men related to the Chouans shared the same mess with those from the Paris Basin, and draftees from the Center were elbow to elbow with men from eastern France.

Regiments with a certain homogeneity, arising from regional

recruitment, were suddenly swamped with citizens from all other regions of France. The 33rd regiment, for example, was composed of men from the eastern departments (Ardennes, Vosges, and Aube); it was transformed by incorporation of draftees from the Ille-et-Vilaine, the Manche, the Midi, and the Nord. In the 34th, the "whites" from the towns and countryside in the West formed a compact body of five hundred men. After the incorporation, they were mixed with men from the Pas-de-Calais, the Dordogne, the Nièvre, the Mayenne, and even from Martinique.

On the other hand there were some regiments where incorporation, far from producing a "little France," made them all the more regional. The 68th became a regiment of Parisians, the 77th of Bretons, the 82nd of Normans, and the 94th of men from Sologne.

The experience of the volunteer battalions was like that of the regular regiments. On the whole, mixture predominated. Draftees from the Allier were put into the volunteer battalions of the Pyrénées-Orientales, the Jura, and the Marne. Those from the Ardennes were distributed among battalions from the Seine-et-Oise, the Nord, the Loiret, and the Var. On the other hand, the volunteer battalion of the Ariège received draftees from that department.

In the letters of draftees to their parents, their individual reactions to incorporation are usually limited to giving an address to which mail could be sent. But some express their feelings, and correct the impression of hostility to incorporation that we obtain from other sources. These draftees reveal the comfort felt by novices at being put with men who could teach them how to overcome their fears. A young abbé from Picardy, taken in the requisition of August, wrote to his parents:

> Our battalion being incorporated with the 3rd battalion of the Meurthe, we now find ourselves at Prisches amalgamated with Lorrainers, but without being separated from our comrades, because each of our companies has come intact into the

company with the same number in the said battalion. Before incorporation, I must admit, we had been living a communal but not at all a military life. Now we are fully initiated. Drills, reviews, duties, everything is in strict order. The veterans are satisfied with our progress, and say that we shall soon be able to assist them.

Not all reports were so positive. In some units the incorporation of too many draftees led to panic. And some sixty battalions of draftees were not incorporated until 1796, so that their military skills were slow to develop.

Some draftees were assigned to the cavalry. A sampling shows that in more than half the cavalry regiments the veterans still constituted more than half their strength. In others, the older and newer recruits were balanced. In four regiments the draftees outnumbered the veterans.

By raising the numbers in each battalion, incorporation made it possible to proceed with the process of amalgamation. But now again, at the level of responsible political leadership, we find the hesitations and indeed the opposition that arose from different political views. In January 1794 Cochon de Lapparent was appointed to prepare a report on the brigading of the infantry. He was a moderate bourgeois and member of the Jacobin Society, who at one time had abandoned the Society and joined the Feuillants. He laid out the arguments against brigading before the Convention. Skillfully drawing on the difficulties met with in the process of incorporation, he argued that the reasons underlying the law of February and decree of August 1793 were no longer valid. He concluded that the projected operation was impossible:

To effect an amalgamation it is indispensable to examine the administration, accounts, and funds of each unit, to take possession of the records and registers of the old administrations and use them in formation of the new ones, to allow for balances due, to verify the service records of all the officers, determine their rank in the new formation, and examine the papers of those claiming military indemnities or admission to the Hôtel des Invalides. For anyone who knows armies it is easy to imagine what delays and difficulties such operations will produce, when they must be carried on in the presence of the enemy and among troops that are continually in active service. . . . It is impossible to deny that the three required battalions will only rarely be found in close proximity, and we shall even be forced to brigade battalions that cannot really be combined until the peace.

Correspondence received by the minister seemed to support Cochon's objections. General Hesse complained to Bouchotte that the required effort was very great, especially in the verification of unit accounts. "Your colleagues," he wrote, "or rather your bureau chiefs, attribute to me the fabulous property of transporting myself everywhere, like Jesus Christ." The commission to the Army of the Côtes-de-Brest echoed him: "The 3rd demi-brigade," he wrote, "which is to be composed of the 2nd battalion of the 9th Infantry regiment in garrison at Belle-Isle, the 3rd battalion of the Maine-et-Loire, and the 3rd battalion of the Loir-et-Cher, has been impossible to form until now, considering that the two latter battalions are geographically separated and have been unable to send any information to Citizen Cachelin, commander of the 2nd battalion, 9th regiment."

In rejecting amalgamation, Cochon also noted the reluctance of men to mix with soldiers of different origin from themselves. Care must be taken, he said, not to dampen enthusiasm and to avoid bringing together men who could not sympathize with one another. Nor did he think amalgamation could be recommended on technical grounds. Incorporation had produced battalions of 1,067 men; if generals needed larger units they could combine these battalions provisionally. And finally, amalgamation and formation of demi-brigades might be fraught with political dangers:

In a Republic it is impolitic and dangerous to maintain armed men in large bodies. The more they are divided the less easy they are to corrupt. A capable but perfidious general can take advantage of large bodies of men and their esprit de corps; he can easily win over their officers, and we know how great the influence of a brave, intelligent, and clever commander can be.

The argument was all the more pertinent because the Convention remembered the treason of Dumouriez and Custine. Fear of the "generalate," as they called it, was on everyone's mind. But there may have been political reasons for this fear, since Cochon also gave assurances that the troops were patriotic.

Another danger that he pointed out was the danger of federalism: "To organize brigades preserves the dangers of federalism, by brigading battalions from the same department. It produces ideas of localism and isolation that might end by leading us to federalism." But neither the earlier steps in brigading, nor incorporation, had given examples of such a danger, except in a few cases.

Dubois-Crancé replied to Cochon's arguments. He used the very language of Cochon's report to show that brigading was a military necessity. "The author of the report has not attacked brigading from the point of view of military operations. On the contrary, he has agreed that the generals would be obliged to brigade their battalions." Turning to the political aspect, Dubois-Crancé pointed to the danger of leaving brigading to the caprice of the generals. He restated the spirit of the law of February 1793: "To break the spirit of the old line army and see that the germs of aristocracy are not perpetuated." He convinced the Convention, which decreed that henceforth "all infantry of the Republic, including the battalions of *chasseurs*, shall be organized in demi-brigades, each composed of three battalions and a company of cannoneers, according to the laws of February 21 and August 12."

Why was there this opposition to amalgamation? Was Cochon really speaking for someone else? Was the principal actor really Carnot? Carnot had shown himself the faithful supporter of Dubois-Crancé in February 1793, and after that of Saint-Just when the latter went forward with incorporations. He kept silent in January 1794, but was Cochon not already one of his "creatures"? Later, at the time of suppression of Babeuf's conspiracy, Cochon was to be his minister of police. Had the organizer of victory been impressed by the opposition to incorporation? Under pressure by some of the local governments, he had agreed to suspend the incorporation of certain battalions, such as the one of Arras. Did he fear a general movement of discontent at the announcement of amalgamation? Did he exaggerate the unavoidable difficulties? Could he have been influenced, as Daniel Guérin has suggested, by the staff officers who surrounded him and who were all military men from the Old Regime? Did he hope to preserve the regiments from Montagnard contamination, from invasion by the *bras-nus*, the bare-armed laboring class, so as to safeguard the future?

On January 10, 1794, the Convention issued its directive for the brigading of infantry units. Demi-brigades would be formed under the responsibility of a representative of the people, assisted by a general officer and a war commissioner. It was recommended that the representatives on mission act rapidly but with prudence. They were to inform themselves on the numerical, material, and moral situation of the battalions to be combined, paying special attention "to their habits and sympathies." No actual movement of troops was to be involved. In cases where battalions scheduled for brigading were distant from one another, the minister of war would take measures to bring them gradually closer together. The directive did not specify whether there should be real fusion, hence amalgamation, or only juxtaposition. It referred back to the laws of February 21 and August 12, both of which had provided for various modes of procedure.

The civil power controlling *embrigadement* assumed also the right to name the commanders of the demi-brigades. They would be chosen by the representative of the people on the basis of their education, zeal, and intelligence. This policy was part of the general program of the Committee of Public Safety, which in the winter and spring of 1794 was on the systematic lookout for talent.

Amalgamation was intended not only to unify the army, but also to provide the government with a better knowledge of its armed forces. It involved a series of preparatory steps that delayed its completion. Each battalion commander began by making a thorough inspection of his unit. Then the war commissioners assembled the administrative councils, or boards of officers, of each unit; verified their procedures; and prepared a report for the representative of the people. The report consisted in a listing of the number and names of the men in each company, to be reviewed in the presence of its captain, the other principal officers, the quartermasters, surgeon-major, and sergeant-majors. The representative of the people examined the physical characteristics of the men, their height, arms, clothing, leather equipment, haircuts, and knapsacks. He approved or disapproved the cases of men on leave, and looked into the professional training of the officers, and their knowledge of discipline and tactics. Files were thus accumulated on the resources and command structure of the battalions. The amalgamation began as a grand survey such as had never been made of the army as it then existed. A huge mass of paperwork resulted, a necessary bureaucracy of which all battalions complained; but in the end the authorities knew, very largely, who was who and what role he played in this or that battalion.

Formation of the demi-brigades went on over a period of more than thirty months, if we include those created in the early stages. Beginning in the second half of 1793, the amalgamation was completed in February 1796, at which time a second process of brigading was being planned. From September 1793 until April 1794—that is, until the opening of the spring campaign—only 63 demi-brigades were organized out of a total that reached 236 by 1796. During the operations that led to the victory at Fleurus (June 1794) the arms of the Republic were still being forged.

Demi-brigades were formed more rapidly in the Army of the North than in the others. Here one-third of those to be constituted already existed in April 1794, and nine-tenths were on a war footing by the end of the year. In the Army of the Rhine the process went more slowly; it speeded up during the summer, but by the year's end one-half of the demi-brigades were still to be organized. In the Army of the Alps and the Army of Italy one-half of the demi-brigades were ready in April, and two-thirds by the winter of 1794–1795. In the Army of the Pyrenees the operation was held back by the lack of regiments from the old regular army; then after victory had been won some battalions were detached and sent for amalgamation in the Army of Italy. In the Army of the West the dispersion of battalions in the hedgerow terrain made amalgamation difficult, and one-half of the demi-brigades were not yet formed at the end of the year.

Brigading was not always synonymous with amalgamation, that is, with fusion of "whites" and "blues" within the smallest combat units. At least one-quarter of the demi-brigades contained only volunteers. In others there was only juxtaposition within the same battalion of companies of different origin, or in some cases juxtaposition of "white" and "blue" battalions. But if we follow the life of these demi-brigades in their registers, we see that, after a few months or a year, the losses were such that commanders mixed the men within the units.

What military experience did these soldiers have? What were their ages and physical constitution? A sampling of 12,682 cases, from all arms, shows that 37 percent were recent recruits. This percentage was higher at the end of the Year II (September 1794), by which time the requisition under the Levy in Mass had produced its contingent. More than 62 percent had received their baptism of fire. More than 15 percent were volunteers of 1793 who had seen the campaign of the fall and winter of that year. More than 23 percent were volunteers of 1792 who had lived through the battles in the Argonne, the invasion of Belgium, and the ensuing defeats at the hands of the First Coalition. More than one-quarter were volunteers of 1791 and soldiers of the Old Regime who had also seen combat for at least two years. The volunteers of 1791 were now only a small minority (4.6 percent). Soldiers of the former royal army still formed 18.4 percent of the total, but real veterans enlisted before 1789 were few, only 5.5 percent.

As a whole, then, the soldiers of the national and revolutionary army, to the extent of nearly 95 percent, were men enrolled since the beginning of the Revolution. By arms, the proportion of men with good combat experience was not the same. In the cavalry and artillery men of the former royal army were more numerous—respectively 34.1 percent and 55.2 percent—than in the light infantry (less than 10 percent) and the battle infantry (14.2 percent). There were also differences between the demi-brigades. In the 26th demi-brigade of line infantry, in the Army of the Ardennes, 52.4 percent of the men were draftees and only 6.3 percent were soldiers of the former army. The 16th, on the other hand, approached the average with 40 percent of draftees and 17 percent of "whites." The armies also differed; the Army of the North and the Army of the Rhine had more experienced men than the Army of the Pyrenees.

The long marches and early engagements had eliminated the men of mature age who remained in the volunteer battalions and in the regular regiments. Some 77 percent of soldiers of the Year II were aged twenty-five or less. The offspring of hard times, they belonged to the generation that had seen, during their childhood and adolescence, bread at two *sous* to the pound, bad soup in cheap eating places, and village unemployment. But there were differences from unit to unit. Men over forty could be counted on the fingers of one hand in the 1st battalion of the 16th infantry regiment, but there were dozens of them in the 3rd, 6th, and 24th. The light infantry, where the proportion of draftees and volunteers of 1793 was most important, seems to have been the youngest arm, with 81 percent of its soldiers under twenty-five. The battle infantry approached this percentage, but the cavalry was far from it, with 66 percent under twenty-five. The artillery had more men older than thirty than the other arms. The Army of the Pyrenees was younger than the Army of the North or the Army of the Sambre-Meuse.

In 1763, in the French army as studied by A. Corvisier, average stature had been 5 feet 3 inches and 1 line, or 1.70 meters.[1] The army at that time, able to select its soldiers, had benefited from the rise in stature of Frenchmen during the course of the century. But, as we have seen, the volunteer battalions, recruiting less selectively in the north of France and in the south, where statures were shorter, were made up of soldiers who were rarely more than 1.67 meters tall. It was the same with the draftees; 65 percent of them were under 1.67 meters, and over a third were between 1.51[2] and 1.65. The shortest men found it difficult to handle a musket, and more than one of their comrades were wounded as a result of their awkwardness.

Heights were higher in the cavalry and artillery than in the infantry. Career officers estimated that cavalrymen should measure at least 1.67 meters if they were to manage their horses properly and be effective in the charge. Only 8 percent in the cavalry failed to reach this height; 75.6 percent exceeded 1.70 and 23 percent exceeded 1.75. The tallest men were found in the artillery, where 90 percent were over 1.70 meters and 8.8 percent over 1.81.[3]

The formation of demi-brigades had created the tactical units needed for command; it had prevented the spread of old regimental esprit de corps and the friction between "whites" and "blues"; and it allowed the Revolutionary Government to obtain better knowledge of its army and better control over it. Amalgamation, resulting gradually from the formation of demi-brigades, answered also to the Jacobin call for national unity. The Jacobins tirelessly taught men from Alsace, the Auvergne, and the Midi that they were all sons of the same country. The army was the instrument of national unity par excellence. The armies of the North, the Rhine, the Alps, and the Pyrenees were crucibles in which local particularisms were melted. Of course, in a general

---

[1] In Anglo-American measurement, 5 feet 7 inches.
[2] Five feet.
[3] That is, 90 percent over 5 feet 7 inches, and 8.8 percent over 5 feet 11 inches, in Anglo-American measurement.

way, the armies recruited in their surrounding areas. Our survey shows, for example, that a majority of soldiers in the Army of the North originated in the departments between the Seine, the Meuse, and the Channel. The Army of the Rhine was mainly composed of men from departments between the Meuse, the Rhine, and Doubs. The Army of the Pyrenees was made up especially of soldiers from between the Dordogne, the Atlantic, and the Mediterranean. The Army of the Alps and Italy drew from departments south of the Haute-Saône and east of the Rhône.

But in all the armies there were recruits from almost all departments. The Army of the North had contingents from the Bouches-du-Rhône, Calvados, Morbihan, Lot, Lot-et-Garonne, and Dordogne. Many examples could be given to show that no army had a specific regional composition, and that in all of them the French language was taught and learned. To become a corporal, sergeant, or officer, a knowledge of reading and writing in the national language was required. The Revolutionary Government so ordered it.

2. THE COMMAND STRUCTURE: OFFICERS AND NCOS

"Obey!" The Committee of Public Safety had shown what fate awaited disloyal generals or those who failed to follow orders strictly. It exerted the same authority over subordinate officers. More than one career officer had grumbled against the amalgamation. There had been talk against the Committee, and some officers had surreptitiously encouraged their men to oppose the formation of demi-brigades. The response of the Revolutionary Government was immediate: imprisonment of officers, prompt judgment, and condemnation to death.

Against both treachery and ignorance the Committee and the ministry carried on the purge. But where could experienced men be found to replace the fallen chiefs? Would commands be given to men who had formerly been in only some mechanical trade? General Krieg warned against such an outcome on August 9. Or would incompetents be seen to shoot "like lightning" from company rank to the head of larger formations?

Carnot, who understood the excesses that sometimes occurred in the purge, intervened to save certain officers. The commander of an artillery battery or a fortification could not be produced by improvisation. Artillery and engineering officers, cashiered as nobles, had to be reinstated. The Committee agreed with Carnot. On January 13, 1794, noble officers of the "learned arms" were reinstalled in their posts. For others, a decree was in preparation by December 16.

The Committee, through the representatives on mission, understood the damage done by pursuit of suspects in the army. It knew that soldiers in many cases denounced their leaders because of old grudges. The result had been the hecatombs of the autumn and early winter.

A good patriot not only had to train his men; he needed a minimum of education, to read and understand his orders; and a minimum of military instruction, to know how to maneuver his troops. Well before the Committee issued orders to this effect some of the generals, such as Hoche, had refused to remove nobles among their staff officers. Colonels and battalion commanders who themselves originated in the Third Estate did the same with their company commanders who had the misfortune to be *ci-devant*. The administrative council of the 95th demi-brigade, for example, made great efforts to keep François Sermizelles, an aristocratic captain who had served for twenty years. In the 101st demi-brigade the council requested not only the retention of a noble officer but his promotion to higher rank.

As between officers who excelled at maneuvers but were politically doubtful, and partisans of the new regime who were without much talent, the Committee took a realistic stand. It put a premium on talent, but sought also to change the mentality of the professional officer. While allowing this "revenge of the talented," the government prepared for the future by creating a school to produce patriots with technical expertise, the Ecole de Mars, for which the pupils were chosen from among the sons of sans-culottes.

By decrees of November 22 and a law of July 19 the Revolutionary Government intervened in the appointment of lower-rank officers and NCOs. One-third of the vacancies in a unit was reserved for choice by the Convention. The choice was between three candidates proposed by the administrative council and battalion or demi-brigade commander. For the other two-thirds of the posts to be filled, the rules of seniority and of election, as modified by co-optation, remained in effect.

Seniority in years of service was denounced by career officers. It brought to the head of companies and battalions, they said, "men who are too old, worn out, and whose minds have become too rigid." Such a system of promotion was unfair "to all officers who had given proof of their talent by seniority in their rank." Anyone who had received early promotion to NCO "would find himself frozen in rank, because subordinates who had enlisted at an even earlier date would have an advantage over him at each step in his career." Hence one would see

> old soldiers, who before their service had been hairdressers or something of that kind, very soon at the head of units that they are not qualified to lead. . . . The administrative councils will consist, in the majority, of men who have no claim except age; without talent, they will bring disorder into the records.

A survey in the registers of officers reveals that these complaints against one part of the law were not always exaggerated. Along with age and wounds received, the files of the demi-brigades show that some officers suffered from disabilities and infirmities. If they had not lost their teeth, or become so short-sighted as to be thought blind, they were affected by double hernias, descents of organs, and rheumatisms that made them unfit for long marches. "They encumber the dépôts," said Carnot, "and they are with the army only because of their own needs. Their services become more dangerous than useful, and they spread discouragement."

It was only in the following year that the rule of seniority in service was replaced by seniority in attained rank. The Revolutionary Government clung to a bad rule because it feared giving offense to old servants of the state, who were annoyed at the use of talent as a criterion in the promotions that could be made by choice. Many protested like the commander of the 6th Hussars:

> If I am reproached for not having much talent I am not the only one afflicted by this malady. I would like to have more knowledge, but at the age of fifteen I did not know that there was going to be a revolution. I know enough to make my men march properly. I have never lost a single man through my own fault, and when it comes to sharing dangers I am always in the forefront.

The Revolutionary Government resolutely pursued its policy of searching for talent, which in part mitigated the effects of promotion by seniority of service. Many old soldiers could not read or write. On February 15, 1794, an ability to read and write was made prerequisite for the ranks of corporal, sergeant, and commissioned officer. In March a vast survey was launched, which continued into July, to ascertain the level of education and military training of all officers and NCOs. Could they not only read and write, but count and draw? Could they read a map, or indicate a terrain on a scaled drawing? Could they readily maneuver a platoon, a company, or a battalion? Did they remain cool in battle? Did they have judgment, and a faculty for quick observation? As someone said in the Convention, it was no longer enough to have been a revolutionary in Paris or elsewhere; it was necessary to know something seriously. Ignorance, and a superstitious regard for force, violence, and severity, would no longer be seen as marks of patriotism or qualify for rapid promotion. Here and there, in the camps, examinations and tests were organized to reveal undiscovered abilities.

The Revolutionary Government favored the professional soldier, but it intended to change his attitude. Jacobins and sans-culottes were shocked by the behavior of some career officers found in the volunteer battalions as well as in the old army. They were heard to speak of "their" company and "their" men. They made some of them into personal servants. They were arrogant and brutal to the soldiers. General Gilot, for example, was accused of treating his soldiers "like slaves."

It was feared that rank might engender a new aristocracy. The Jacobins explained to the military chiefs that, as in civil society, "to command is improper, for, however much the law is observed, it is not commanded." The army was the offshoot of civilian society; in the army as in civilian society the Republic placed its citizens according to the public good. In whatever posts they were put, citizens should respect the general will as expressed by law through the Convention. The soldier owed no loyalty to his chief; he owed all his loyalty to his country.

The chief was, for the moment and by will of the Republic, the first among equals. He should model his attitude on that of the people, which possessed the true patriotic virtues. He should imitate the common soldier and the representative on mission in teaching the following syllogism: the people are virtuous, the soldiers are of the people, therefore the soldiers are virtuous. It was among the soldiers that courage, heroism, unselfishness, and love of country reached sublime heights. By acting like the soldier, the officer would be in communion with the people. By this unity he would develop the qualities that made him worthy of the place to which the Republic assigned him.

The officer should show by his apparel the austerity of the Jacobin or the sans-culotte—no more oversized epaulettes or overload of gilt. In camp, his good morals should be evident—he avoided prostitutes and ordered them driven away. In the evening, his duties over, he did not spend his time with the bottle—he was never seen "tipsy." He received soldiers as brothers, and was scrupulously careful, in conversation, to avoid any tone or expression that might suggest haughtiness. When on duty, he must always remain calm. A certain colonel Boyer, who sometimes insulted and mistreated the hussars under his orders, was subjected to an investigation. In his defense he said that he struck the men not as a colonel, but because he was of an impetuous and hot-blooded temperament. He promised to mend his ways.

Sacred equality obtained without distinction of color. On this ground the commander of the 13th regiment of mounted *chasseurs* was severely rebuked: officers in his unit had mistreated some blacks in their company.

In camp or away from it, the officer should read the patriot press, informing himself especially on the laws, and making them known to his men. Every day he should prepare himself for combat, learning from more capable friends. On the battlefield he should prove himself a patriot by deeds, not words. Master of himself, he was to give an example of bravery, never accepting surrender or retreat, pursuing and destroying the enemy.

The officer who failed thus to behave himself should be reported by his subordinates. In the military, as for the sans-culotte and Jacobin, delation became a civic duty. "We believe in the generosity and virtue of the soldier," wrote Saint-Just. "Tell them for us that we hope they will turn in those they believe culpable, and that we have high expectations from the heart of the French soldiers."

But the soldier must be careful to avoid slander, which would be firmly punished. An officer of patriotic demeanor should be strictly obeyed; like a magistrate, he was clothed with the authority of the law. So while the Jacobins educated the leaders, they taught the troops to accept and observe the discipline necessary for victory.

For the most part, the officers learned the lesson. When making nominations for promotion in their administrative councils, they presented candidates as men of proven civic rectitude, jealous of the public good, and exact in maintaining order. Captain Leydier of the 6th battalion of the Ardèche was regarded by all as a model of the patriot officer: pleasant and affable in society, rigid in his duties without giving offense, he knew how to adopt the tone of

command without forgetting the tone of friendliness and fraternity.

But not all adapted to the Jacobin model. Many career officers
continued to act as in the past, and some, as we shall see, managed
to circumvent the laws. What most of them absorbed from the
Jacobin policy was the restoration of discipline.

How was the command structure modified by the purges, the
losses due to war, and the promotions effected by the Committee
and its representatives? Who were the officers that led the soldiers
of the Year II to victory? Four examples give us an indication.

The first was named Despeaux. He was born in 1761 in a parish
in the Ile-de-France. His father was a farmer, and he himself had
begun by guiding a plow. At the age of fifteen, from need or impulse, he enlisted in one of the king's regiments. In the Year II he
was a general.

The second, Pierre Girardon, was born at Saint-Pierre near Bar-
sur-Aube in Champagne. His father was a merchant tanner, who
in middle life had retired to the country to manage some property
in which he had invested the gains of his business. Pierre was a
boy "given to foolishness," and when his schooling was over his
father thought to settle him down by placing him in the army.
This was in 1789; the Bastille had been taken, riots broke out in
the countryside, and the first Jacobin clubs were opening in the
provinces. Pierre made himself known to the lesser bourgeois of
the town, who conceived "the highest regard for his enlightened
views, through the intelligence, clarity, and judgment that he ex-
hibited in various discussions of the Society." In April 1792, giving up his property at Chalvaudet and another property acquired
from the convent of the Cordeliers at Bar, he left it to his father to
deal with his debtors, and became a hussar. He did well under fire,
and enjoyed good relations with his superior officers, including
General Lamarche. He knew also how to abandon friends when
they became suspects. In the Year II, a brave patriot, wounded
several times, and well esteemed by his administrative council, he
had risen in two years from sub-lieutenant to captain.

L. Glence came from the world of artisans and small retailers. Born at Quimper in 1756, his father was a hairdresser who gave him some education. He escaped from a trade troubled by excessive competition and depressed conditions. He joined the army, but despite his talents, and under the aristocratic reaction, could rise no higher than noncommissioned officer in fourteen years. As for many others, the Revolution gave him his revenge. He mounted the steps of the military ladder in a few years, and in the Year II was a colonel commanding the 54th demi-brigade.

The fourth was named Gudin. In the Year II he was forty-one years old and in command of the 95th demi-brigade. Born at Ouroux in the Nièvre, of a family of lawyers, he was one of those *bourgeois à talents*, or middle-class professionals, who had made the Revolution and owed everything to it. Head of a tax office in the Creuse, he gave up his tax registers in 1792 and volunteered in the 2nd battalion of the Creuse.

These men were typical officers of the Year II, when two out of four were professional soldiers. With the generals the proportion was higher, with 87.3 percent of them having been in the army before 1789, and a majority (67 percent) having at that date seen thirteen or more years of service. The Old Regime, within the limits of the aristocratic reaction, had recognized their talents; of these generals, 22.9 percent had been NCOs and 41.8 percent officers in 1789. Commanders of demi-brigades and battalions were also men with military experience; 86.9 and 73.1 percent, respectively, had served before 1789. More than 46 percent of the demi-brigade commanders, and 43 percent of the battalion commanders, had seen thirteen or more years of service before 1789. Among the brigade commanders, 39.7 percent had been officers in 1789, and 41 percent had been NCOs. From a survey of more than 20 percent of company-level officers in the battle infantry, we find that half of them had known the trade of arms before 1789. Of the captains, 59.6 percent had frequented the camps of the old monarchy, half of them for nine years before 1789. The lieutenants (46.2 percent career soldiers) averaged more than nine years with the colors in 1789. Fewer of the sub-lieutenants were military professionals (43.9 percent), but most of them had had more than four years of service at the dawn of the Revolution. These company-level officers owed their rank to the Revolution, because only 4.6 percent of the captains had been officers in 1789, and most of them (54.8 percent) had been only corporals.

There were differences between arms of the service. The cavalry had the largest number of professionals, with more than 80 percent having served before 1789. Of the cavalry captains, 60 percent had more than thirteen years of service in 1789, and a majority were then already sergeant-majors or officers. In the artillery 84 percent of the captains, 73.7 percent of the lieutenants, and 80.8 percent of the sub-lieutenants knew how to serve an artillery piece before the Revolution broke out. Most of the captains had practiced their trade for more than thirteen years. Engineer officers counted the largest number of experienced men.

Differences existed also between one army and another. The Army of the North and that of the Rhine, in the battle infantry, had more career officers than the others. Inspectors found all of them qualified in tactical maneuvers, and 60.9 percent of the captains in the battle infantry were well grounded in the military art. They were not unschooled; 85 percent of the captains, 81 percent of the lieutenants, and 78.7 percent of the sub-lieutenants could read and write. Some could also make computations, 54 percent in the Army of the North.

Because these professional soldiers had enlisted at a young age, their average age was no higher than that of the nonprofessional officers. The generals commanding divisions were not as young as a tenacious legend, based on a few individual cases, would lead us to believe. But a majority of the divisional as well as the brigade generals were between twenty-one and forty-five. We find the same relative youth among the colonels; 30 percent were under thirty-five, and 58 percent under forty-five. In the battle infantry half the captains were under thirty. Officers of such ages possessed a vital drive and dash that carried their men along.

We take as an example an action of Lieutenant Jean Repp, on October 18, 1793, at the head of the 10th mounted *chasseurs*. His horse was frightened by a shot, and he was thrown out of his stirrups. Four Austrian hussars fell upon him. One of his comrades cried out for him to seize the horse's tail and escape. "No," he answered, "the nation has entrusted this horse to me, and these four slaves will not get it until I am dead." He managed to get the animal up, mounted it, and fought a duel with the Austrians. With his body criss-crossed with wounds, and his left wrist slashed half through, he ended up by dispersing his adversaries.

Another incident, among thousands, will show the republican officer who knew his trade as a swordsman and leader of men. There was Macquart, who from a common soldier became a general in the Revolution. When the scouts reported seeing the enemy he announced, "Let's go. I'm going to dress like a beast." He stripped to the waist and exposed a torso as hairy as a bear's, jumped on his horse, waved his sword, and charged forward yelling horrible insults. The whole regiment followed him.

The youth of the officers is explained partly by the action of the Committee of Public Safety, when it modified the law of February 1793 by reserving a third of appointments to be made by the representatives on mission, who were empowered to dismiss and promote officers as they thought best. There was also the attitude of old soldiers, some of whom (voluntarily or under pressure from their comrades in arms) refused the promotions to which seniority of service entitled them. Thus Henri Hubert Maugrein, aged fifty-five, with thirty-nine years of service, a color-bearer in 1786 and captain in 1792, declined the post as battalion commander to which he had a right. His health was not good enough, he said; the fatigues of war had impaired it. He asked to remain at his post as captain until his retirement.

Though a process of selection was at work, there remained in the Year II a strong nucleus of officers who had "grown old in harness." Their small numbers should not lead us to underestimate their importance in the transmission of ideas and attitudes from the camps of the monarchy. Two agents of the ministry, in their report of December 1793, declared that these old-timers had "the Old Regime imprinted in their very bones—drunks, fanatics, and girl chasers." They were nonetheless bearers of a mission that gave them larger dimensions for all time.

Among these veterans was General Oudart. Born at Liège, seventy-six years old, a dragoon since 1739, he boasted that his father had been an officer under Louis XIV. Another, named La Badie—whether his age was seventy-one or seventy-three is uncertain—had already been a lieutenant when Louis XV entered upon his personal rule. A general of brigade, he did not retire until June 1794. At that date the dean of the French army was still on active service, Captain Jantron of the 1st Hussars, who was eighty-two!

These all belonged to that group of the wounded, sick, and infirm that the historian is astonished to find still present in the actual campaigns. With health undermined by long marches, unbalanced diet, and poor hygiene, a line of the gouty, the asthmatic, the consumptive, the epileptic, and even the insane formed with their younger fellows the great procession of this epic time. In the infantry 1 to 18 percent of the company-level officers were chronically ill; in the cavalry and artillery the rate was 20 to 30 percent. Counting the lame, the deaf, the one-eyed, and the bilious, the historian can measure the pain of these sacrifices willingly made.

Despeaux, Girardon, Glence, and Gudin, whose careers we have summarized, were typical of the officer corps in their social origin. Of the four, one came from the peasantry, one from the lesser or white-collar bourgeoisie *à talents*, one from the bourgeoisie of business affairs, and one from the retail and shopkeeping circles that produced many Jacobin and sans-culotte militants.

Few among them were rich. To explore this aspect of social reality would require regional surveys, using marriage contracts and inventories after death, which the absence of information on place of domicile usually makes impossible. Their letters show a deprivation that is attested to also by the representatives on mission.

Their civilian occupations also reveal the modesty of their conditions.

Officers from the peasantry were more numerous in the Year II than earlier in the Revolution, being of the following percentages of the officer corps:

	Battle infantry	Light infantry	Cavalry
Captains	22.3	24.3	33.8
Lieutenants	24.4	26.6	32.8
Sub-lieutenants	27.3	19.4	33.4

Many of these ex-peasants called themselves *cultivateurs*, a term generally indicating a needy rather than a well-to-do agriculturalist. Among these captains in the battle infantry, 61.7 percent were *cultivateurs*, and the percentage of *cultivateurs* among lieutenants and sub-lieutenants of the various arms was nearly the same as for captains. Those who called themselves *laboureurs* formed 23 percent of the captains of battle infantry originating in the peasantry, and the percentage for lieutenants and sub-lieutenants of all arms was almost the same, except in the cavalry where the percentage exceeded 40. Of the *laboureurs* many came from the Midi, where the word signified a day laborer and not a more well-to-do peasant as in the Ile-de-France. Finally, more than 4 percent of captains of battle infantry, of those issuing from the peasantry, were of the more humble category of *ménagers*, *jardiniers*, and *manouvriers*. This percentage rose to 10 for lieutenants and sub-lieutenants of the same arm. Only 6.5 percent of the peasant captains of battle infantry designated themselves as *propriétaires*, and some of these must have possessed only small parcels of land.

The world of the workshop was well represented among these officers, a milieu of artisans dependent or independent, of those who worked at home or before the eyes of their customers and of those who handled the cold chisel or the shuttle. Percentages for this class were as follows:

	Battle infantry	Light infantry	Cavalry
Captains	25.8	28.1	
Lieutenants	33.6	28.1	about 23
Sub-lieutenants	35.1	37.4	

The most numerous were workers in leather, textiles, and wood, whose trades were hurt by the economic depression. When a minimum of education became a requirement for promotion, the poorest were excluded. Wage workers, domestic servants, and lesser employees never provided more than 5 percent of company-level officers in the battle infantry, and the percentage in the light infantry and cavalry was only 2 or 3. It was the levies of 1793 preceding the Levy in Mass that allowed these few men of humble condition to achieve the epaulette.

The bourgeoisie supplied from a third to a half of the company officers, in percentages as follows:

	Battle infantry	Light infantry	Cavalry
Captains	44.2	42.1	38.2
Lieutenants	36.5	38.4	39.0
Sub-lieutenants	32.4	37.7	35.7

And in the artillery, 23.7 percent of the captains. Most of these men were of modest status: schoolmasters, surgeons, artists, clerks, and office workers. The most compact group in this *bourgeoisie à talents* was made up of former students, sons of master craftsmen, and the like. The business bourgeoisie was represented in most cases by only 7 to 13 percent of the company officers, with small retailers or their sons more numerous than the larger merchants.

Most came from regions near the French frontiers. The Nord, Pas-de-Calais, Somme, Aisne, and Ardennes, along with Alsace and Franche-Comté, provided the largest percentages. The garrison towns were located in these regions since the Old Regime, and young men of the artisan and lesser bourgeois class had been tempted to enlist by the proximity of military installations.

Nobles, priests, and foreigners formed a suspected element. We have seen how the Committee, after the purges under sans-culotte pressure, restrained the expulsion of noble officers from the army. Carnot protected those in the artillery and engineers. Even Saint-Just kept nobles in their posts, such as the squadron leader d'Hautpoul, a *ci-devant* marquis, or the brigade commander Rabinet de Mervielle, or the *ci-devant* marquis de Mariscot. D'Hautpoul was liberated by Saint-Just in consequence of a petition from the soldiers in his regiment asking unanimously that he be retained. How many others were thus saved from the purges by the zeal of their companions in arms? It is hard to say, because most of them kept quiet about their social status during the investigations.

Not all kept silent. Nobles accounted for 2 to 3 percent in the several arms, with the cavalry having the most. Take the case of Captain Charles Lavillette. Born at Gap in the Hautes-Alpes, he entered the service in 1782 as a sub-lieutenant in the Soissonnais regiment. He remained three years, then left to take his chances in the colonies as steward for another noble. He was unlucky, went to Bordeaux, lived a while in Paris, and then returned home. His parents sent him away. He sojourned at Toulon, and enlisted as a naval cannoneer. Clearly our man enjoyed quitting a job that he had sought only the day before. He left Toulon and was a workman in the manufactures at Rouen for fifteen months. In 1792 he became a lieutenant in a legion of mounted *chasseurs*. What was he? A noble? A man of the people? Not knowing his true position himself, he replied to the questionnaire from the Committee: "I am a *rentier* . . . a *ci-devant* noble." The administrative council of his unit recognized him as "a good soldier, a good republican, zealous in his duties. . . . He deserves to keep his place."

Another example: Montpezat was twenty-four years old in the Year II. As a noble he had entered the old royal military school, and obtained a sub-lieutenancy when the Revolution began. Discharging his duties well, and with a good knowledge of mathematics, he was thought by his comrades not only to deserve to be kept in the army, but to be promoted to a higher rank and sent to the Engineers.

"We entrust ourselves to the tricolor flag and the hand of the Most High spreads above us as our shield against the hatred of tyrants." Such words come from fathers whose sons were *défenseurs de la Patrie*. Many soldiers, setting out to face death, rejected dechristianization. They wanted to keep the priests who might help them with their pastoral ministrations at the supreme moment. These priests had often left home with them as chaplains in the volunteer battalions. Such was Christophe Hamel, chaplain to the 2nd battalion of the Ardennes, who had been an officer under the Old Regime and chaplain to the Royal Picardy in 1776. The Convention forced him out in October 1793.

Priests threatened with eviction concealed themselves inside their companies by agreement with the volunteers. They became ordinary soldiers. Some were elected to replace NCOs or officers who were lost. Thus Pierre Augustin Gabarnais, born at Les Salles in the Var, holder of a benefice at Ricquen in 1790, became chaplain to the 1st battalion of the Basses-Alpes on May 8, 1792, a corporal on May 22, 1794, then a sergeant in June, and sub-lieutenant in September.

Others were willing to abandon the priesthood to obtain positions of command. One of them was Charles Renaudy, born at Guillestre in 1763. First a teacher of physics and rhetoric, then in 1792 chaplain to the 1st battalion of the Hautes-Alpes, by 1793 he was quartermaster of the 69th demi-brigade.

Some continued to say the Mass, as one of them admitted in an inquiry of 1795. Sans-culotte militants feared such men, "who announce principles of fanaticism all the more dangerous if established in the armies." Militants thus multiplied their precautions and controls. On 29 Prairial Year II the war section of the Committee of Public Safety advised the military police of Paris against admitting priests among *défenseurs de la patrie*, even if they possessed certificates of good citizenship and papers certifying abdication of the priesthood. Local administrators and popular societies were sometimes ahead of the Committee. But the contrary pressure of local communities remained. In the Indre-et-Loire draftees prevailed on the departmental authorities to include priests, curés, and vicars in the requisition. On September 1793 Citizen Diray, curé of Châtellerault, appeared before the assembled draftees of the district. He said that he would have been willing to remain at his post, but that "in doing so he would have chilled the zeal of his brothers." Hence he announced his intention of departing with them, and signed the register, "Diray, district chaplain."

Still others professed such patriotism that it would seem unjust to deny them the enlistment that they solicited. A priest named Cazes explained:

> Enveloped since birth in all the prejudices of the eighteenth century, I was destined by my status to propagate them. But I have always used the language of reason and truth with my contemporaries, and been full of zeal to expound the rights of Man and Citizen to them, and I swear to you that I have never tried to bind them to principles that I could not understand very well myself. But do not think that I wish to make a profession of atheism. Liberty and Equality are the deities that I adore. I detest superstition, federalism, and royalty. . . . I would wish with all my soul that all thrones in the Universe might be overturned and broken up, to make a great bonfire around which all the sans-culottes in the world could dance and warm themselves.

So some of the clergy departed with the draftees. The abbé Cognet, in minor orders, was incorporated in the requisition of September 1793 in the department of the Aisne. Elected a sublieutenant, he held this rank until incorporation of his battalion into the 35th demi-brigade.

The other suspicious category was the foreigner. The Frenchman, who made war on kings, not on peoples, nevertheless came to distrust men who, for so long the mercenaries of tyrants, had been corrupted in their service. But here, too, there were contradictions between the intransigence of the militants and the needs of war. The latter were felt most deeply by men in responsible positions, who allowed a small group of foreigners—a little more than 4 percent of company officers—to remain in the armies of the Republic. The largest group (13.2 percent) was in the light infantry, into which the foreign legions of 1792 and 1793 had been incorporated. To expel foreigners from this arm was to rob them of talents and render them ineffective. Some battalions were officered almost entirely by Germans, Belgians, or Swiss. Even in the cavalry, where leaders could not be improvised, foreign officers were relatively numerous, at 5.3 percent.

The Belgians, whose territory was annexed to France in 1795, formed the most important group among the foreigners. Then came the Germans, mostly from the Rhineland; then the Swiss, and the Dutch. A few exceptional cases are found—a Canadian and a Senegalese.

The class of NCOs, so important in every army as the backbone of the troops, was of high quality in 1794. This was the opinion of Gouvion Saint-Cyr a few decades later. Was it correct? A sampling of the results of the survey by the Committee of Public Safety, and of some tests conducted in the demi-brigades of battle infantry and in the cavalry regiments, brings out three traits in which the NCOs resembled their superiors and augured well for renewal of the office corps. These traits were youth, habit of command, and level of education, which was relatively high because many NCOs came from social levels close to the bourgeoisie.

The NCOs were young. More than 62 percent in the battle infantry, and more than 65 percent in the cavalry, were under thirty. Less than one in ten were over forty, and a fifty-year-old was an exception. There were of course differences from army to army. As with the officers, the armies of the Alps and of the Pyrenees had more youthful sergeants than those of the North, the Sambre-

Meuse, and the Rhine. The demi-brigades also differed. While the 48th approached the norm with only 4 percent of its NCOs in their forties and fifties, the 24th departed from it widely with 14.6 percent of its sergeants over forty. There were similar differences in the cavalry, where the 3rd Hussars had older men than the 9th. The cause of these disparities was usually the irruption into the units, in greater or less numbers, of the volunteers of 1792.

These young men were also robust. Very few claimed or were reported to have a delicate constitution. Young and strong, they were also experienced in arms. Most of them, having begun as volunteers, had now made two campaigns. Some 44 percent of the NCOs had come to know, in the camps of the old monarchy, men who were now officers commanding them in the Year II. There was indeed a difference between the two groups: men who had served under Louis XVI and were officers in the Year II could for the most part take pride in seven or eight years of service, and had gained the rank of corporal or sergeant on the eve of 1789, whereas the NCOs of the Year II were former fusiliers of the line who had barely won their first chevron. Does this mean that the NCOs had shown less ability than their superiors? Some notes gathered from the questionnaire issued by the Committee of Public Safety might give the historian this impression. Although only 4 percent were held to be poor tacticians, the officers when interrogated maintained what seems a revealing silence on the level of military education of 38 percent of the NCOs. We find in reports of the Year IV, submitted by inspectors of demi-brigades of the second formation, a recommendation made a hundred times to the officers: assemble your NCOs and teach them the art of moving forward on the battlefield, on which they seem to have only vague ideas.

It would therefore be false to believe that it was the NCO in the Year II who taught the military trade to the new officer recently arriving from his town or village. Teaching was reciprocal. In one place the chevroned sergeant, after the amalgamation, revealed the fine points of tactics to the officer of 1793. In another, the former sergeant, now an officer, instructed the soldiers and the sergeants.

Education of NCOs was at a relatively high level. Only 14.7 percent of those in the battle infantry were recorded as not knowing how to read or write. More than half knew not only how to read and write but also how to calculate. Some representatives, like Goupilleau with the Army of the North, took care to assure that there was "no faking" in such reports. A reading of inspectors' reports of the Year III confirms that those unable to read or write were a minority. Most of these were elderly soldiers who continued to complain against the law that blocked their advancement. Martin Bide, for example, aged fifty, son of a *laboureur*, twenty-seven years in the service, was illiterate. He said of himself: "Always in the army, he could neither read nor write, but he enjoys his work and is good at tactical movements."

Those NCOs originating in the peasantry were a minority in both the cavalry (30 percent) and the infantry (23 percent). Here also the most important group came from the world of the workshop, retail trade, and the lesser white-collar bourgeoisie. Sons of artisans or small shopkeepers, one in four NCOs of the Year II had studied letters or law, and became a lawyer's clerk, or some kind of legal practitioner, or some kind of office employee.

The patriotism of the group is shown by the fact that 21 percent of the captains had enlisted voluntarily in 1791 when the Revolution was threatened, and 28 percent in 1792 when the country was declared in danger. The survey made by the Committee of Public Safety included a question on the patriotism of officers. The reply was to be confirmed by certificates from the municipalities, the districts, or the committees of surveillance, then verified by the unit administrative councils and the emissaries of the government. A majority of the officers was found to be composed of "well-informed patriots."

The fact remains that most of officers and NCOs were military men by occupation who, well into the Year II, accepted the changes ordered by the authorities with something less than wholehearted agreement. The Jacobins concluded that for officers and NCOs, as for the draftees, a political education was necessary. "The soul of the Revolution," under direction of the Committee of Public Safety, was to be made to infuse the army.

CHAPTER VIII

• • •

The Army as the School of
Jacobinism in the Year II

Officers in the summer of 1793 still tried to imbue their men with a love of glory and the honor of belonging to their unit. These "virtues" of the Old Regime nourished an esprit de corps that might be harmful to the public interest, because they made the troops potential instruments in the hands of generals avid for power. "For the State to be free," said Robespierre, "the public forces must uphold the general will; otherwise the State is agitated and enslaved." The camps were too often, said Saint-Just, "like fairs where the country is up for auction." The fighters must be unceasingly taught the revolutionary meaning of the struggle. "The war" (Robespierre again) "is the clash between two prose-lytisms." Military honor, the sign of the mercenary, should be re-placed by the honor of being a revolutionary. The vanity of be-longing to a combat group tested in battle should give way to pride in forming the vanguard of the Nation. The physical strength of the soldiers, redoubled by good morale, "would nec-essarily produce advantageous results for the Republic, and the energy of patriots would overcome the perils." By February 12, 1794, Saint-Just had formulated the thought by which the Revo-lutionary Government would continue to be guided:

It is not by numbers and discipline alone that you should expect victory; you will achieve it only as the republican spirit
makes progress in the army.

For the Montagnards the army was to be not only an instrument of war but a school of Jacobinism. The Jacobin spirit, imparted to the soldiers, would be spread by them to the rest of the
country with which they were in correspondence. But this political education, as launched by the Jacobins, was to find a more or
less concealed opposition within the Committee of Public Safety
itself, in the person of Carnot. From April 1794, when the war
ministry was suppressed and replaced by an executive commission,
Carnot undertook, by manipulating the bureaus, to restore esprit
de corps to the troops and contain them within their military mission alone. He only half succeeded, for the spirit of the Revolution
had penetrated the army too deeply to be quickly or completely
expunged.

The spirit of the Revolution was Equality, which as a right
given to all determined the character of Liberty and rendered imperative the struggle against aristocracy. It was also Fraternity, a
duty of mutual aid, accepted within a community in which each
man's right to existence depended on his own willing contribu-
tion.

1. The Educators

The educators first of all were the members of the Convention
who served as representatives on mission. Assisted by the Jacobin
network throughout France, they had the duty to watch and punish, but also to give instruction and reward patriotism. While they
had to discover and arrest traitors, and bring before the Revolutionary Tribunal any army man who had aided, favored, or advised a plot against the liberty and security of the Republic, it was
also their task to distribute to the troops the bulletins, addresses,

proclamations, and instructions of the Convention, and in general to maintain the republican spirit in the armies.

To arouse and sustain the political consciousness of the soldiers, the Republic had to show itself ready to sacrifice all else to its armed forces. To take shoes from the "dandy" so that the infantry-man need not march barefoot, to take blankets from bourgeois beds so that volunteers could keep warm in their camps, to divide up "fraternal bread" among the citizens, all such actions were to keep alive the principle of mutual assistance, the foundation of republicanism. In letters to the Committee of Public Safety, in addresses to the popular societies, in the order books of staff offi-cers, in the general correspondence of the armies, everywhere the historian finds evidence of the day-to-day activity of representa-tives on mission to the armies, and their constant concern to trans-late the language of democracy into concrete terms and give it wider publicity. Milhaud and Soubrany with the Army of the Pyr-enees, Dubois-Crancé with the Army of the West, like Ruamps, Borrie, and Guyardin with the Army of the Rhine, upheld the principles of equality and discipline among the troops by first trying to relieve their material wants. No one doubtless did so with so much intelligence and goodwill as Saint-Just. One of his historians, J. P. Gross, has shown how Saint-Just established in the Army of the Rhine a system of social welfare unknown until then, "extending well beyond the traditional limits of military in-stitutions." He sought to validate the basic principles of the Rev-olution "by having the soldier exercise his civic and political rights, within an institutional framework, through a real possibil-ity of having a part in the work of revolution." By liberty he meant the assured right to have a part in the selection of leaders and in the administrative and political control over them; and to confirm it he listened to the soldiers before ordering any removal or ap-pointment. By equality he meant distinguishing and rewarding heroic action by the common soldier as well as by the man who wore epaulettes, and punishing the leader and the subordinate with the same rigor. In a justice that was both equitable and severe the army saw that the representative honored his promises. Saint-Just wished also to create a force of partisans, that is, in the words of Gross, "a handful of determined revolutionaries, worthy of confidence, and able to inculcate republican spirit at all levels."

Besides the representatives on mission, the Committee had its own agents, dependent only on itself, to act upon the army. At first they had police functions, assembling files on public functionaries and denouncing suspects. They had also to stimulate and oversee the patriotism of the troops. The representatives on mission disliked these competitors, and made their feelings known.

Army magistrates were educators of another kind. Military justice was rendered by military criminal courts, which judged the gravest offenses, and on which "militarized" civilian judges sat. They replaced the more purely military judges created by the Legislative Assembly, who had neither independence nor authority apart from the generals. The mission assigned to them by the Committee was a delicate one. It required exceptional personnel, able not only to enforce the law but also to explain it to the soldiers. The idea was that instilling love of country and hatred of tyrants in the troops would prevent derelictions. It was to educate, so as not to have to punish. Thus the magistrates went through the army, speaking to the soldiers of their duty and reinforcing their attachment to the Republic. For example, a military prosecutor with the Army of the Rhine, named Clément, drew up proclamations and fraternal notices that he arranged to have put on the orders of the day, anticipating directives from the government. The magistrates became the great moralizers of the army, working to prevent the corruption of minds and reappearance of abuses. They were under orders to report on the spirit of the army to the Committee of Public Safety every ten days.

These army magistrates had for the most part formerly been lawyers, justices of the peace, or otherwise experienced in law and administration. Few in number, they were selected by the Committee of Public Safety or by representatives on mission, who chose them from among Jacobin circles. Such were Dejean, an administrator at Mons, Derche, a justice of the peace at Wissembourg, and Bruat, who worked in the Army of the Rhine. The Committee of Public Safety kept close watch over them, and recalled them when they seemed negligent or when their talents for education were not much in evidence. Thus, Legier, military prosecutor in the second district of the Army of the Rhine, was suspended from his post after only two months. Following their activities through the War Archives, one is struck by the unity of outlook among these men. All shared in the ideal of protecting and defending the Jacobin Republic. Zealous agents of the Jacobins, they gave lessons on the law and assured respect for it; they considered that the justice they rendered was a principal means of making the soldiers feel an emotional attachment to the Republic. We can see them minutely examining the dossiers on the accused, inquiring into the exact circumstances of an offense, informing themselves on the background, the education and the level of maturity of the men that they had to judge. The prosecutor Clément wrote:

> Because offenses vary in seriousness according to their nature, the application of a penalty should necessarily allow for the circumstances that determined them. Often a passing incident, mistake, or weakness has been the cause. We must not suppose that all actions leading to the same offense are the same. We must look into the habits and opinions of the accused, see whether he is the victim of the moment, and learn whether his previous conduct has been irreproachable.

In the Army of the West a soldier who stole a wallet was punished with five years in irons because he was found fully responsible, but a soldier who was absent without leave was acquitted because he had gone to bring help to his wife and child. In the Army of the Ardennes a soldier who had robbed a local resident of a few pieces of cloth and half a dozen dishes was condemned to ten years in irons, but at the same time deserters, if within the interior of the country, were only put in two months' detention and then set free, on the ground that they were ignorant of military law and had only gone home to take part in the harvest. In the Army of the North the theft of a hat could be punished by death, if the guilty man was proved to have understood the laws concerning pillage; but, on the other hand, flight in the face of the enemy might draw only a reprimand if the guilty men were young recruits whose conduct was explained by "lack of experience."

Justice and probity were the order of the day. Magistrates aware of the implications inspected the prisons, "delivered the innocent languishing in chains," and speeded up their judgment of the guilty, since "obvious impunity confirms evil-doers in indiscipline and even in crime."

The army magistrates, like the representatives on mission, thus demonstrated to men who were often rough and simple-minded what the regime was that they were defending. Like other agents of the government, they preached by both words and deeds. They issued proclamations that they widely publicized. They were like schoolmasters teaching republican morality. For example, the prosecutor of the second district of the Army of the North, in January 1794, warned his brothers in arms of the two scourges of the army—drink and loose women:

> The reign of good morals as well as courage has arrived. Remember that despots favored debauchery and depravity, the better to debase men and lure them into a foul servitude. Today the people, in which sovereignty resides, requires of all its members that they be pure, virtuous, and incorruptible. How can anyone who loses his reason for an instant be responsible for himself or for his actions?

Prostitutes who followed the army were a "plague." "They not only undermine the warrior's courage but corrupt the source of the purest French blood." The virtuous warrior would receive the reward he deserved, and the army prosecutor expatiated on the Jacobin promise:

You will rejoice in a cherished wife and companion, and, when peace comes, in possessing the fields abandoned to us by émigrés and cowards. You will till them with your victorious hands, and produce a robust generation worthy of supporting your reputation, your labors, and the Liberty of the Republic.

At the time of the fall of Hébert and his friends, the army magistrates explained the motives of the government in striking them down, declaring that there had been a plot against liberty, that vigilance was required, and that the treason that had surrendered the lines at Wissembourg still existed in the camps.

2. THEMES AND METHODS OF EDUCATION

Themes and methods of education were numerous. It was thought necessary to strike the imagination first, then to offer explanations and appeal to Reason. In the spring of 1793 commanders reported with alarm that indiscipline was making their armies useless. "With the enemy," wrote General Deville, "everyone is at his post. With us, everyone comes and goes as he pleases." Carnot reported on June 1 of that year:

The conduct of the soldiers is a mixture of actions, some fine, others disgraceful, which show the flighty and temperamental but undeniable character of the French. Nothing can resist our first attack, but then confusion breaks out everywhere. . . . We could take Ostende by main force. With well-ordered troops we would feel no hesitation, but we must fear, with ours, that once they had made the assault they would scatter into the houses, and get so drunk that in two hours some of them would be slaughtered like cattle on the street corners.

It was a question whether discipline was to be restored by appeal to reason or by training of the body. To learn the trade of arms had always involved coercion, a yielding of one's body to leaders who would shape it and give it the necessary reflexes. In the eighteenth century the soldier had become "something manufactured. You produce the machine you need from a formless paste and inept body; you gradually readjust its postures; a calculated constraint slowly takes over each bodily part, becomes master of it, bends the whole, and puts it perpetually at your disposal." The professionals of war well understood how to impose this training. We shall see that revolutionary tactics were more complex than is often said, requiring movements that had to be executed together. Attack in columns to utilize the *furie française* was ineffective unless the men knew how to carry their weapons and march in step with a firm cadence, "keeping the knee stiff and the toes pointed down and outwards," as the oldest drill books expressed it. But such a military discipline that turned men into automata was contrary to the wishes of patriots, who meant to make soldiers out of wide-awake, vigilant and responsible citizens. The soldiers of the Republic, said the patriots, could not be slaves like the soldiers of tyrants.

The Jacobins therefore, civilian and military, looked for a compromise between political requirements and the necessities of war. An instruction book for all grades in the infantry, drawn up by a military man in 1794, acknowledged that the old drills could be made useful if they were brought up to date. While helping in the formation of warriors, they could also serve to inculcate the first elements of republican virtue. From physical exercises moral lessons would be drawn. The citizen-soldiers should submit voluntarily to the various orders given in their military evolutions, for they would thereby learn to understand their own bodies and use them properly for their own self-preservation, which was important for the triumph of the Republic. To augment his strength, the soldier should feel the obligation to observe good bodily and alimentary hygiene. His superior would make him understand that cleanliness was of concern not only to the individual fighting man but to the whole social order: "The soldier who is not clean jeopardizes his health. If he is dirty when wounded he runs the risk of an incurable injury, and may even die." This would "be unfair to the social order by jeopardizing humanity, which is its principle." More than any other citizen, the soldier should practice temperance. Addiction to the bottle would make him unfit on the battlefield, and compromise his own life as well as that of his brothers. As a model citizen the soldier should advance himself by the social virtues. "Intemperance or drunkenness degrades the man and assimilates him to wild beasts."

Leaders were invited to interrupt physical exercises with moral lessons, to prepare soldiers to listen to readings of the great revolutionary texts, and to understand them. Directives written to create machines had to be revised. "We must suppress all those trifles that are far from good principles," wrote General Schauenbourg. To get at essentials meant eliminating "the little futilities in the manual of arms and the eternal details mistakenly demanded by ignorance." But it meant also making the recruit understand the usefulness of certain gestures and positions. The lives of all could depend on the soldier's keeping his place in the ranks. He must know the various posts in close-order formations. Some exercises were thought especially valuable. In the change of formations, for example, the recruit could best be taught "why he must take long or short steps, incline to the right or the left, and hence maintain his place when marching in battle line or in column."

Time was organized as well as space. Inspection was in the morning, instruction in the afternoon; idleness, the source of "marauding and drinking bouts," was thus restrained. The recruit instructed in this way would lose his physical awkwardness and develop his intelligence at the same time. The young soldier would grow in devotion to his duty and in republican pride, and so move into the higher classes of his platoon. The leader would then deliver the message of *la Patrie*. "Every *décade* the corporal will read to his squad the Rights of Man and the list of military crimes and misdemeanors." He would impress upon his men the truth that "the soldier's obligations are no heavier than those of the citizen; that like the citizen he is required only to obey the laws; and that in the military state as in any private condition, anyone refractory to the law is a dangerous person against whom the law should take stern action." One battalion commander wrote in a letter:

> Nothing is so natural as obedience to the laws, because they are an emanation of our will and in obeying them we only confirm decisions made by us, and also because the laws are made for the general happiness and whoever disobeys them declares himself the enemy of the public happiness. When a soldier obeys his superior, it is certainly only the law and not the individual that he obeys, for his superior cannot order him except in execution of a law. . . . The soldier who disobeys his superior is in an inconsistent position, in view of the law to which he has consented, and is culpable with respect to society, by troubling its harmony.
>
> With discipline, republican *sans-culottisme* always triumphs over royal *culottisme*.[1]

By drilling bodies and opening them to reason, the school of the soldier could regenerate "egotists and intriguers, shameless single men and youths married before the age of reason to escape the draft, indolent *rentiers* and rich merchants, the whole swarm of idle and useless people, all the aristocracy of munificence." Under the reign of despots, it was said, the army had been a kind of imprisonment to "rehabilitate the indigent," whose misfortune was thought to be due to vice; but the sans-culotte and the Jacobin proposed a grand confinement of aristocrats of wealth in the republican army, and their gradual assimilation into the national glory. Good soldiers would be found in "the dandyish mob," and they could be put to good use if dispersed in the republican battalions:

---

[1] That is, republican trousers always triumph over royal knee-breeches.

When the rich have the honor to see themselves as comrades of sans-culottes, they will have only one course to follow—to put themselves on terms of cordiality.

Equality means that all measures affect everyone without distinction. Where the poorest open the way the rich should follow; they should themselves deign to fight for the preservation of their persons and property. The useful laboring class will be respected and treated with consideration; the idle and comfortable class will be actively employed.

Instruction and discipline were thus regarded as a means of moral leveling. "Known, placed, and classified so as not to escape surveillance," citizens would learn in the army this republican virtue: "Always act in the open."

The Terror invaded the camps. It too was a means of education. Strong measures were indispensable for repressing what Barère called an "alarmist" spirit. In the Army of the Sambre-Meuse, by an order of 15 Floréal (May 4, 1794), the military court was authorized to suspend the military penal code. The courts were transformed into special revolutionary commissions. From 20 Floréal they were no longer required to use a jury, even a jury composed of members of the popular societies. Le Bon, organizing a revolutionary commission on 16 Floréal, filled it with some twenty "good patriots." Traveling commissions visited the army and examined the conduct of officers whose units had been routed. Where a fault was found, the penalty was death. Desertion, insubordination, and pillage were rigorously punished. The findings of these commissions were used to show the troops how severely the Republic took action against those who knowingly "isolated" themselves from the body of the nation by cowardice, treachery, or rascality. For the soldiers, dishonest employees and suppliers were bloodsuckers, as monopolists and speculators were for the citizens. "You will obtain the judgments rendered against them," Bouchotte wrote to a division chief in the war ministry. "Six thousand copies will be printed and sent to the armies and garrisons." In April 1794 the Committee demanded the widest possible publicity in the camps for these judgments.

Application of the sentence was the occasion for veritable ceremonies. The guilty were brought before the assembled troops; the sentence was noted and sometimes commented upon; the execution was public. Thirteen men of the 6th battalion of the Seine-et-Oise who had thrown down their arms and abandoned their post in the presence of the enemy were shot before the eyes of the whole battalion. Jean Népomucène Evrard, commander of a demi-brigade, was convicted of abandoning his men when they were under attack by the enemy, taken to Lille, publicly stigmatized before the troops, and shot in their presence. Yet the death sentences were not numerous. Of 660 accused and brought before the court in the Army of the Rhine from October to May, only 62 were condemned to death.

The Terror was revolutionary justice, and like the god Janus it had two faces—severity for the criminal and favorable treatment for the innocent. With one hand it wielded the sword; with the other it pointed out the man of valor. It punished vice and rewarded virtue. This was the meaning of Saint-Just's action of October 23, 1793, when he proclaimed to the Army of the Rhine: "We are determined to seek out, reward, and promote merit, and to prosecute all crimes." At the very time when traitors in the 8th *chasseurs* were punished, two captains distinguished for bravery and good citizenship were officially honored before their units. Rapid and conspicuous promotions on the one hand; on the other, executions by firing squad. "The psychological impact on the troops was intense."

There were other marks than promotion by which the Nation could show recognition of its soldiers. Since individual decorations were a sign of "feudalism and aristocracy," old pre-Revolutionary soldiers were invited to give up their crosses of Saint-Louis, which thereupon flowed into the Convention. But could not a republican decoration be created? In 1792 citizen Dufour, of the Théâtre français section in Paris, had proposed striking a round medal with the insignia of patriotism, a Phrygian cap surmounting a triangle surrounded by the fasces, or rods, of a lictor. The reverse would show the place and date of the action for which the medal was awarded. An employee of the Committee on Military Legislation, himself an old soldier, made himself the spokesman for veterans who regretted the loss of medals showing their years of service. He proposed a medal bearing a republican stamp: "On seeing it, the young man admiring this proof of national recognition, and striving for the same favor, will say, 'It is by fighting to break our chains that he won this mark of gratitude.'"

In the end the Revolutionary Government refused to create medals, but it used other kinds of rewards, such as gifts of money, gifts in kind, and collective congratulations decreed by the Convention. All had the same meaning, to give concrete expression to republican solidarity.

The government bestowed "arms of quality" on the valiant. These were most often arms captured from enemy officers. In the hands of patriots they became symbols of the struggle against aristocracy. To possess them was not to advertise a personal glory, but to attest a courage that only the fraternal cooperation of fellow soldiers made it permissible to display. Such arms were conferred by preference on common soldiers. Under the Old Regime, it was said, "the colonel took upon himself the honor for successes won by his men; under democracy, the man who performs the gallant action gains the prize himself." When a battalion commander—for example, the commander of the Indre battalion in December—received a sword of honor, he wore it in the name of the whole battalion.

Representatives on mission rewarded military men with money. Saint-Just, by way of General Pichegru, sent a sum of 1,000 livres to two cannoneers and a volunteer "of whose bravery he had received a favorable report." A week later he granted 3,300 livres to citizen Raffi, captain of the 5th company of horse artillery, "who lost an arm on September 12 and on the same day lost all his possessions."

These actions must be seen in connection with the social policy of the Jacobins for the army, as for the whole country. As early as February 21, 1793, the National Convention had earmarked property confiscated from émigrés, to the extent of 400 million livres, for payment of pensions and bonuses to men in the army and to their widows and children. Throughout 1793 there were repeated proposals to set aside nationalized properties, of almost a billion livres in metallic value, as a fund from which either land or cash annuities could be granted to soldiers or their entitled survivors. Barère in 1794 renewed such promises of government aid, no doubt in part for reasons of expediency, at a time when the government was concerned to hold the support of the army after the execution of Hébert and his friends. But the social policy toward the army had a larger purpose. It was consistent with the measures taken by Saint-Just and other representatives on mission in dispensing immediate cash aid to soldiers and their families. Such gifts were more than military awards; they were a demonstration to everyone of the social and humanitarian foundation of the Montagnard republic. The society of ordinary people, as envisaged by Saint-Just, "would be valid only on a basis of solidarity and goodwill." But the fund of nearly a billion livres was never realized. Three years later the Directory received angry reminders of the "billion for the soldiers" that had been promised.

Solidarity was expressed finally in the highest award that the Convention could confer in the name of the French people: to declare that a particular army had "deserved well of the country"— *avait bien mérité de la Patrie*. This proclamation was always preceded by a rehearsal of its conspicuous deeds, with the orator contrasting the cool behavior of patriots with the agitation of mercenaries, the courage of the former with the cowardice of the latter, the enthusiastic march of soliders of Liberty supported by the whole people with the dejected movement of the satellites of tyrants. The solidarity of Nation and army, and of the armies with one another, was emphasized by Barère on May 6, 1794, when he concluded a report to the Convention on successes against the Spaniards and Piedmontese with these words:

> This news, honorable for the armies of the Republic, must not remain sterile in our hands. The armies are solidary, and there exists among them an exchange in glory and honor to which the national representation today should give new means of communication. Let the cries of victory in the south reecho in the Army of the North. Passing through the National Convention, these proclamations of victory will have a terrible and happy effect, of which the Republic is in need on the frontier where the ruins and ashes of Landrecies call upon republican valor.

To show the solidarity of the armies, and of the people with its soldiers, the Jacobins had another resource, already created by the people—the civic festival. The first such festivals to mix citizens and soldiers dated from the Constituent Assembly. They remained improvised affairs until the time of the Convention. In the spring of 1793 the patriots of Chambéry, to show their friendship with soldiers, invited them to a festival. There was dancing around a tree of Liberty, singing of the Marseillaise, burning of traitors in effigy, then a farandole about a bonfire to the sound of the Carmagnole. Sometimes there was a pause to break the bread of fraternity, take a few glasses of wine, or just to chat, while some said that defense of the country was a duty, with others insisting that discipline must always be observed, while all laughed at the stupidity of enemies of the Republic. Then the sound of fife and drum would call them to form the rounds of the dance again. Song and dance were the essentials of such a festival. In pure joy and elation, said the sans-culottes and the Jacobins, citizens and soldiers would see themselves as equal sons of the same country.

As the Revolutionary Government gained in authority, these festivals became more regulated. "The great people of Rousseau and Robespierre" (in Mona Ozouf's words) "could not be enchanted by its own spectacle in a state of confusion. A festival required a plan, by which an elementary distribution of roles could be organized." At first the role of the military was to be present at festivals marking the stages of life. In the towns soldiers took part in republican baptisms, or invited members of the Jacobin societies to such "purifications" of army children. At Ambérieux, on March 30, 1794, there was a patriotic *fête* for the marriage of a poor girl, at which the national flag was unfurled, and the march to the *autel de la Patrie* was opened by a military band. The *fête* of the *décadi* was the occasion for distribution of provisions or monetary aid to the most destitute families, many of which had a breadwinner absent in the army. At such affairs soldiers joined the crowd in singing patriotic songs and in "civic dinners," after assisting in distributions to the poor, "to enable them to share within their families in the joy that we owe to the valor of their children." At Strasbourg, Colmar, Landau, Besançon, and Wissembourg, the military joined the citizens in parades to mark the reception of the constitution, the anniversary of the fall of the monarchy, the commemoration of the martyrs of liberty, and the anniversaries of July 14 and August 10. Each battalion sent a few dozen officers and men as delegates, who met with the local officials at the altar of the motherland or at the tree of Liberty.

The ultimate union of the Nation and its army was the presiding idea in the staging of these events. An example is the *fête* inspired by the Jacobins at Collioure on July 25, 1793. It was to celebrate the presentation to the people of the new constitution (the one soon suspended). Two military detachments led the march. They were followed by a delegation of civilian militants, bearing a flag on which was written, "All unite for the triumph of the Republic One and Indivisible." A third group, composed of officials from neighboring village communes, carried a banner announcing "In union there is strength." Then came an infantry detachment, the justice of the peace, the municipal officers, and the national guard, above whom floated a banner declaring, "We will die for the Republic One and Indivisible." A group of children carried a pennant with the words, "We are learning to defend it."

They were followed by four old men carrying flags on which could be read: "War on tyrants, anarchists, and federalists," and "Rights of Man, Equality, Liberty." Then, marching in step to a drum, came a fusilier, a corporal, a sergeant, a sub-lieutenant, a lieutenant, a captain, and a colonel. Then, on a little platform decorated with the tricolor and borne by two veterans and two young recruits, appeared the Constitutional Act. The representative of the people, accompanied by a few generals, escorted it to the altar of *la Patrie*. The altar, in the center of town, was surrounded by troops deployed in the shape of a horseshoe. The Act was placed on the altar. Copies of the constitution were read aloud at different points in the public square. A general approached the representative of the people, and said: "The army receives the constitution and will defend it until death." After the Act had been entrusted to the oldest soldier present for safekeeping, the civilians and the military exchanged the fraternal embrace, *l'accolade*. Finally, there were discharges of muskets and artillery, accompanied by songs, oaths of fraternity, and declarations of hatred of anarchy and federalism. All participants gave assurances that the Convention was the only rallying point.

Festivals in commemoration of victories, though assembling soldiers in larger numbers, were never purely military events. They too were political ceremonies, intended to convey the Jacobin message of unity. Typical in this sense was a festival in Paris on December 30, 1793, "in memory of the victories of the French armies and especially of the recapture of Toulon." The parade, which lasted an hour, was opened by cavalry, sappers, cannoneers, and infantry, with officers and NCOs mixed together, so that the unity of the four arms and the new relationships of ranks were clearly manifested. Next came the popular societies, with their civil committees and surveillance committees, and the police commissioners and justices of the peace. Military detachments marched between such groups. Members of the law courts, the commune of Paris, the department of Paris, and the provisional executive council were followed by the Conquerors of the Bastille, the Men of August 10, and the paramilitary "revolutionary army," an instrument of the popular Terror. There were also cars carrying wounded men, surrounded by girls clothed in white and bearing laurel branches. Finally came deputies from the Convention, preceding the last vehicle in the parade, which bore an image of Victory, surrounded by fifty retired soldiers and a hundred sans-culottes wearing red caps.

The ceremony exalted the bravery of soldiers. It was meant to show, above all else, the integration of military victories with the prior successes of the revolutionary people. It affirmed that the exploits of citizen-soldiers had been made possible only by the close alliance of political militants with the armies, by the bonds that joined them to the central and local governments. The democracy in arms was sustained by the Terror, by members of surveillance committees, judges, police agents, the revolutionary army—all acting as a coercive force without which there could be no victory over the aristocracy.

As well as being actors and spectators, the soldiers were sometimes called upon to be authors of festive celebrations. The formation of a demi-brigade might be observed in a "civil communion." When the 141st was activated all the citizens of the nearest town and the constituted authorities assembled. The representative of the people reviewed the troops, drums rolled, and flags and arms were arranged in a cluster. The representative harangued the men, portraying the advantages of fraternity, the horrors of despotism, and the strength and good fortune of the republican government. The troops broke ranks, and all present mixed together with embraces and cries of *Vive l'union des Français! Vive la République!* More drums rolled, and the men resumed their places. The representatives named the staff officers, returned the flags to their units, and after more beating of the drums administered the oath:

> You will swear to uphold Liberty, Equality, and the French Republic One and Indivisible. You will swear obedience to the law, respect for properties, and maintenance of military

discipline. You will swear hatred of tyrants and all their accomplices.

The troops repeated in a thousand voices, "We swear it," to the acclamation of the whole gathering.

On June 23, 1794, a festival was organized by the military at Granville. Its purpose was to commemorate the heroic defense of that town, which had been besieged by the Vendéans. Here, as at Paris, the cavalry, the force of extermination after combat, led the parade. It was followed by the population, divided by age: the old men; the children of the two sexes in two lines, led by their teachers; the adolescents; and wounded men carrying laurel branches. A car drawn by six war-horses supported a funerary urn decorated with oak leaves. At the foot of the urn was an assemblage composed of a musket, a sabre, a pike, a gun rammer, and an anchor, symbolizing the fraternity between the armed services and the revolutionary people. To this assemblage was fastened also a scarf, symbol of the town government, stained with the blood of Clément Des Maisons, a martyr of Liberty. Children of the wounded men, riding in the car, placed one hand on the urn and with the other held a tricolor cord fastened to the assemblage. Garlands floated from each side of the car, which dragged the attributes of royalism and fanaticism behind it. At the middle of the procession flags enclosed the busts of Lepeletier and Marat. Next came the representative of the people, administrators, generals, officers, and soldiers, all mixing together and surrounding the children of citizens killed during the siege.

Reaching the outskirts of the town, the procession stopped before a pyramid built by the army. On one side of it could be read: "Year II of the Republic, 24 and 25 Brumaire, the garrison at Granville triumphed, with a representative of the people sharing in their peril and their glory." On the second side: "We died in defense of Liberty. Live for your country." On the third side: "On 28 Brumaire Year II of the Republic the National Convention declared Granville and its garrison to have *bien mérité de la Patrie*."

And on the fourth: "This pyramid was constructed from the debris of buildings committed to the flames by the inhabitants to assure the public safety." When the funerary urn had been deposited on the pyramid, the representatives of the people asked all present to take an oath to the dead to persevere in the fight, and then, turning to the officers and soldiers, invited them to express their republican sentiments. Choruses intoned funereal dirges. Then suddenly the ceremony changed from sadness to joy. The car carrying veterans moved along the wall of the city amid songs and dances. A libation was offered to all. Cannon thundered. A band played, and martial airs were followed by music for the dance. A ball was improvised and lasted until late at night.

Whether devised by the army or by the civil authorities, such *fêtes* served to unify the citizens and reinforce their unity behind the Convention and the Committee of Public Safety. But the Committee was disturbed when the army organized festivals in honor of Reason. The cult of Reason raised political dangers for the Revolutionary Government. It might be a tactic of the advanced wing of the sans-culottes to increase its penetration of the army. In the proponents of dechristianization Robespierre saw preachers of atheism, and for atheism he felt a horror, not only, as Mathiez said, "because he believed a faith in God to be a social necessity but because he feared that such preaching would destroy the basis of a moral life for a people poorly prepared to hear it."

The affirmation by the government of belief in the Supreme Deity and the immortality of the soul, in May 1794, was favorably received in the army. The cult of the Supreme Being was observed by the Jacobins in the camps as well as in the towns. The republicans of the 4th company of the 5th artillery regiment, for example, announced that they had celebrated this festival with enthusiasm, and had planted a tree of Liberty in their redoubt with cries of *Vive la République! Vive la Montagne!*

In the army as in the rest of the country the cult of the Supreme Being brought together, in support of the government, patriots disoriented by the drama of Germinal, in which Danton, Hébert, and so many others had gone to the guillotine. In the manifestations of this cult, as in other festivals, there was no separation between civilians and the military. All the civil ceremonies were accompanied by military pomp, and those in the camps adopted a symbolism copied from observances in the towns. Military reviews, activation of units, and ceremonies of amalgamation all took place before the eyes and with the participation of the people.

With the cult of the Supreme Being went the cult of the martyrs of Liberty, which relieved the anxiety of soldiers in the face of death. The cult of the martyrs of Liberty arose spontaneously within army units, whose control registers piously preserved the memory of brothers who died as heroes. The government gave it a decisive impetus by ordering a collection of the heroic and civic actions of republicans. Several numbers were published until July 1794. The fifth and last number, read aloud in the Convention, rehearsed the heroic acts of soldiers in the Army of the Rhine. The *Journal de Paris* reproduced large extracts beginning on July 28.

The patriot, whether young or old, was expected to remain unmoved in the face of death, and to reject pity. Pictures were multiplied of the young Bara, a boy of fourteen who died at Cholet at the hands of the Chouans. The same was done for Viala, who, at the age of thirteen, died heroically resisting the insurgents in southern France. Their remains were brought to the Panthéon. Another case was that of citizen Rochon at the siege of Mainz, who when a bullet crushed his leg amputated it himself, "to prove to the enemy," he said, "that to lose a leg is nothing for a republican, and that he was ready to sacrifice the other in defense of the country." Brought to the rear, and seeing his end approaching, he called the war commissioner and presented him with 52 livres for the expenses of the siege. The story was told also of Mathieu, who, in the Vendée, received a serious abdominal wound and refused to be taken to the rear. "I die content," he said, "because you have defeated these cowardly persecutors of a righteous cause."

Suffering, according to the Jacobins, was a matter of indifference to the patriot soldier, and death had in it nothing to surprise him. In dying he transmitted his virtues and courage to his comrades in arms, and when the blood he shed "passed into their veins the enemy would soon see the effects." The republican hero

> is not lost in an eternal nothingness. His remains are precious to the country, his name is dear to humanity; they will last, like the example of his virtue, as long as the world itself; and his soul, even more immortal, will surely enjoy the place reserved for the martyrs of liberty, the defenders of the rights of the human race.

These words were written by the commissioner who sent the remains of Viala to the Panthéon.

The erection of monuments was a more special form of homage to the military. It is not in the aftermath of World War I that this kind of cult of the dead first appeared; it was born in the Year II. A journalist at Reims was the first to assemble, to make them known to all, the names of volunteers of his city who had died under the colors. On May 8, 1793, he published an appeal for this purpose to all relatives of the deceased. The popular society of the city supported the idea. Rauxin, a professor of philosophy at the college, made a speech to the society in which he proposed that a pyramid be erected on the pedestal where the statue of Louis XV had been overturned and replaced by a statue of liberty. The pyramid should bear "various inscriptions in the common language [not Latin] in memory of our brothers who have died in defense of the country." The monument was inaugurated on August 10, 1793. Lists of names were also posted on the walls where municipal assemblies met. At Chinon the municipality opened registers to receive the names of soldiers killed by the enemy. At Vesoul a pyramid was erected to the memory of the fallen. In other communes monuments were built to the memory of all soldiers who had helped to save the country by their victories. At Valence, in the department of the Drôme, an altar was built in stone and dedicated to *la Patrie*; on it was raised an obelisk of triangular cross-section, one of whose angles pointed toward Toulon. At the base were attributes designed to recall the recapture of Toulon and the sacrifice of one particularly courageous soldier. On the sides it read: "The people of the Drôme to the conquerors of the combined forces of England, Spain, and Italy," and the names of the brave men of the Drôme lost in the war.

Military symbolism was also a mode of political education. The foremost symbol was the flag. The flags of different units varied in their colors. Even with the tricolor attached, they recalled the days of despotism and symbolized esprit de corps. The battalions of volunteers and draftees had flags in the three national colors, but the arrangements of the colors were different. On the folds of a flag was written the regional origin of the men assembled beneath it. A continuation of local spirit that might lead to federalism was thus encouraged. The volunteers had also wanted to inscribe on their flags their feats of arms or participation in popular uprisings. Those of the 103rd, 104th, and 105th regiments, who had formerly been in the Gardes françaises or the national guard of Paris, had expressed the intention of putting on their standards in gold letters: "Conquerors of the Bastille." Others had received their emblem from a popular society with an inscription testifying to fraternity. The 1st battalion of the Doubs had a flag made for it by the female patriots of Besançon, who inscribed it with a couplet:

> Nous venons des despotes couronner les vainquers.
> Des femmes patriotes ils possèdent les coeurs.[2]

And on the reverse: "Presented to the 1st battalion of the Doubs by the women citizens of Besançon."

All such distinctive signs and inscriptions were denounced as new "armorial bearings." The only one for the French to adopt should be *Patrie et Liberté*. When the Revolutionary Government decided upon amalgamation it decided also to unify the flags, to

---

[2] We come to crown the vanquishers of despots.
They possess the hearts of patriot women.

make them cult objects, and for each demi-brigade to have three of them. The central flag of each demi-brigade, the flag of the 2nd battalion, would be the same throughout the army, white with three bands in the national colors in its upper part. It played the role of the old colonel's flag that had traditionally shown the location of the commanding officer. The flags of the 1st and 3rd battalions were alike, but varied from one demi-brigade to another in the arrangement of the three colors. A special flag, "Palladium of the Republic," was awarded by the Convention itself to units that had several times "deserved well of the country." "Fruit of the soldiers' courage and confidence," it was another testimonial to the unity of army and government in France.

The wearing of the tricolor cockade was widespread. Marks left on weapons from the Old Regime were eradicated and replaced by those of republicanism. Sabres, no longer engraved with the fleur-de-lys but now with a fasces or a sans-culotte cap, were decorated with tricolor tassels.

Printers' ornaments on the letterheads of administrative papers were another vehicle of Jacobin thought. At first they were little pictures of battle scenes: a soldier lighting the match to a cannon; or a soldier charging with his bayonet against enemies who fell on their knees, while cavalry in the distance pursued those who would not surrender. Gradually these designs added political symbols: a cock beside the soldier, watching over the *salut de l'Empire*;[3] a lion seated beneath the tree of Liberty; or a fist holding a bludgeon, signifying the force of the people. In the end Liberty dominated the scene, represented in different ways. She took the form of an angel, with wings deployed, soaring over a camp with pike in hand. She was also a young woman at a roadside, meeting a peasant with a sack on his back and a tricolor cockade in his hat, and inviting him to join his brother. Or she appeared in sterner guise, seated on a Mountain, and ordering the movement of armies to crush tyranny, symbolized by the double-headed eagle of

---

[3] *Veillons au salut de l'Empire* was a widely known war song of the Revolution.

Germany, the British leopard, the tiara, and crowns and scepters. Finally, placing the horn of abundance on flags and cannon, she was the promise of better days to come with the peace. Along with Liberty appeared Equality in the form of a carpenter's level. Even more of a favorite was Equality shown as an agricultural worker at his daily toil. "Of all the occupations of man," explained the engraver, "there is none more worthy of respect, more touching, or more endowed with virtue; none in which man is more happy or more removed from corruption, because he is closer to nature."

Passwords were another means of transmission of Jacobinism in the army. Within each unit three words were chosen and renewed every day; the troops used them to recognize each other at night. Those employed in the Army of the Sambre-Meuse referred mostly to virtue and examples from ancient Rome: "Virtue, bravery, triumph." "Love virtue and cherish it." "Rome, Cato, Virtue." They specified the various forms of republican virtue: modesty, rejection of flattery, suppression of intrigue. They taught that all citizens should practice frugality and simplicity of life, and that the soldier should especially cultivate the courage, alacrity, firmness, and constancy that along with vigilance would make him invincible. The theme of union was often heard: "Love, brotherhood, strength." "Armed force, friendship, fraternity." A related theme was obedience to law and to the Convention: "Paris, Convention, rally." "Frenchmen, Convention, trust." "Revolution, Convention, obedience." "Love, respect for laws." "People, friend of order." To obey the orders of the Convention imposed respect for discipline: "Soldiers, obey your leaders." But if the leaders wished to use the army against the Convention they must be resisted: "Caesar, tyrant, death." Disciplined and subject to the law, the soldier must respect property: "Pillage, republicans, horror." "People, property, respect." And the meaning of the struggle must always be kept in the memory: "Kings, tyrants, conquer." "Thrones overturned, repose." "Pursue tyrants without respite." "Peoples, oppressed, revolution." The republican was contrasted with cowards that he should scorn. "Heroic actions rewarded." "Marat, Lepeletier, friends of the people." "Bara and Viala immortalized."

The theater should also become "a school of morals and a warm hearth to which all should return to be steeped again in republicanism." Saint-Just, during his mission in Alsace, took care that officers and men should not attend trivial comedies. We have little information on theatrical productions staged in places near the camps. But we know that at Besançon and at Metz such plays were performed as *Bara*, *Brutus*, *Perfect Equality*, *The Republican Wife*, *The Republican Widow*, and Sylvain Maréchal's *Last Judgment of Kings*. We have no information on the participation of army men in these spectacles intended to heighten their patriotism.

Finally, the Jacobins, like the sans-culottes, made use of the press as an instrument of political education. Among journals there was the *Bulletin de la Convention*. As early as October 15, 1792, the Convention ordered the war minister to send the *Bulletin* daily to the armies. Pache then had 6,000 copies a day distributed. After April 4, 1793, distribution was effected by the representatives on mission. The *Bulletin* used the petitions and addresses received by the Convention to develop public spirit and propagate republican instruction and morals. The minister issued precise orders that, in each army, there should be several places where the men could read the *Bulletin* at stated hours. In March 1794 the *Bulletin* became an organ for liaison between the army and the Committee of Public Safety. At that time the Committee obtained authorization "to use the *Bulletin de la Convention* to distribute information that it believes must reach all points in the Republic promptly." In their struggle against the factions Robespierre and the Jacobins made use of the *Antifédéraliste*. One of its editors, Claude François Payan, a delegate from the popular societies of the Drôme, and head of the correspondence bureau of the Committee of Public Safety, was one of the men closest to Robespierre. Gournay's *Journal militaire*, which had appeared since early in the Revolution, contained matters on the composition and action of the public authorities, and hence all that concerned the military. It was a kind of official bulletin for the army, a connecting link in the operations of military administration. In 1794 it published decrees concerning general policy. But despite the mass of copies dispatched, these government journals were sometimes in short supply. Some officers took it upon themselves to have them copied and reprinted. Some generals had their own journals printed, like Dugommier, who created the *Avant-Garde* in the Army of the Pyrenees, with the help of a hundred good Jacobins from Marseille.

In competition with the Jacobin press, journals of particular armies multiplied. The *Bulletin des Côtes-de-Brest*, born in summer of 1793 and lasting only until that October, dealt only with the war, camp life, and soldiers' duties. Conveying a traditional idea of military hierarchy and discipline, it invited the soldier to obey his leaders, and it justified command authority not by conformity of the commander's decision to the interests of the Republic but by his own qualities of courage and rapid observation in the battlefield. This sort of enterprise was a means used by certain leaders to limit or obstruct the introduction of politics into the army, by developing an esprit de corps as an antidote to Jacobinism.

Carnot thought to utilize the press for the same purpose. With Valcour and Camilla, two employees of the Committee of Public Safety, he launched a journal called the *Soirée du camp* on July 20, 1794 (2 Thermidor). It was issued in 10,000 copies. He had submitted the proposal for such a journal to the Committee on July 8, at a time when Robespierre was no longer attending its meetings. To outwit Saint-Just and his friends, Carnot represented the journal as a substitute for Hébert's *Père Duchesne*, designed to combat ultrarevolutionism in the armies.

Like Hébert's journal, the *Soirée du camp* took the form of a monologue, addressed to the soldiers by the veteran Va-de-Bon-Coeur, who "had lost a wing and had only one window left." It used familiar language, in a conversational tone as if between old companions in arms, raising questions about their joys and woes, their escapades and memorable actions, and at the same time denouncing the friends of *Père Duchesne*, "who wanted to counter-revolutionize the army by degrading the French soldier so as to bring back the Old Regime." In fact, under the cover of anti-Hébertism, the *Soirée du camp* laid the way for the fall of Robespierre on 9 Thermidor. On 6 Thermidor it announced:

> Friends, the order of the day for you is always victory. There are scoundrels here whose order of the day is lying and deception, but they are known and they are really cowards. . . . Every day they invent new devices to succeed in their horrible plots, and the old friends of the Brissots, the Dantons, the Héberts, and the Chabots, frightened by their own crimes and fearing vengeance, do all they can to obstruct the national justice and block the march of government. Is this race of rascals indestructible?

"Rascals" was the word used to characterize Robespierre and his friends on the night of 9 Thermidor. The *Soirée du camp* taught also that a man could be a tyrant without assuming the fancy dress of monarchy. "Can liberty and a tyrant exist together? Hardly! They are like fire and water. It is like trying to join day and night, existence and death."

Carnot postponed announcement of the events of 9 Thermidor. He was concerned to consolidate the position of the Thermidorians before presenting the army, whose reaction he feared, with an accomplished fact. It was only on 14 Thermidor that he announced what had happened and denounced Robespierre:

> Never was the national representation and the whole republic in such great danger. Everything that the worst rascality could imagine for the loss of liberty was combined with the most perfidious cunning. Monsters who tried to destroy the country appeared to be its most ardent defenders. Weren't they above suspicion? . . . Robespierre . . . forever infamous . . . traitor who deceived your fellow citizens and abused the

confidence you had inspired to serve your own ambitions and criminal designs.

Now for the first time the press was used massively for direct address to the soldiers. Carnot was the first to tell the army again that it was a body distinct from the Nation, with its own problems, way of thinking and acting, and its own particular ethic. Warriors shaped by life in their camps, by dangers encountered and fears overcome, possessed distinctive virtues of their own. The image that he sought to popularize in the army was no longer that of the political militant, but of the "old-timer" or professional soldier who knew all the fine points of his trade and shared them with men who were not brothers but comrades. Carnot's attitude toward the army prefigured that of the Thermidorians, who saw men in arms as an army, more than as citizens.

But was this not to prepare the birth of a power that would counterbalance, contest, and soon overturn the government?

Did the propaganda carried on for more than a year by the sans-culottes, then by the Jacobins, remain without effect on the troops?

Did they not absorb something of the message of Jacobinism?

3. The Effects of Political Education on the Army

To judge the transformation in the collective psychology of the soldiers, the historian has, first of all, the reports of enemies and of populations liberated by "the messengers of Liberty." For example, the Belgians: attracted by soldiers who seemed affable, cheerful, jaunty, and irreverent, they approached them and began to talk. Then the soldiers became more solemn; the Marseillaise resounded, and they forced the spectators to kneel on hearing this patriotic hymn. Or again, five years after the Year II, an Austrian describes his amazement at examples of French equality:

In the presence of the general everyone kept his hat on. A lieutenant walked around the room, wearing his hat and whistling some air of his country, while all the others sat drinking, and a secretary took down in writing the peasants' replies to the general, who spoke very good German, and dictated his answers in French. There was a knock on the door, and the village officials came in, with their hats in their hands and bowing deeply to ask the general to be kind enough to spare their locality. The general ordered them to put their hats back on.

The historian has also the letters written by volunteers. Many of them have been published, and many still remain in cartons in the archives. We must ask whether such letters constitute valid evidence for the researcher, whether their authors told freely what they saw, whether they may have practiced a self-censorship so as not to be seen as lukewarm patriots in the eyes of their fellows or of the friend who often actually held the pen. It is a question also whether official censorship, as we have known it in recent wars, was absent in the Year II. We have evidence of its existence in the letter of a soldier, Margetta, to his mother:

> I wrote you a letter from Condé eight months ago that did not reach you. I have not written more because it was forbidden. Letters we wrote were stopped, for fear of giving out bad news. It was forbidden to give any details of what had happened or was still happening.

There were also stereotypes. The soldier who acted as a scribe, writing to the dictation of others, used the same style and similar formulas in all his letters. There are examples of this procedure in letters of soldiers from the Puy-de-Dôme.

But from a reading of several hundred letters we can see that the censorship was very sporadic, since many letters showed no hesitation in depicting trouble and adversity. Most of them were not afraid to show attachment to Catholic worship, then officially frowned upon. "Ready-made" letters are in a minority. The style of most of them expresses the patriotic mystique and virtuous sensibility proper for sincere revolutionaries.

But do a few hundred letters offer a good sample of the state of mind of hundreds of thousands of men? Those that we have do not all come from the same army or operational sector; some are from soldiers of the line, others from volunteers and draftees.

Some letters are from soldiers who were avowed political militants. They reecho, more or less naively, the song that carried them at the moment of combat, the Marseillaise. As a man named Bourgognonaux wrote:

> They are trembling, those *féroces soldats*,[4] and thanks be to heaven, the Republic triumphs. Better die than yield an inch. Our cause is just, and we will uphold it, as we have always upheld it, to the last drop of our blood.

Others recall former times to contrast them with the republican era. From a letter by a battalion commander from a place near Amiens:

> You were not assembled by orders of an intendant or a sub-delegate puffed up by this ridiculous function, who took soldiers by measurement and obtained strength and courage by a lottery. Our country calls us, and good children obey their mother. With such a title, honor will guide us. . . . Born in a village, we have known better than townspeople the horrors of the feudal system. We were "villains." So! We will teach these one-time "great" people that villains and sans-culottes will no longer let their crops be eaten by rabbits, and will pay no more tithes.

A soldier named Jacques Tuzot assured his parents of the promise made by the authorities: with the feudal aristocracy ruined, and liberty won, peace would prevail forever in the fields:

> I will tell you that all is well in the armies of the Republic, and that the tyrants will soon be confounded. When the ene-

---

[4] Cf. the Marseillaise: "Entendez-vous, dans ces campagnes, Mugir ces féroces soldats?" where the *féroces soldats* are the invaders of France in 1792.

mies of the Republic are defeated I shall have the happiness of coming to embrace you, and to remain, if it please heaven, in the bosom of my family. It is there that I shall taste the torrent of delights brought by liberty and equality to free men. It is there that the worker will peaceably till his fields, taste their sweet fruits, and enjoy liberty and equality. Evils will be no more, they are in the past; amidst the greatest dangers the cries of our country have resounded to the four corners of France . . . and the Republic has been saved.

Bertrand Verdier, of the first battalion of the 54th demi-brigade, said much the same:

There are over 8,000 men before Mainz, sharing in innumerable and extreme hardships, but we must hope that they end and that we shall return to our homes after dethroning the tyrants. The aristocrats of the country will have the shame of yielding to a liberty they so much detest.

Militant soldiers wrote of the decisive support that they derived from the Terror. At Lyon and at Toulon they proclaimed their adherence to a regime that rid them of the enemies they had faced. One man said, when Toulon was recaptured from the British:

Our general brought together all the inhabitants and made them stand in two rows. He asked which of them had sold out the town and betrayed the country. He found two hundred, who were shot on the spot. I can assure you that our general led them in a merry dance.

The hardships of their daily lot never blunted their faith:

Sleeping always on the ground, we bivouac under the nose of the enemy with never a moment of relief, always in wet mud up to our knees. I don't know how I keep alive, losing the rank I had in my company, losing also the booty I had taken, and suffering two sabre blows from the enemy. But I will tell you that I still have eyes to weep, legs to march, and arms to support my country.

Cosney, a drummer boy of grenadiers, wrote from Mainz:

It is now almost four months that I have been sleeping outdoors despite the rigor of the season. But in serving my country the discomfort changes to pleasure, and I know that I will remain at my post to end up by exterminating our enemies.

There were the two Primault brothers, one in the Army of the Rhine, the other in the Army of the Pyrenees, who both complained of the lack of food and clothing, and who both ended their letters by invoking the "Republic one and imperishable." Finally there was Joseph Rousseau of Châteauroux, who reassured his parents:

You told me to have courage, and be sure that I will not lack it, and far from being like those cowards who abandon their country I burn with love of the Republic and I will die before abandoning it. I have taken an oath not to abandon my flag before driving from French territory all the satellites of crowned despots allied against us.

They tried to convey their ideal to the communities from which they came. They invited their fellow citizens to be vigilant toward royalists. They lectured them when some showed a reprehensible tendency to federalism. They visited them when the hazards of war made visits possible, and encouraged them to keep their patriotism "burning," and renewed with them "the oath of fidelity to Liberty and Equality." Their letters give evidence of common feeling between the interior of the country and the battalions. One commander, Couture, wrote of the comfort that both he and his men drew from home, in a letter to the officials of the city of Amiens:

Our battalion, equipped by your efforts, animated by your liberty, guided by your counsels, and strengthened by your confidence, has received the paternal embrace that you charged its emissaries with bringing to us. What you have told them, and what you have written to me, the worries that agitated the city in dangers that seemed all the greater from inexperience, the touching interest that these dangers inspired as shown by your feelings and your tears, are all consoling proofs that the existence of the battalion is closely tied to that of an immense family.

In moments of discouragement the soldier knew that he could count on the moral support of his parents, who remembered the patriotic enthusiasm that they shared. A modest farmer in the Meuse wrote to his son:

The fever you had is only a slight indisposition for a republican who knows how to fight and die for his country. I know that these are your sentiments, and they are those also of your father, mother, brothers and sisters. . . . While you fight the satellites of despotism your brothers are busy in the convoys supplying their comrades in arms with food and forage— nothing is too much when it comes to saving the country. . . . Take courage, and never go against the principles I have instilled in you. Know how to bear hunger, thirst, cold, and heat. When you suffer, know that it is for your family and your country. When you march into combat, never forget that it is for your father, mother, brothers, and sisters, and know how to prefer death to disgrace.

Sometimes more militant voices were heard, as in a letter by Gilbert Sulfour to his parents in April 1794:

When we had no more ammunition we had to surrender. The damned rogues took all we had, including our hats; they wanted to take our grenadiers' epaulettes but we said they could kill us first. We had only eighteen ounces of bread a day with a little vermicelli soup. That didn't prevent us from always singing *Ça ira*! We were quartered in a church, with a badly paved yard where we planted a tree of liberty in spite of them. They threatened to beat us, telling us we are no longer in France and must say "Monsieur" and not "citizen."

Of course not all soldiers of the Year II, many of whom had been draft evaders, became republican heroes by the magic of Jacobin education. The researcher may deceive himself by too much reading of virtuously patriotic language. Like the militant sans-culottes of Paris, who numbered only a few thousands, the Jacobins and sans-culottes in the army may have been a minority. For example, of about a hundred letters from soldiers from the Indre, now in the Archives de la Guerre, only fifteen give evidence of pure republican virtues, the others telling more of fear, fatigue, and despair. Such demoralization is clear in the letter by young Guillaume Ollier, who wrote from the Army of Italy, operating in the Alps in the winter of 1793:

I will tell you that I am in these mountains, facing the Piedmontese, and that we can get neither bread nor wine, and if a few casks of wine arrive it sells for 40 *sous* a bottle. Perhaps we will be on the way to Turin, perhaps we will leave these accursed mountains where our only consolation is to receive an Austrian or Piedmontese bullet to put us out of our misery.

Or another soldier, named Montvallot, or Bellegarde:

I take the opportunity to send this by Meliodon, who is departing for Riom with a crippled arm, due to a gunshot. He is lucky in this misfortune to get out of this frightful war. I would be glad to be out of it at so little cost; I really wish it. We are overwhelmed with troubles, in bivouac night and day, and after all our struggles we may have to give up the siege of this town. Good-bye, I am cold, I am frozen, and going on guard duty.

Or this cry from an artisan:

I am getting impatient to return to work. I've grown up a little, and the shuttle wouldn't be so bad!

Some did not wish to listen to the Jacobin lessons at all. They preferred to forget, to forget everything if only for a moment. To drink, until rolling under the table. Some were driven to desperation, and some were clever operators that thought only of the maximum profit to be gained from the adventure into which they had been thrown. Jean Suchard told his parents of a little business he had contrived:

> I joined forces with a comrade to sell wine and other provisions, but someone stole part of my profit and took a sheep that had cost me 20 crowns.

Others were what the sans-culottes denounced as "bloodsuckers." Lieutenant Michel, son of a hardware dealer, thought of a way of playing on the value of money and price of goods:

> If peace should come, and money fall to a suitable level, one could buy in Paris and sell in Strasbourg. . . . Or one could buy in Mannheim, where there is a glut of merchandise, and only thirty leagues from Strasbourg and navigable [sic].

There is no way to know how many derided the principles of equality. In the Army of the Rhine there was anti-Semitism, with all Jews regarded as low speculators who lived by trickery.

Civic education met with a different reception from one army to another. The Army of the Sambre-Meuse, thought to be more "military" than the Army of the Moselle, later showed a republican spirit that contrsted with the Army of the Rhine-Moselle. In reading the letters of soldiers from the Puy-de-Dôme we see that differences remained between volunteers and draftees. The former forgot their troubles and thought of the public good, the latter continually lamented their fate. Rivalries between units did not disappear. Quarrels continued to break out between "old-timers" and those they disdainfully called "contingent men"—that is, draftees. Royalist propaganda worked upon these rivalries and exploited the demoralization produced by hardship. General Leclerc noted, in March 1794, that his troops were infiltrated by "liberticide pamphlets." At about this time a "counter-revolutionary clique" formed within certain cavalry units, especially the hussars. A captain, a lieutenant and two sub-lieutenants of the 9th Hussars, were arrested and brought to justice.

Agents of the war ministry, such as Bruslé and Verjade with the Army of Italy in January 1794, sometimes stressed the inadequacy of the purge and saw danger in favoring the abilities of career officers. General Brunot had been dismissed and executed as a suspect, but his friends still filled the staffs of the Army of Italy:

> Obliged to render homage to the Mountain, they do so with such poor grace that one easily sees their displeasure. They form a kind of coalition in clubs where they have won influence, and try to weaken our revolutionary measures.

These suspect officers cared too little for the material condition of their troops, who, at all times in the snow, were almost without clothing, food, and munitions. The result was seditious talk, and even sometimes revolts. Maurice Requiers, a sub-lieutenant in the battalion of the Var, declared that he would mount guard no longer and invited his subordinates to refuse also. Anyone was a fool to obey orders, and why should anyone fight with his fingers and feet frozen, his stomach empty, and his nights without sleep?

While the officers were not insensible to the advantages of Jacobinism, which had restored their authority over their men, some of them reacted like military professionals in objecting to supervision by the state, especially in matters of promotion. Some of them found means of concealed resistance by using the administrative councils of their units.

From August 1793 to March 1794 these administrative councils were composed of officers, NCOs, and soldiers taken from among those with the most seniority in the demi-brigade. A law of March 9 restored the right of election. The councils were then formed, at the battalion level, of the commanding officer, a captain, a lieutenant, a sub-lieutenant, a sergeant-major, a sergeant, a quartermaster-corporal, and five privates. Each member except the commander was elected for six months by men of the same rank. At the demi-brigade level the council was formed of six officers, six NCOs and nine privates taken from those composing the battalion councils.

The councils were democratic organs, each a kind of military muncipality, whose function was to manage the funds, supervise clothing, equipment and armament, and appoint the officer in charge of clothing, the quartermaster-treasurer and his assistants, the adjutant, the drum major, the musicians, the chief armorer, and the tailors, cobblers, and baggage master. The councils also made the nominations for promotion. They gave assurance that there would be no improper favoritism, that the rule of seniority was observed, and that candidates presented to the Convention would have the necessary merit and abilities. These "military republics" functioned to the general satisfaction, especially, as we shall see, of company-grade officers.

But a study of the registers of these councils, as found in the war archives, shows that in certain demi-brigades the officers managed to dominate the councils. The proportion of enlisted men elected by their comrades was not always as high as the law stipulated. Officers once elected remained in place. For example, in the 113th demi-brigade, two sub-lieutenants promoted to lieutenants continued to sit on the council without having been elected by the other lieutenants. The commanding officer of the battalion or demi-brigade did not always conduct himself as chairman of the council, but acted rather as was his daily habit in matters of command. This caused some soldiers to complain.

To discover the attitude of officers sitting on these councils I accumulated a file on all officers in a dozen demi-brigades. With a knowledge thus gained of the age, rank, and years of service of each officer, it became possible to analyze the work of the councils. It became evident that some failed to give notice of vacant positions. Others tampered with the service records. Some overstated the years of seniority or altered the date of an election. Sometimes there were illegal elections, in which not all those qualified to vote were assembled. Candidates not wanted by the council might be recorded as illiterate. The council might refuse to hear or transmit the complaint of an aggrieved soldier. Or if soldiers asked to see the minutes of the council, so as to bring their grievances before the representative of the people, the request might be rejected. If it was not granted, and the civil authorities opened an inquiry, the procedure might be subjected to indefinite delay.

In some cases, when a council presented only one candidate, the Convention could not exercise its power to choose one of three candidates for an appointment. Or if three were proposed, they might be such that only one choice was possible. There were even cases where units never informed the Revolutionary Government on promotions. The 117th demi-brigade was such a case.

There were, then, here and there, officers who worked behind the scenes to limit the power of the government over the armed forces. On the whole, however, their efforts did not prevent Jacobinism from making its mark on the army. Jacobinism instilled the principle of unity, its essential watchword. There were no more "whites" and "blues," no more draftees and volunteers, no more Alsacians, Auvergnats, and Gascons, but only Frenchmen fighting in the cause of Liberty against aristocracy.

By this principle the army was led to accept in turn the liquidation of the *enragés*, the elimination of the Hébertist and Dantonist factions, and the fall of the Incorruptible and his friends. The Thermidorians used it to rally the army after Carnot had prepared it psychologically for the disappearance of Robespierre.

Yet the events of Thermidor produced occasional signs of discontent in the army. General Meunier, commanding a division in the Army of the Rhine, wrote to General Michaud on 14 Thermidor that "news of this latest conspiracy will surprise all brave republicans." Some soldiers understood, in the fall and winter of 1794, when the subsistence crisis struck both the army and the people, that the former Jacobin government had been able to assure citizens of "their right to existence." Like the sans-culottes, some soldiers called for a return to the Terror. Some never stopped doing so, and Napoleon Bonaparte would have to get rid of those he called *septembriseurs* (from the September Massacres of 1792), and who despite purges remained sufficiently numerous in the army to form secret societies, such as the Philadelphes.

CHAPTER IX

• • •

War in the Year II

1. STRATEGY AND TACTICS

The Revolutionary Government transformed the art of war. The Committee of Public Safety gave notice on February 2, 1794, that "the general rule is always to act in mass and on the offensive, keep the troops ever on the alert, seize every opportunity to employ the bayonet, and pursue the enemy until his complete destruction." On May 27 the Committee wrote again: "Attack to avoid being attacked." And on August 21: "To disperse the troops along a long frontier makes us weak everywhere, and means that the enemy, by combining his forces at one point and attacking by surprise will make a breakthrough wherever he pleases." So: "Attack by surprise like lightning."

There would be no more of the old campaigns in which a general brought the enemy to a terrain of his choice by ingenious marches and countermarches. Revolutionary France had a mass army, a young army, an army of patriots. The problem was to utilize these three elements for a strategy of mass and speed. An "economy of forces" replaced the old "economy of directions."

Organization into divisions was necessary for application of such a strategy. By the regulation of 1791, a field army was divided into an advance guard composed of grenadiers in battalions and a right and left wing composed in part of battalions of *chasseurs* and in part of cavalry in regiments or brigades. Each of these three groups was commanded by a divisional general. The central group, under the direct authority of the general in overall command, consisted of a variable number of infantry brigades.

Even before 1794 a more flexible divisional organization had begun to replace this classical eighteenth-century formation. The need of separating for procurement of supplies led to the introduction within each army of permanent divisions, each containing elements of the three combat arms and provided with services so as to be able to remain in place, march, or operate apart from the others. The division came gradually to be constituted of two brigades of battle infantry or light infantry, a regiment or brigade of cavalry, and a company of cannoneers and in some cases of "flying" artillery—that is, of twelve infantry battalions, four to twelve cavalry squadrons, and thirty-two to thirty-eight artillery pieces. At full strength, the division comprised 13,000 infantrymen, 700 to 1,200 cavalry, and 400 to 500 artillerymen. It was under the single command of a divisional general who knew his troops well, and was known to them.

To gain the advantages of this divisional system it was necessary to conduct operations in such a way as to satisfy two apparently contradictory conditions: first, the need of maneuver, which required an extension over large areas; and second, the need of forceful action, which demanded maximum concentration for battle. To reconcile these two needs, the forces had to be so distributed spatially that they could adapt at any moment to the demands of an extremely variable situation. A commander had to estimate these demands at their true importance, so as to meet them by strictly measured out means. This judicious employment of forces under all circumstances received the name of "economy of forces."

In the absence of a commander who knew how to seize the divisional instrument firmly, such organization by divisions could lead to miscalculations. Divisions of the same army acted without relationship to one another, and so engaged in a war of minor engagements yielding only partial successes. In its early applications the divisional principle contributed to an excessive dispersion of the troops. At Neerwinden the army of Dumouriez was deployed along a twelve-kilometer front; that is, with 45,000 men it covered a front twice as wide as Marshall Luxembourg had occupied a century before with 70,000. The results were a juxtaposition of engagements that were hard to orchestrate and a gap in the center that was exploited by the Austrian reserves; while Dumouriez's right wing was on the point of winning its part of the battle, the reserves overwhelmed his left wing.

Beginning in August 1793 E. A. Berthelmy, appointed as adjutant-general by Custine and put at the head of Houchard's staff, extended the divisional system to the Army of the North. He organized into "active masses" what had been only a crowd of men exerting no force because they were dispersed without order. Against Bouchotte's incomprehension and Carnot's lack of interest, the reform went forward in the various armies. It made it possible, by strategic movements, to bring a mass of forces greater than those of the enemy into action at the principal point of operations.

But strategic progress was not accomplished in a day. Well into the Year II the comings and goings of French troops in the north copied the movements in previous wars more than they innovated. It has been found that shortly before the French victory at Fleurus, in June 1794, the French dispositions were strategically mediocre. The force at the disposal of the commander in this theater was too weak to contain the enemy center and to attack on the two wings at the same time. The wings were too far apart to combine their action. If the enemy had been quick enough to maneuver on interior lines between the two wings, he could have destroyed them both, one after the other. The French left wing, incautiously placed near the coast, was in danger of being taken on the flank at any moment and pushed into the sea. The French groupings, in the words of a recent historian, Henry Lachouque, were "disposed in a uniform way with the same number of divisions, and apparently established more by some systematic idea than with a view to maneuver. The strength of the left, charged with taking Ypres and initiating a grand battle, was no greater than that of the center, charged only with defense."

It was not until Bonaparte's first Italian campaign, in 1796, that it was possible to see what a general of genius could do with the possibilities offered by the divisional organization.

During his conquest of Piedmont Bonaparte understood how to maneuver in a central position. His center of gravity, where his command post, reserves, and supplies were located, was so placed as to allow him to be constantly in a position to concentrate his army, by a few hours' march, at any point that was menaced or where he wished to make an effort. Taking a calculated risk, he managed always to be stronger than the adversary at the decisive point, so chosen that "all the rest remained accessory." "It is the same with systems of war as with stationary sieges," he said. "All fire must be concentrated on one point. The breach once made, and the balance broken, everything else is unnecessary. The place is taken."

This concentration of effort made it possible to combine a frontal attack, holding the adversary in a fixed position, with a wider movement against his flank and rear. As the battle developed, Bonaparte applied not only the strategic advances of the Year II but also the progress of that period in tactics.

There had been important changes in tactics even before the Revolution. The speed of musket fire (three shots a minute) had allowed the arrangement of men in three ranks instead of seven or eight. As weapons became easier to handle, men in the same rank could be put elbow to elbow. This "light order" made the infantry more maneuverable. The line of three ranks was divided into platoons. The men in each platoon could turn to the right or left to form a column of platoons "at full distance." The line produced a maximum intensity of fire; the column, rapidity of evolutions. As for which was better, column or line, there were disputes throughout the eighteenth century between upholders of the "light" order and those who preferred the "deep." Those, like the chevalier Folard and Mesnil-Durand, who assigned greater importance to maneuver, recommended the thin line or light order. Only toward the end of the century did the truth emerge with adoption of the "mixed" order, which combined the light and deep orders to obtain the advantages of mobility and firepower. It remained only to perfect the evolutions by which line could change into column, and vice versa. These were the innovations made by Guibert and de Broglie.

The need was also recognized in the eighteenth century to employ skirmishers to test the enemy's nerves, feel out his placement of troops, and take possession of difficult spots, such as wooded areas or pieces of broken terrain. At the moment of battle, shielded by such skirmishers (*tirailleurs* or special marksmen), the front would suffer less danger from the openings and irregularities that sometimes appeared in its formation.

As the infantry became more mobile it exerted more power than ever before. It was learned from Frederick II how to move an army against an enemy flank under protection of an advance guard, and how to deploy so fast that the adversary could not rearrange his dispositions. For the best-trained troops, a single command sufficed for forming the line by turning left-face, after which, by turning right, the battalions formed the "oblique order."

The oblique order made possible the use of infantry for movement on the flanks, for which cavalry had been customarily employed, and which fell upon the adversary, surrounded him, and took him in the rear. With a new suppleness of maneuver for infantry and artillery, and with heavier firepower, openings could be allowed in the line of battle without risk of infiltration by the enemy. The army thus presented itself in battle, not as a rigid and compact block but as a mechanism of articulated parts, each capable of various movements.

The material designed by Gribeauval for artillery was the most recent in Europe, and the most effective. The cannonballs were heavier, carried further, and could be more accurately aimed. The creation of horse-drawn batteries, by Narbonne's report of January 11, 1792, permitted an augmentation of firepower against a point chosen for attack or defense.

There has been uncertainty whether the army of the Year II, reconstituted in depth and commanded by former NCO's, possessed the qualities of a readily maneuverable force. Until 1902, military historians saw the armies of the Revolution as incapable of complex movements. They held that the republican soldiers, until the Italian campaign of 1796, attacked in columns with bayonets raised and revolutionary songs on their lips. In 1902 Captain Jean Colin published his work on *La tactique et la discipline dans les armées de la Révolution*. He, too, held that the armies of the Year II failed to understand the techniques of combat developed a few years before. But he found that in 1793, in the Army of the North, for example, the troops had fought in lines, or as individual *tirailleurs*, rather than in columns, precisely because of "their inexperience and lack of solidity."

It is in fact a singular error [wrote Colin]

> to suppose that ardor and inexperience led infantry units to adopt formation in columns for the attack. Battalions that had received no training were at first used as light infantry, but they were a minority. Others were formed in lines for battle.

Colin broadened his conclusions to the army of 1794:

> Accounts of different engagements, even when they make no explicit mention of the formation, are unintelligible unless we suppose that the men were deployed in line. This order, the simplest of all, was the only one possible with green troops.

It is true that formation in columns could be adopted only by trained men, as is abundantly proved by the accounts used by Colin and by the inspection reports submitted to the ministry of war. But Colin was mistaken in not sufficiently distinguishing between the two halves of 1793, and completely in error in generalizing to the Year II his findings that were valid for the first months of 1793. Late in 1793 and at the beginning of 1794 the training of troops received the constant attention of responsible political and military leaders. Abridgments of the regulation of August 1791 on infantry drill and maneuver were distributed to officers and NCO's, who were urged to digest their contents and use them in the instruction of the draftees. By the late summer of 1793 a training camp was operating at Cambrai, and a little later one at Launac, which, with assistance from the popular society of Montpellier, undertook the training of draftees in the southwest. The camp at Cambrai, installed by Custine, was put in charge of General Meunier. An officer, an NCO, and a drummer from each battalion in the armies of the North and the Ardennes proceeded to Cambrai, where they were occupied in daily drills. The drummers learned how to beat a rhythm of eighty paces to the minute, while the officers and NCO's learned how to train for this pace and apply it on the march. In July 1793 one soldier per battalion was detached to Cambrai to receive lessons that he then taught to his companions in arms. Another camp was opened at Maubeuge, and then, after the arrest of Custine, at Gravelle. The commissioners Varin and Cellier reported that the battalions drilled every day with "inconceivable" activity. They assured the ministry, in the summer of 1793, that in two weeks "the army has doubled its strength without increase of numbers." The soldiers, they said, drilled indefatigably and many battalions maneuvered with a precision worthy of troops of the line. New recruits were exercised twice a day both in firing and in movement. "No one should be surprised," as one soldier said later, "at the extreme fatigue caused by drilling, when it is remembered that at our age, and at that time, the regulation musket with its bayonet weighed thirteen or fourteen pounds."

Training went on repeatedly under Houchard, with battalions maneuvering from eight to nine o'clock in the morning and from two to four in the afternoon. Jourdan wrote to an adjutant in January 1794: "Issue orders to drill the troops every day, and make the unit commanders responsible for instruction in the battalions and regiments." The brigade generals were to make visits of inspection. General Vandamme also reported the activity in the camps; the whole month of February 1794 had been spent in training. As the spring season opened, Pichegru increased the hours of drill, and Macdonald issued reminders to subordinates who had relaxed their attention to such matters. Speaking of the draftees, a Sergeant Brault wrote: "We give them hardly any free time; with three hours of drill in the morning, and three in the afternoon, they will not get bored."

An American researcher, John Lynn, has sifted the reports and correspondence of the Army of the North and produced a statistical study of the battles it engaged in. From his work it is evident that the army profited from the instruction received in the camps.[1]

A clear improvement was shown by the success at Wattignies in October 1793, which marked a turning point in the state of military education of the army. It may be remembered how the plan first worked out by Carnot—a frontal attack executed on the two wings, followed by an attempt to pierce the enemy center to push through to Maubeuge—had failed. Now Carnot could rely sufficiently on the discipline and skill of the troops for them to slip from the left wing and center to the right. For the first time the army maneuvered well, and the battle can be called modern in the extent of its front, its general form, its duration, and the division into three phases: establishment of contact, frontal combat, and decisive attack on the wing.

But at a tactical level, it was not really until the spring and summer of 1794 that the troops were able to employ all the resources of their art. In the Army of the North they had enough skill to use a line formation in both attack and defense. The column was also used successfully for the attack. The cases assembled by John Lynn (forty-two out of more than a hundred) confirm the importance of this technique of attack in June 1794. Massed columns won a

---

[1] John A. Lynn, *The Bayonets of the Republic: Motivation and Tactics in the Army of Revolutionary France, 1791–1794*, Urbana and Chicago, 1984. This volume is mainly an intensive study of the Army of the North.

victory against both infantry and mixed forces. In several cases, in the spring and summer of 1794, columns proved their superiority even against cavalry. It was a sign of the high level of training in some of the demi-brigades.

It was also in the spring and summer of 1794, in the Army of the North, that the infantry successfully employed another formation that is said not to have been perfected until 1796—that is, the formation of a square by a single battalion, allowing a stronger defense, notably against cavalry charges. The new role of light infantry must also be emphasized. In a "primary attack role" the light infantry prepared, sustained, and protected the principal attack delivered by battalions of battle infantry. There were many cases where *tirailleurs* acted in conjunction with attack columns and supported them. Light infantry, acting alone, carried on veritable small battles to attack and take a wooded area, a redoubt, or a village. The best grenadiers were used to form small shock forces in the "indirect style" of combat, falling on the enemy's rear to disorganize his communications and create panic.

Revolutionary warfare thus employed innovative tactics more than has been said. The new tactics can be reduced to two essentials, a flanking movement and a strong general assault. Both were appropriate for an army of superior numbers, which made it possible to engage the enemy along the whole front while striking him on the wings. Keeping the whole front in a state of suspense, the French army could direct its efforts against the point believed to be weakest. At Fleurus the army turned the enemy's flank while Jourdan held a reserve in the center that he could use at his discretion. In such maneuvers the army developed a system depending surely on numbers, but also on the agility and vigor of the men— in short, on their suppleness in movement.[2]

[2] With the Levy in Mass the French army by the end of 1793 reached a strength of about 700,000. The Emperor, fearing an inferiority of numbers, made a proposal to the German diet on January 20, 1794, to proceed with a general arming of the German people. His proposal was not accepted. In Prussia the peasants were refusing to pay their seigneurial rents, and the agitation persuaded the king of Prussia to reject the mass enrollment proposed by Austria.

Yet it must not be forgotten that combat in the Year II, as in the following years, was not always carried on by learned maneuvers. It varied from one army or theater of operations to another. For more than half the men involved the war was a succession of small encounters in which they fired quickly on an enemy after a lengthy search. In the wooded areas of the Vendée and Brittany, as in the heights of the Pyrenees, the war consisted of hundreds of separate engagements.

Thus we must not extend the findings of John Lynn to all the armies. And especially, by attending too much to the statistics of combat, we may forget that behind the tabulations of attack by the light and the deep order there was a human reality not always reflected in the staff reports. It is to be found in letters, marching journals, and the records of military justice. The reality was often fear and panic. Then as now, panic was the main adversary of command. It broke the lines, shattered the columns, and made maneuver impossible. It might spread among the best regulated troops, and the veteran was no less subject to it than the draftee. It invaded a unit on either the offensive or the defensive. In one case, the newly formed 7th battalion of the Gers, composed almost entirely of inexperienced men, received its baptism of fire without flinching and attacked under the worst conditions. In another case, the best soldiers of Pichegru broke into a rout on hearing false rumors of treachery from a few carters.

An example is given by the troops under General Declaye, near Bouchain in the autumn of 1793. Marksmen were feeling out the retreating enemy. The advance guard was in good spirits, count-

---

The soldiers of the coalition were mercenaries, most of them well trained. In August 1793 the commander-in-chief of the Austrian army, Coburg, had 110,000 men at his disposal between the North Sea and the Meuse—Austrians, Prussians, Hanoverians, Hessians, and a small number of British. The king of Prussia marched on Mainz with 42,000 men and held 33,000 in reserve in Westphalia; he was supported by 24,000 Austrians and 14,000 Germans. England subsidized 20,000 Sardinians and 6,000 Neapolitans. In April 1794 England paid for 62,400 Prussians. Spain had 50,000 men under arms, and Portugal one division.

ing on an easy victory. But the enemy was only feinting, hoping to turn the French flank. This being perceived, the advance guard began to withdraw through a cramped space between low hills. Some horsemen appeared; they were French cavalry causing a commotion as they moved back. Their sudden arrival set off a panic through the whole unit. The disorder stopped when a few officers, remaining cool, and by using both threats and patriotic exhortations, reassembled a few dozen of the fleeing men. No sooner was a line of resistance formed than calm returned.

We have here a type case for most of the panics that we have examined. Panic always struck a unit that had long suffered from hunger, thirst, and fatigue. With physical resistance worn down, moral faculties were also weakened, and men in combat were unable to react properly to unfounded suspicions of treason.

We come then to the problem of supplying the army, which, if inadequately solved, could disorganize it. Carefully calculated maneuvers required a reserve of firepower that was sometimes lacking. And maneuvers could be brought to a halt because an army had, at any cost, to be fed and clothed.

2. The Material Basis of Combat

Parthenay in the Deux-Sèvres, like many other municipalities, had a complaint to make in January 1794. There was simply not enough military apparel for the draftees. The officials wrote:

> We have just seen the arrival of fifteen young men eager to depart in defense of the country. But what condition they have come in! All come only with caps, not hats; some in wooden shoes, others barefoot, and still others in plowmen's clogs; their jackets torn, and many with little bottles slung across their shoulders in which they carry water given to them by people along the way.

It was hard to procure uniforms in the extreme shortage of blue, white, and scarlet cloth. So draftees were authorized, "in the absence of uniforms," to wear "trousers with leather between the legs and a woolen jacket. . . . To obtain uniformity the jackets and trousers should be as nearly as possible of the national blue." In the Gers red cloth was so scarce that the districts called on the magistrates to part with their robes and hoods:

> Thus these hoods, which paraded the importance of these red-robed seigneurs and gave the municipalities of the towns an air of supremacy over those of the countryside, and these red robes of judges, which symbolized the gold and blood of litigants on which they gorged themselves, would serve to clothe the brave fighters who are to deliver us from the oppression of kings and seigneurs.

Arms were as scarce as clothing. On September 30, 1793, the 2,600 men in three Saint-Quentin battalions were about to depart, but only 600 muskets and 200 cartridges could be found to equip them. On October 17 the 2nd battalion of Vervins arrived in the camp at Boherie. Not 1 of its men was armed. In the absence of guns, pikes were assigned to the draftees at Saint-Quentin, Ribemont, and Fresnoy-le-Grand. Hunting guns were collected in the district of Sainte-Menehoud; there were enough for only a quarter of the companies. At Boulogne arms were taken from the national guard to give to the draftees, with resulting anxiety over how the town might defend itself if the need should arise. In November La Rochelle had 584 muskets to distribute to its recruits, but a third of them were soon found to be useless, and 1,000 draftees left for the frontiers armed only with sticks. In the Somme the local officials asked the representatives on mission "what to do in the absence of guns," and Elie Lacoste replied, "Arm your men with pikes, and if there are no swords use axes and pickaxes." At the same time agents of the Committee of Public Safety stationed with the Army of the North recommended arming with scythes and pikes, and with axes and pickaxes instead of sabres. Representatives on mission multiplied their warnings to the civil powers. "Again I say," wrote Bernard from the Jura, "it is not men we lack, but weapons!" Pflieger reported that generals in the Army of the Rhine were sending back battalions of the new levy because, arriving unarmed, they were a useless encumbrance.

Not only the draftees, but soldiers already engaged in operations were inadequately equipped. At the beginning of 1794 the Army of the North had a shortage of 10,000 muskets; the Army of the Alps, 2,000; the Army of the Eastern Purenees, 20,000; the Army of the Western Pyrenees, 6,000. All told, one soldier in ten had an unserviceable gun. Did some then fight with the pike? We do not know. What is well attested, however, from more than one report by unit commanders, is that formations of pikemen did exist in the army. At the end of 1793 Jomini noted a whole division of pikemen in the camp at Reunion-sur-Oise, and General Beauregard wrote to his subordinates:

> I will send you information as soon as possible on the drill and use of the long pike. If you think it wise you may issue the pike to all the levies that will be arriving, for it is the only weapon now appropriate considering the short time needed to teach its use.

Pikes were carried not only in training but also by soldiers on guard duty.

By the end of 1793 there were 700,000 men to be clothed, armed, and equipped. Never in any European country had a government faced such a situation. France was essentially an agricultural country, and although industry had developed during the eighteenth century, it was mostly in a system of small workshops rather than in factories of hundreds of workers using new sources of energy. Industry suffered also from the state of the roads and the lack of transportation to move raw materials and finished products. It was thus a gigantic effort that the Revolutionary Government undertook.

The Committee of Public Safety, subordinating the Commission on Powder and Arms to itself, became the center for mobilization of supplies. It surrounded itself with scientific men as advisers, including Monge, Berthollet, Hassenfratz, Vandermonde, and Chaptal. It nationalized the manufacture of arms. It created forges in the open air. "In distributing forges in great numbers in public places," wrote Carnot, "the Committee has had the object of inspiring the people's confidence in their own resources, and making them the overseers of the problems that such a great manufacture may involve." Shops making musket barrels were set up in the Luxembourg gardens, at the Tuileries, on the esplanade of the Invalides, and at the Place de l'Indivisibilité (formerly the Place Royale, now the Place des Vosges). The manufacture at Saint-Etienne was put under control by the central authorities, and the workers were requisitioned. At the end of the Year II (September 1794) it was producing 3,000 muskets and 600 pistols every *décade* of ten days. Much the same was true at Charleville, Tulle, Moulins, Autun, Clermont-Ferrand, and Bergerac.

Cannon were produced at the works of the Périer brothers at Chaillot, at Romilly, Indret, and Le Creusot and at Douai, Strasbourg, Metz, Saint-Lô, and Villedieu. Some were produced also in the south in the neighborhood of Toulouse, Lyon, and Toulon. Bells were removed from the church towers, because the metal in them could supply half the material needed to make bronze for cannon. At the beginning of the Year III these establishments were furnishing about 7,000 pieces a year.

The Office of Gunpowder and Saltpeter, created in 1775, received authority, by a law of August 28, 1793, over all sources of saltpeter throughout the Republic. By a report by Prieur of the Côte-d'Or, on December 4, 1793, all owners or tenants were ordered to scour their cellars, stables, and cowsheds to collect saltpeter. Sans-culottes learned how to produce gunpowder in shops in the sections of cities. In the summer of 1794 Barère announced that 6,000 such shops were fully active throughout the Republic. Toward the end of the Year II the shops delivered 450,000 pounds of saltpeter; in the period through 10 Thermidor, they had delivered 8 million pounds, or double the production of the Office in 1788.

A special administration under the ministry of war was organized for military clothing. It dealt with private enterprises, whose products could be accepted or rejected by war commissioners. Fraudulent administrators risked the death penalty, and a few were executed before the eyes of the troops in the Army of the North. The sections of Paris opened shops to produce garments for the army.

A decree of October 25, 1793, ordered every shoemaker in the Republic, for a period of three months, to produce five pairs of shoes per *décade*, and as many more for each journeyman working with him. Leather was delivered to shoemakers by municipalities at the controlled price, and the shoes were likewise paid for at the price set by the law of the Maximum. On December 8 shoemakers were placed under a requisition to produce exclusively for military needs during the period from December 21 to February 8.

While these measures were having their effect, the representatives on mission confiscated shoes from civilians and especially from the rich. Like Saint-Just in Alsace, Milhaud and Soubrany near Perpignan requisitioned "all shoes with a double sole in passable condition." Citizens possessing only one pair had to wear shoes of wood. When even these were lacking, as at Saint-Geniès, the population went barefoot for several months. In the Haute-Loire it was decided not to wait for the shoemakers to finish their task, so that footwear was made of wrapping canvas, of the kind normally used to "pack cotton from the Levant."

Despite the effort put forth by the whole nation, the army was still short of arms and clothing. The general correspondence of the army reveals incessant cries of alarm. "We have whole battalions without guns." In May 1794, in the 139th demi-brigade, 7 percent of its weapons were unserviceable. At about the same time a quarter of the muskets of the 15th demi-brigade of light infantry had to be replaced. In June 1794, in the 140th demi-brigade of battle infantry, about a third of the muskets, 940 out of 3,024, were scrapped. In the summer of 1794 only half the muskets were functioning in the 11th demi-brigade of light infantry, a quarter in the 4th, and a tenth in the 14th.

If arms were in short supply it was not always because of faults in production and transport but also because they were badly used. The new draftee maintained his weapon poorly. It must be said, in excuse for him, that the necessary grease and oil were often unavailable, so that gunlocks dried up, wore out, and had to be replaced, "their repair being impossible." As the storekeeper Doizy explained, "When the barrel is dirty the rust reduces the caliber and so makes it hard for the cartridges to go in. When the soldier hurries too much in pushing in the cartridge, he allows too little time for the powder, the ball, and the paper to take their places; he moves them in all at once . . ."—and the musket finally goes off in the unfortunate man's face. For proper firing, it was necessary not only to keep the barrel clean, but also to have priming needles, wad extractors, and flints. These were sometimes lacking. Finally, there had to be powder and balls, and the younger the soldier the more excessively he consumed them. Receiving his "baptism of fire," he sought to protect himself by an extravagant shooting that soon reduced the firepower of his battalion. The fight sometimes stopped because powder was exhausted. The bayonet charge might come as much from the lack of other arms as from the doctrine of the schools stressing the inexperience and impetuosity of the combatants.

It was the same with clothing. Prints of the time, especially those originating beyond the Rhine, have given us pictorial evidence of the medley of uniforms in the French army. Some men still wore the old white, others the new national blue, and others a civilian costume of "gray jackets with trousers of the same color." The fabrics were of poor quality. One soldier complained that

> the jersey was so bad and the lining so mediocre that geese could have nibbled through holes in them, and the pockets so tight that a soldier could not put in his handkerchief and snuff-box. The coats were so small that after getting wet they shrank so much that they could no longer be worn.

Soldiers from private to general made similar complaints. In January 1794 Philoxème Leulier wrote that badly built shoes, with ill-fitting heels and uppers, made walking difficult and gave the men corns, bruises, and calluses from pressure of the buckle. Uncomfortable hose and breeches interfered with movement and did nothing to prevent varicose veins in the legs. "The flaps and facings on the uniform are useless. The coat does not come down far enough to cover the lower belly; yet this part of the body must be kept warm if it is to perform its functions."

The hat was inconvenient, with its corners reaching so far beyond the shoulders that the soldier was in danger at any moment of having it knocked off by a comrade wielding his musket. The helmets gave more trouble than protection; the men threw them away; "roads and fields seemed to be paved with them." As General Hoche wrote later:

> The cut of the uniform was designed in 1787 by a war committee that had never seen an army drawn up for battle. Let us no longer have our men wear useless lapels that leave the thighs and abdomen uncovered, or breeches so tight that they have to unbutton them on the march, or wretched poorly made gaiters that no one wants. We should give our infantry a head covering that holds its shape and can protect the soldier's head from sabre blows by the enemy cavalry.

Even defective shoes and other clothes were hard to obtain. The dishonesty of suppliers is not a sufficient explanation. The sad state of the troops was sometimes due to faults in organization and distribution. We may cite an example from the minutes of the administrative council of the 1st battalion of Phoceans (from Marseille), which on January 4, 1794, tells us that the unit was in urgent need of 200 pairs of shoes, 200 shirts, 300 jackets and breeches, and 300 hats. Three weeks later the council revised its figures; now it was 654 coats, 674 jackets, 500 breeches, and 300 pairs of shoes that were needed. The council appealed to various authorities, who had no idea where such equipment was to be found. It then turned to the representative on mission, who obtained a delivery of coats, which arrived without buttons. The council had to find a button merchant and someone to sew them on. In March there were still no shoes. It was decided to dip into the battalion funds to buy leather to be made into shoes by a local artisan. In May there was a new crisis: five hundred men had coats in rags, no shirts, and no stockings. There were hasty purchases of shirts and stockings, but as for the coats, no one knew where to turn to obtain them.

Soldiers who had a shirt looked in vain for soap to wash it. They wore them soiled, and the health officers denounced the conditions that led to disorders of the skin. The itch was an omnipresent enemy. A doctor at the military hospital at Auxerre wrote:

> The soldier is in his clothes most of the time and seldom changes his linen. Hence there is a blocking of the slow perspiration necessary to maintain life, a congestion of the cutaneous glands, and finally the exudation of acrid sweat that produces the foul and contagious malady called the itch.

For some victims the number of sores, overlapping and suppurating, was so great that the itch was intolerable.

Above all else there was hunger. The garrison at Lille alone, for example, "required 36,000 rations of bread a day, for which 400 or 500 quintals of flour were needed." For three months this meant finding 23,000 sacks. The Army of the North, in 1794, had a daily consumption of 2,120 quintals of wheat and rye. Or 70,000 to 80,000 a month! How could they be found when part of the country was in a state of insurgency, and big farmers were concealing their grain? "Revolutionary armies," hosts of sans-culottes, scoured the countryside, forcing the rich to open their barns, but transportation was often lacking and movement of foodstuffs was slow. Each army had a territory reserved for its provisioning, but on failing to obtain what they needed the armies encroached on adjoining ones, and the supervising commissioner was helpless.

In the Year II the soldier's daily ration was set at 1.75 pounds of bread, 500 grams of meat, 1 ounce or about 32 grams of rice, and 2 ounces of dried greens. When all went well the soldier rose at five in the morning, confident that after a puff on his pipe he might take a sip of gin. After drill, review, or guard duty, he made a meal of bread and meat, had some vegetable soup, and swallowed a glass of water with a bit of vinegar to drive away bad humors, or a glass of wine if his mother had sent him a little money. He might have extra bread with an onion if the merchant respected the price controls. It was enough to last until evening, when a piece of cheese given by some peasant might relieve the monotony of the army mess.

The soldier's pay, from which he might obtain some improvement to his diet, was very low. After deductions for food, clothing, equipment, upkeep, linen, and shoes, until July 1794, only 9 *sous* 6 *deniers* were left. The paper money continually lost its value, so that soldiers complained of paying 13 livres for a bottle of wine, and bad wine at that, 20 livres for brandy, and 40 *sous* for a half-pound loaf of bread. They were asked to pay 20 to 30 *sous* to have a shirt washed.

When the food furnished by the authorities failed to arrive, it was impossible to count on one's own resources for subsistence. And although, on the whole, the Revolutionary Government managed to feed its troops, under a thousand difficulties, it could happen that some units could expect empty stomachs. In the Army of the North, in March 1794, the volunteers of the 1st Seine-et-Marne battalion were on the road for three days with less than a pound of bread. In July in this same theater the supervising commissioners were afraid to go outdoors for fear of being attacked by the soldiers. The men had received moldy bread and fasted for three days.

Marauding was inevitable in such lean times, despite orders received and penalties imposed. The Revolution had proclaimed "War on the châteaus, peace to the cottages." But pressed by necessity the soldiers sometimes forgot the Revolutionary slogan. A

certain Corporal Demonchy described his entry into Belgium in
October 1793:

> We took horses, colts, cows, sheep, pigs and animals in gen-
> eral after these forays, and after entering a peasant's house we
> ate up his food, drank his wine, had fun with his women, and
> made off with pieces of gold and silver. That is how we treat
> these Imperial gentry. They do worse with us. They act with
> cruelty, while we French always act humanely.

The soldiers justified their behavior by explaining that peoples liberated from the feudal yoke should contribute to the struggle
against aristocrats. Those who failed to do so willingly were suspects and even allies of the former seigneurs. According to soldiers
of the 2nd battalion of the Tarn, in camp in Spain in 1794, "the
people of Spain are not like others in Europe. The peasant's cottage should no more be respected than the palace of a *seignor* [sic]
because the popular class is as much an enemy of the French as
those who wear monks' hoods or velvet mantles." A higher officer
in March 1794 recalled that the Spanish hatred for the French had
been stirred up by priests and incited by émigrés. He concluded
that "the only thing to do is to devastate their territory, for I think
it impossible, considering the ignorance and superstition of these
people, to change them except by Terror."

Some generals who were career officers, reviving the practices
of the Old Regime, held for ransom the towns and villages that
fell into their hands. The Committee of Public Safety had created
evacuation agencies to remove from conquered areas whatever
might be useful for the progress of agriculture and industry in
France. These agents sometimes personally urged the military
chiefs and their subordinates to carry out such extortions.

But along with these acts of pillage and marauding we should
note the attitude of other generals, such as General Vignes, who
ordered the return of stolen animals to their owners, or of soldiers
who shared their meager ration with the poorest villagers in the
occupied countries.

The deficiencies of food and clothing had consequences for operations. Sometimes they made the generals and their troops advance more rapidly so as to abandon an area exhausted by requisitions. Sometimes commanders feared to carry on an offensive too fast, lest their men should not find enough subsistence. Short intervals of carousing, punctuating the ordinary frugal mess, caused maladies that raised the number of men in the hospitals.

3. CASUALTIES, ILLNESSES, AND HOSPITALS

How many soldiers of the Great Nation, from 1792 to 1794, lost their lives on the battlefield, or in hospital beds, or in the prisons of the Coalition? Historians still dispute the figure. Their differences have sometimes been animated by partisan spirit. For some, like Taine, the point was to demonstrate that the Revolution—and after it the Empire—had so devoured men as to stunt the growth of France.

The first estimates come from the early nineteenth century. For the wars of the Revolution and Empire they give figures of over a million and a half. To accept them, we would have to believe that the entire French army created from 1792 to 1815 was swallowed up between the hills of the Argonne and the steppes of Russia. Other estimates, like those of Bodart, are less fantastic; they reach a total, for example, for the period from September 1793 to February 1795, of 108,400. But Bodart did not always clearly distinguish between the number of the dead and of the wounded, and sometimes he did not indicate the sources he consulted.

Historians have not always had, nor could they have had, the conscientious concern of official compilers of vital statistics, and they have mixed the dead, the hospitalized, and the missing under the heading of "losses."

One scholar, Meynier, in 1930 and again in 1937, put the losses of the Revolution at 600,000, of whom 126,000 were classified as "disappeared." More recently Louis Henry, working on the death statistics by age and sex as established by the Statistique générale de France, arrived at an estimate of 438,000 losses, of which 203,000 were from 1792 to 1794 and 235,000 from 1795 to 1799. But here, too, "losses" do not mean dead soldiers. His figures include the navy and civilian populations suffering from the war. It would be desirable to know also the number of deaths by the year, and even by the month.

Hence, we have examined the troop registers, but with disappointing results. All too often the quartermaster from 1792 to 1796 was unable to record the fate of men in his unit. When the French army was too pressed by the enemy, or when on the contrary it was successful in a continuing offensive, the quartermaster had no time for writing. When he sometimes found time he no longer knew the date or cause of the departure of a particular man, and simply wrote "removed from the list," which makes statistics impossible and obliges us to group together the losses of several years. Finally, the scribe who kept the register could not tell whether a given man was dead or a prisoner of war, and either noted both possibilities or left the place in the register blank.

Using the registers that give the best information, and comparing them with inspection reports (series Xb in the Archives de la Guerre), one can see that the war was especially deadly in 1793, but it is hard to offer numbers that have any validity. For 1794–1795, one can estimate that 200,000 men disappeared, and for the whole period 1794–1797, at least 320,000 and at most 400,000.

What is obvious is the numerical importance of deaths in the hospitals. In the 2nd battalion of the Ille-et-Vilaine, the losses were 18.3 percent in 1793, in which only 4 percent were at the place of combat. In the district of Mamers, for which we have a list of citizens dying in the war, two-thirds expired in the hospital in consequence of wounds or "the fatigues of war."

Soldiers' letters testify to the hecatomb caused by exhaustion, cold, and bad diet. Here is one from a soldier of the 99th demi-brigade: "The demi-brigade was composed of 2,000 men, now it has only 500, more than 1,500 are sick, and not many will ever go home." Sometimes the number dying in hospital was so great that the attending personnel could keep no exact count. When the administrative council of the 6th battalion of the Oise inquired of the hospital at Maubeuge, hoping to get information on the death of its comrades there, it received the reply that "the great number of wounded arriving at the same time at the said hospital, and dying a few days later, made it impossible to record them on the registers of entry and exit."

We do sometimes find statistics compiled by hospital directors. They confirm the high rate of mortality in the hospitals and the greater number of deaths from sickness than from wounds. In September 1793, for example, the hospital at Béziers attributed 68 percent of deaths to fevers, scabies, and venereal disease. At the hospital at Nantes, in the winter of 1794, where 16 percent of the patients died per month, those dying of wounds accounted for from 30 to 40 percent from one week to another, with the rest afflicted by fever or venereal maladies. At the Hôtel Dieu at Saumur, out of 88 cases for which the cause of death is recorded, only 2 died of wounds. The hospital was the antechamber of death.

Despite the efforts of the Revolutionary Government the number of hospitals was insufficient and their condition often deplorable. Here, too, everything was to be done. In 1793 convents with their chapels were hastily transformed into hospitals, but their capacity was limited. For the army of the Eastern Pyrenees, in 1794, the hospitals at Lodève, Aniane, Gignac, Clermont, Montpellier, Pézenas, Sète, and Béziers provided for a few more than 4,000 beds for an army of 15,000, which sometimes had more than 30 percent of its strength on the sick list. It was worse in the Armies of the North and of the Rhine, where there was no room if the average number of sick and wounded rose above 13 percent of effectives, and where at a time of general offensive the number of hospital cases suddenly reached 20 or even 30 percent in each demi-brigade. In May and June 1794, in the Army of the North, the 85th battle infantry had 28.9 percent of its effectives in the hospital; in the Army of the Rhine the 140th had 31 percent; in the Army of Italy the 169th had 31.3 percent and the 56th had 32 percent. Two health officers, Tissot and Petetin, inspectors of military hospitals at Besançon, wrote in the Year II that

> the corridors were full of patients, most of them lying on the floor. Contagion has raged for a long time in the military hospitals at Besançon and all others of the sixth military division that we have visited. It is caused by the shocking disproportion between the size of the wards and the number of soldiers in them. We consider these hospitals to be arsenals of contagious miasmas, more deadly to the human race than the most lethal instruments of war.

At crowded moments the sufferers from the itch were pitilessly turned away. They were sometimes made to go two hundred leagues to find a hospital that would admit them. To prevent overcrowding of the hospitals commanders tried to create small field stations at the battalion level, under supervision by the battalion surgeon.

Overwhelmed by a throng of sick and wounded, the hospital personnel were unable to maintain the premises properly. Soldiers complained of lying on soiled and vermin-infested sheets. The hospital orderlies defended themselves by saying, to take one example, that "with the arrival of two hundred patients without prior notice the confusion had made them guilty of this negligence." At Montpellier in the Year II a provisional health officer found the patients indiscriminately piled up in badly aired rooms, two by two in beds that were too narrow, and with the feverish and the convalescent mixed together. Everywhere there were complaints against the "service." At Pézenas there was only one orderly for fifty patients. Physicians and surgeons were too few in number and of mediocre ability; some had recently been students who had passed hasty examinations.

Sometimes the hospitals were unable to provide meals. The rise in prices in the Year II, despite the controls, led to a reduction in purchases of the meat and vegetables necessary for making soups. The situation improved after a decree of February 1794, and by the spring and summer a military board of health brought the hospitals under better supervision.

Many of the sick were afflicted with a diarrhea due to polluted water. The basic medical treatments were enemas and broths, together with bleedings. Here is an example from a report sent to the ministry, and judged by the inspectors-general to be "an estimable statement of principles conforming to sound doctrine":

> For fevers accompanied by diarrhea the enema should include without fail a half-ounce of poppy syrup. Note too that in complicated maladies such as pneumonia, stroke, pleuresy, and wounds of different kinds, this treatment is always successful and relieves the fever.

To cure venereal diseases:

> Take one or two *sous'* worth of saffron in a spoonful of olive oil every morning two hours before or after eating. The simplest remedies are often the best. One of our kings was cured of a dangerous malady simply by a decoction of boxwood, which is also a sudorific. The itch can be cured in a week by rubbing oneself with a mixture of sulphur flower and fresh butter.

We should not laugh too much at these prescriptions, not all of which resembled "old wives'" remedies. As recently as thirty years ago, enemas containing opiates were sometimes used to relieve diarrhea. The army doctors not only made many observations but sometimes drew from them quite justified conclusions. They were urged to do so by the army health board. In the Archives de la Guerre a few evidences can be found of discoveries that seem modest to us but which doubtless helped to save more than one life. Thus Citizen Housset, physician at the military hospital at Auxerre, after devoting himself all day to his patients, found time in the evening to write up the conclusions to which an examination of hundreds of cases had led him. He recognized that many intestinal troubles came not only from polluted water but also from a badly unbalanced diet, as when too much starchy food and not enough green vegetables were eaten. Like many of his colleagues, he opposed an excessive bleeding that exhausted the patient, and he insisted that his patients should keep absolutely clean. Like certain civilian doctors, he understood that lemon and nitrous fluids could be useful in some cases. It is also amazing to see the skill with which surgeons could amputate a gangrened limb or operate successfully for hernias.

Among the missing there were many prisoners of war. Some were immediately shot: Jacques Perdreaux, of the 149th demi-brigade in the Army of the Sambre-Meuse, reported in the spring of 1794 that sixty of his comrades had been captured in a small affair, of whom five were shot for refusing to cry "Vive le roi!" General Dellarch, made prisoner at the same time (he was then only a company officer), declared in his memoirs that of sixty soldiers captured with him twenty-seven were put to death and he himself owed his life only to the protection of two hussars. If he remained alive, the French prisoner often had a pitiable experience. If he could give information, he was interrogated and sometimes tortured. Whether or not he talked, he was sent with a convoy of prisoners into the interior of Germany, Austria, or Hungary. The civilian population, incited by enemy soldiers, might meet the prisoners in the streets of towns and villages, kick them, strike them with sticks, or throw stones. Prisoners made journeys of several tens of kilometers without food or drink.

Arrived at their destination, prisoners were crowded into jails where the food was bad and they were again beaten. According to some who escaped, such treatment was the common lot of all prisoners. To quote Dellard again:

> It was the same everywhere, in the circles of Germany and in the Austrian and Hungarian states. Whatever was foul and fetid in the way of prisons was our destiny, from our departure from Tournay as far as the borders of Turkey. The straw that we had to lie on, squashed down by criminals before us,

was alive with vermin in most of the places assigned to us. No complaint was listened to, however well founded, and whoever complained was answered with corporal punishment.

The situation was equally frightful in Prussia. From another report:

> Bad and often insufficient food; old rags in place of the clothing taken from them; no linen to escape the vermin produced by infected and rotten straw. They were hardly permitted any air; a small courtyard hardly different from the prison itself was the only place to relieve a painful existence for a few hours of the day. When they were almost ready to give up, their strength exhausted, they were dragged off to hospitals less suited to restore nature than to dissolve it by new infirmities.

And it is a fact that the mortality of French prisoners was very great; a register preserved at the Archives de la Guerre (series Xz9) indicates the death in captivity in Austria of 11,517 men from 1794 to 1796, while the total estimated number of prisoners was from 40,000 to 50,000.

A few sporadic testimonies provide brighter touches to this somber picture. French soldiers were not always and everywhere mistreated. P. Dobris, of the 1st battalion of the Indre, wrote to his mother on February 17, 1794, that he had been made prisoner by the Prussians and that they had taken his knapsack and wallet but otherwise done him no harm. Sergeant Dumey reported in April 1795 that he had seen 665 returned prisoners, captured eighteen months before by the English and the Imperials:

> Whatever may have been said of the English they were not so barbarous to them as we have been led to believe. The Emperor's people treated them humanely. They had to suffer, it is true, but it was usually at the hands of some British and émigrés who took the opportunity to insult them.

At Frankfurt, a doctor named Ehrmann gave himself unstintingly to sick prisoners throughout the war. He was present when they died, took their names, and wrote to their families to apprise them of the sad news. All prisoners testified to his humane conduct.

With time, agreements were made between the two sides for exchange of commissioners to visit prisoners and bring them aid in clothing and sometimes food. The commissioners sent to Spain, in their reports so far as we have them, found that on the whole the prisoners were not too badly treated. Their situations differed according to places and personalities of the guards. Conditions were very difficult at Malaga but good at Gerona, where the prisoners worked in the town.

The extreme deprivation to which prisoners were sometimes subjected was occasionally used as a means of inducing them to serve in the enemy armies. Claude Pigeron of the 2nd battalion of the Allier testified later that, when detained in Austrian prisons, he and his comrades had been visited by French officers wishing to recruit them for émigré regiments. They enlisted in the hope of finding a way of eluding their new chiefs. Others, even before being sent to a prison camp, frightened by what they had heard of the conditions of detention, agreed to follow the enemy recruiters. Joseph Schwickarthe, chief musician of the 81st demi-brigade, denounced such cowardice among his fellow soldiers. But such cases were exceptional.

Most French prisoners dreamed of escape, or waited to be exchanged, rather than collaborate with the enemy. After escaping the prisoner was expected to report to the military authorities. But alerted by the discovery of spies among the escapees, the French authorities subjected the ex-prisoners to a veritable court of judgment, at which witnesses were called from the men of the demi-brigade of which the escapees claimed to be members.

French officers often had to give their word not to bear arms against Austria, Prussia, or England in exchange for their liberation. A decree of June 22, 1793, relieved them in advance of such promises, and declared them "cowards and deserters from liberty" unless they immediately resumed their rank in the troops of the Republic. Lists exist at the Archives de la Guerre showing that some ignored the decree, although most accepted it. A battalion commander, Dupont, for example, considered fidelity to an oath to be a primary human virtue. On the other hand, a Lieutenant Bidat, more recent in his career as a soldier, held that the first oath he meant to keep was his word to live free or die, and that hence he would again serve the Republic. "Perjury is a virtue," said a Lieutenant Gauthier, "when the oath is a crime."

4. DESERTERS

How many soldiers deserted in 1793 and the Year II? To find an answer, we have followed the same method as for the losses. Instead of taking a sounding of all the demi-brigade registers, not all of which indicate the cause of disappearance, as already noted, and which having been initiated at the end of 1793 and early in 1794 give no record of desertions in 1793, we have chosen to take a 10 percent sample from the registers of seventy-two volunteer battalions not yet amalgamated, which give information on desertion. These battalions served in all theaters of operation. We have chosen these registers of volunteers, rather than those of amalgamated regiments, because they allow us to obtain easily the figure for effective enrolled strength, whereas the registers for the regiments, initiated in 1786, require a long and perilous gymnastics to separate men present and men absent in 1793. Nevertheless, so as not to lose the advantage of comparison between "blues" and "whites," we have made an exhaustive study of three regimental registers. We have thus obtained a card index of 5,000 names.

In 1793 deserters represented 8 percent of the effectives, or 40,000 to 50,000 men roaming the countryside or hiding in the towns. Desertion was more frequent in the first half of the year (76 percent of deserters of 1793), a time of defeat and enemy advances, than in the second half, which was marked by French victories as well as by the installation of a better network of popular surveillance to bring the faint-hearted back to their duty.

Coercive measures and political education had their effects in 1794, since the proportion of deserters fell from 8 to 4 percent. Here also we see differences between the two halves of the year. There was more desertion after the fall of the Revolutionary Government in July, which brought a slow-down in political education and increasing food shortages in the camps. The political factor thus played a part in desertions, but it is hard to measure. Other factors explain the departure of soldiers for points inside of France. There was more desertion after the fall of Robespierre than before it because it came at the time of year, as the men well knew, when it was easier to find agricultural employment, and easier to conceal oneself in the horde of migrant harvest hands and vineyard workers that crowded the roads in search of jobs.

In all units it was the draftees who were the first to leave the battalions in bands of several men. They did so less often where men of different origins were mixed in the same combat unit. It was as if men refused to depart unless they had enough fellow travelers in whom they had confidence. Those who resisted desertion the longest were the volunteers and soldiers of the former regular army. Patriotism and esprit de corps combined to hold them close to their flags.

But though in small numbers in the Year II, desertion did occur. There were soldiers who were not susceptible to the Jacobin appeal. One explanation lies in hunger and deprivation. We have seen how the efforts of the Revolutionary Government to feed its troops were long impeded. In November 1793 the civil authorities of the Ariège reported that "if the draftees desert it is because no one gives them bread." Later the municipality of Lavelanet offered the same account:

> All the volunteers give us the same reply. They say that five days' pay is not enough to get a morsel of bread or sip of wine. "We hoped that the Convention would do something

to help us," they say, "but it has not done so although it has raised the pay of all public officeholders in the country. We can't live, and are quitting. . . ." Just this morning three volunteers of the Montlibre division that we had taken back to their unit told us the same story, and added that whole companies were returning to the interior with their captain and drummer in the lead. Only a month ago there were 8,000 men at Puigcerda, now there are only 4,000.

It was poverty that pushed Julien Simon, for example, into desertion. On receiving a letter from his wife he took off from his comrades, saying that he must rejoin his family immediately; his children had too little to eat and the roof of his house had fallen in. He returned to his unit willingly. Brought to justice, he said, "I did not think I did anything wrong." Others were like him in denying that they had really deserted.

Royalist agents tried to play on these motives to induce desertion in the Year II, claiming that the pay and food were better in the enemy armies. But desertion to the enemy remained in fact very exceptional. The troop control registers provide only a microscopic number of such cases. Refractory priests, writing to their parishioners, also attempted to persuade them to desert.

To these principal causes of desertion were added others. First of all was a man's feeling that his rights had been flouted. This had been a motive for desertion even under the Old Regime, but it was now different. Formerly enlistment had been a contract, resembling the "feudal contract"; if his chief failed him, the soldier considered the contract broken and that he had a right to leave. Under the Republic a man was a soldier in response to the law, but the law protected him against arbitrary action by his chief. If, beyond the normal limits of the service, an officer enforced a discipline to which the soldier had consented only as a man at arms, or if the officer committed acts that gave offense to the dignity of the citizen, a crime against the law existed and desertion was simply the exercise of the right of rebellion guaranteed by the constitution. Thus, if there were so many desertions in the Army of Italy at the end of the Year II, it was in part because of "various vexations that officers inflicted on the volunteers when they made a few complaints." This response showed the continuation of a state of mind formed in 1793.

Desertions were also a consequence of the amalgamation. The representative on mission to the Army of the Alps, writing from Nice, informed the Committee of Public Safety that the process of brigade formation was causing "considerable" desertion. Joseph Le Bon, representative in the north, explained that the law had caused dissatisfaction among the officers, who were granting permissions to all comers to "remove themselves from the army and take a vacation." Men of the 4th *chasseurs* deserted because the amalgamation obliged them to mix with German-speakers. Some men from the Midi did the same to avoid associating with Lorrainers whose language and customs they did not understand. Soldiers newly assigned to a battalion were often "abused." Caselli, an agent of the central administration, recalled four years later that many desertions had been caused by rough jokes perpetrated on newcomers.

Desertion was also a way out for men who could not lift themselves to the new status created by republican law. Some saw themselves less as citizens than as members of a "clientele." If the chief with whom they had signed up left the army, they abandoned it with him. Others considered themselves not as bound to the Nation, which it was everyone's duty to serve, but as engaged by contract with their home community for a limited time. If the community stopped paying the agreed upon indemnity, the contract was void.

Then there was the case of returned prisoners of war. Some, after capture by the Chouans, were released after taking an oath to fight against them no longer, and had their heads shaved as a guarantee against their breaking the oath; then, on return to their camp, if ordered to go out again against the same enemy, they deserted. Others declared that their having suffered wretched conditions in enemy jails gave them the right to go home.

There were a thousand ways of regaining one's home without being too much disturbed by the gendarmerie. The most usual was to obtain a hospital certificate attesting to a benign malady or supposed infirmity. Since the hospitals were overloaded, the health officers readily signed permission for soldiers to receive the necessary care at home. A year later, the representatives Reubell and Rivaud at the Army of the Rhine-Moselle wrote to the Committee of Public Safety: "It is certain that our battalions have been alarmingly reduced by failure to execute the law ordering the return of absent soldiers, and by the ease with which others can avoid service by taking refuge in the hospitals, and then in the interior."

Hospital personnel soon began to sell tickets of convalescence, and there were even little shops in which they were forged. Men really sick or wounded, once they were cured, did not return to their battalions. For safety in escaping, they made false declarations of the whereabouts of their company; from one military district to another they pretended to be lost, and received food and resting places as they zigzagged all over France. It was even safer to pass as a civilian, but the needed clothing cost too much. In some cases the families of soldiers brought civilian clothing to the gates of the camps. The captain of the 6th company of the 9th battalion of the Seine-Inférieure denounced this practice in 1794.

Mixing with the floating population of laborers looking for work, or of villagers displaced by the war, the deserter made his way toward his native place. Hiding in the woods, earning something to eat by "carding wool," a fusilier named L'Heureux managed to reach Paris after deserting from the Army of the North. Another soldier, of the 48th demi-brigade, after covering the two hundred kilometers that separated him from his home in less than two weeks, fell into the hands of the gendarmes. Others moved from town to town in a *tour de France* that they could never have accomplished as artisans. The desertion of Philippe Dole became a thousandfold adventure. After having served in the old royal army for twelve years, he enlisted in the 7th Hussars in 1791, and he deserted in 1793. He was arrested and thrown into prison at Valenciennes. When this city was besieged, he was put into one of the defending battalions. When he could leave the town he was taken to a hospital. There he recovered his health and was given permission to leave. He started for home and "forgot" to return to his unit. He found employment as a carpenter at La Chapelle, then at Maubeuge. He was trapped in Maubeuge when the enemy laid siege on it. Taken prisoner, he enrolled in the Rohan Infanterie, an émigré regiment, and remained in it for five months until captured by the French. He was condemned to death and executed.

Men did not generally go alone when they deserted. They went in bands, which were not numerous in the Year II, but of which the existence is known in the Rhône valley, Lorraine, Normandy, the Pas-de-Calais, and the Pyrenees. After leaving the frontier zones, pursued by the mobile search columns, they headed for the mountainous regions of the Massif Central or the forested areas of the Paris Basin, playing tricks on merchants along the way. If caught, and in the absence of attenuating circumstances, the deserter was punished with five years in irons. But the time would come, after the fall of the Revolutionary Government, when with the scarcity of manpower mass pardons were granted.

Conclusion to Part Two

Before 1793 the Revolution had three armies at its disposal: the former royal army, the army of the volunteers of 1791, and the sans-culotte or popular army of 1792. They differed in all respects: in their manner of recruitment, their command structure, and their discipline. Misjudging the transformations and politicization in the old regular army, the Jacobins persisted in denouncing a conspiracy of generals in the old army. In 1792 Lafayette had served as their target, and the facts proved that their suspicions were not unfounded. At the beginning of 1793 Dumouriez had appeared as the ambitious general ready to turn his troops against Paris. His treason once again showed the need for vigilance by the civil authorities over the "generalate." In July 1793 Saint-Just justified the May–June insurrection by announcing a conspiracy against the Revolution by General Arthur Dillon, brother of the General Theobald Dillon murdered by his own troops; he was supposed to have formed a military organization to which many generals lent their support. With their troops, they were to liberate the young Dauphin, proclaim him as Louis XVII, and install Marie-Antoinette as regent. As for evidence, none was ever produced.

This divided army, which might offer leverage for manipulation by generals, had been turned into a national and revolutionary army in only one year. As a national army, it henceforth recruited its members in all sections of society by requisition, since military service had become a duty for all. As a national army, combining the three armed forces, it had a single pay scale, the same discipline, and the same mode of recruitment and promotions for all its members. As a revolutionary army, it had been taught by militants both in it and outside it the meaning of the struggle in which it was engaged: the equality without which liberty was a snare, the need for unity of all Frenchmen against aristocrats, the duty to unite behind the Revolutionary Government as appointed by the Convention, which was the representative of the people. Citizens, citizen-soldiers, and citizen-generals all owed total obedience to the laws. The arm of the Revolution would no longer be gangrened; factious generals had been exiled, imprisoned, or executed as allies of aristocrats.

Hatred of aristocracy was the strongest force, and would long remain so, that bound together the army of the Year II. But there were contradictions within the new military society, as in the civilian society of which it was a projection. Of course there was a mixture of social classes from top to bottom of the hierarchy. Among the officers a Murat, son of an innkeeper, consorted with a Kléber, an architect, with a François Lejeune, son of a well-to-do merchant, and with a Jean Lichague, son of a baker. Among the common soldiers the lesser bourgeois rubbed shoulders with the ordinary workman. But the great majority of the troops was composed of men of minimal income—day laborers, occasional workers, and servants. They received a legacy of equalitarianism in the Year II. It was an equalitarianism, as we have seen, that showed itself in the call to the colors: there would be no more favoritism or exemptions; rich and poor, municipal officials and plain citizens would all march to the frontiers. It was also an equalitarianism by which citizen-soldiers demanded and obtained relief for their families in need and the promise of easy access to the ownership of lands. Equalitarianism was manifest also, within the army, in laws that gave revenge for talents against merit,[3] that is,

---

[3] On the French *talent* see Chapter III, n. 2. Where *talent* suggests ability, *mérite* suggests the just deserts of long service. "Revenge" or *revanche* suggests the resentment felt by capable men before the Revolution.

against mere length of service and bravery. It became evident in the relations within the army hierarchy: the citizen-soldiers had too long considered their leaders as their equals in right, as mandatories of the sovereign people of which they were part, for them easily or lightly to be converted to the policy preferred by the Revolutionary Government. And were not the orders of this government in any case contradictory? Soldiers were asked to obey their superiors without discussion, and at the same time urged to be vigilant, to watch them, and to denounce them if necessary.

At the command level most officers were of the lesser bourgeoisie, but, what was of more importance for their future reactions, they were also regular soldiers from before 1789. They had grumbled at the prospect of being mixed into a national army. They had shown sometimes an open opposition, and always a passive resistance, to turning the army into an itinerant political club. They had yielded to the Revolutionary Government in the Year II. But this government had given them, as a net result, what these men, like those of the lesser nobility, had hoped for before 1789: an army that was an effective instrument of war, capable of revenge upon Europe, and especially upon Prussia. These officers were also sons of the Revolution, to which they owed their present rank and posts. The idea of revenge taught in the camps of the army was blended in their minds with a revolutionary spirit that made them hate the aristocrats and the monarch who had slighted them. If some of them went along with the demands of the sans-culottes, they all agreed that such demands should not overflow from the civilian into the military society.

The army was coming to resemble professional armies, through the joint action of Carnot and the career soldiers, by the fact that the war zone was increasingly distant from France, and by its taking in fewer and fewer new recruits as time passed. Only its revolutionary heritage made it different from other armies. The danger was that, as the civil power exerted less control over this army, its chiefs might use the ideal of the Year II to manipulate the troops and draw them into the paths of Caesarism.

From the National and Revolutionary Army to the Army of the Coup d'État of Fructidor (Year III to Year V)

In the battle of Fleurus, on June 26, 1794, the Austrians were defeated and the French began their second conquest of Belgium. Three months later, Pichegru was master of Holland. The Army of the Sambre-Meuse crossed the Rhine, taking Cologne and Coblenz and besieging Mainz. In Spain the French occupied Catalonia, Navarre, and the Basque provinces. In the southeast the republican forces crossed the Alps and marched on Turin. The First Coalition fell to pieces. On February 19, 1795, the grand duke of Tuscany signed a peace treaty at Florence; on April 5 Prussia accepted the conditions of the first treaty of Basel; on May 16 the new Batavian Republic allied itself with France; on July 22, 1795, Spain reached an understanding with the victorious Republic in the second treaty of Basel. In France, the insurgency in the West was pacified at the beginning of that same year.

These victories left England and Austria isolated. They were the fruit of the effort made by the Nation under the Revolutionary Government. The institutions that this government had set up were dismantled by the Thermidoreans, piece by piece. The royalists thought their moment had come, and a White Terror spread through the Midi. Convalescent soldiers on the roads were assaulted and murdered by bands of the Company of Jehu.

Bread was scarce in the winter of 1794–1795. Nor were there firewood, oil, vegetables, or meat for the sans-culotte who was attacked in the streets by *muscadins*, or "dandies." But the shops were replete with such items for those who could afford to pay the prices. We quote a police report of April 25, 1795:

> You will be no less shocked if you look at the displays in the pastry shops. Everything seems offered to the sensuality of the rich; butter, eggs, white flour are all laid out, worked over, and transformed into some dainty substance to appeal to their appetites. Such a contrast in what can be seen only a few steps apart should be of concern to the authorities.

Insolent wealth insulted the poverty of the people every day. Popular uprisings erupted on 12 Germinal and 1 Prairial of the Year III (April 1 and May 20, 1795), against which the military were called out. The uprisings were put down. The threat from the left was followed by one from the right, when the royalists attempted a *coup de force* in Paris. The army, under the orders of Bonaparte, suppressed it, annihilated the royalists, and saved the regime on 13 Vendémiaire, Year IV, or October 5, 1795.

On October 26 the Convention held its last meeting and gave way to the Directory. The new regime was unable to end the financial disorder or assure bread for the multitude. The new rich made pleasure "the order of the day." Some Jacobins, mixed with friends of Baheuf, and attempting to create what has been called "the first communist party to take practical action," formed a secret directory to overthrow the government. They tried to form cells in the police and the army. They worked in vain, for the conspirators were arrested, brought to trial, and guillotined. "Anarchists" continued to agitate in the army and tried to raise a rebellion in the camp at Grenelle near Paris. A military commission ordered the mutineers shot in September 1796.

Carnot devised a plan of operations against Austria. Two armies were to march toward Vienna, one under Jourdan by way of the Main valley, the other under Moreau along the Danube. In Italy an army entrusted to Bonaparte was to make a diversion. It was this army that won the victories, marched on the Austrian capital, and forced the envoys of the Emperor to sign the preliminary peace of Leoben on April 18, 1797.

The royalists in the spring of 1797, under color of legality and disguised as moderates, won the elections. The new majority elected Pichegru to the presidency of the Five Hundred and obtained the election of a monarchist, Barthélémy, as a member of the five-man Executive Directory. The other Directors, alarmed, called on the army, which was ready to act. The armies of Bonaparte and of Hoche had already made it known that they would not allow internal enemies to seize power. On 18 Fructidor of the Year V (September 4, 1797), the Directors Reubell, La Réveillière, and Barras had Barthélemy arrested, and forced their colleague Carnot to flee when he disapproved of their *coup de force*. The elections of the preceding spring were annulled in forty-nine departments.

Against Jacobins and sans-culottes on the one hand, and royalists on the other, the representatives of the republican bourgeoisie had prevailed in both cases only with the support of the army.

By 1797 the army was under the exclusive control of its generals, who had freed themselves from supervision by the State, and transformed their armies into a docile "clientele." In the occupied foreign countries they had learned to exercise civil authority and diplomacy. They could now exert pressure on the State, and take the first step toward a militarization of society by the Jourdan law on conscription in 1798.

But for the generals to achieve this domination over their men was a gradual process. It lasted for three years. The troops were not as easily cut off from the national realities as has been said. They began to withdraw into themselves in the Year IV, but even when they became tools of the generals they remembered their legacy from the Year II.

CHAPTER X

. . .

The Armed Forces from
the Year III to the Year V

1. NUMBERS

The army continued to receive contingents of draftees from 1795 to 1798, but its numbers were diminished by war losses and, above all, by desertion. While less numerous, the rank-and-file became an image of the technicians of war, the NCO's and officers who commanded them.

Under the Thermidorian Convention and the Directory, the army lost its mass basis. From an estimated figure of 732,474 present in August 1794, the minister Petiet reported only 484,363 present in August 1795, 396,016 in August 1796, and 381,909 in 1797, or about the figure reached on the eve of Valmy, five years before.

Most historians explain these reductions not only by losses but by the total cessation of the requisitions (under the Levy in Mass of August 1793) after the fall of Robespierre. An examination of the troop registers contradicts such an affirmation. A close study reveals the existence, at a minimum, of 29,210 draftees inducted from August 1794 to August 1795, of 30,550 draftees from the summer of 1795 to the summer of 1796, and 22,800 draftees from the summer of 1796 to that of 1797. As in the Year II, the frontier departments produced the largest contingents: in descending order of importance these were the Nord, Pas-de-Calais, Bas-Rhin, Haut-Rhin, Moselle, and Isère. Paris continued to furnish an important number. Conquest augmented the number of foreigners, which was 3 or 4 percent per year.

The new draftees were not always of the legal age. With variations by year, 4.8 percent to 5.2 percent were under the age of eighteen, and 19 percent to 31 percent were over twenty-five. More than in the Year II the local officials, for fear of stringent enforcement in their communes if the number of evaders was too great, took measures, with money if necessary, to induce men to enlist to fill their vacancies. Others simply shut their eyes when well-to-do draftees purchased replacements. It has been claimed that the quality of recruits was not as good as before. The only index that we have, which measured stature, gives no confirmation for this opinion. In the battle infantry 60 percent of draftees of the years III through V reached a height of 4 feet, 8 inches or more,[1] and so were comparable to their predecessors of the Year II.

The requisition originating in the Levy in Mass thus did not come to an end, and this fact is one of the first elements in modifying the idea that the soldiers of the Year II became completely detached from the Nation. But if the requisition continued to operate, it must be admitted that its yield was limited. The draftees of the Year III made up at best only 6 percent of the mass of the army. This reduced flow from the requisition can be explained by the disappearance of civic education, or indoctrination. The meaning of the struggle was no longer explained in the towns and rural areas where the number of the indigent was increasing. Who should fight? And why? In 1796, at Mamers in the Sarthe, young men invaded the hall where the departmental directory was deliberating. They were armed with sticks, and cried out:

> It's only the poor that support the Republic. They are the only ones forced to join the armies because they don't have the money to get exemptions. We will not go . . . unless all

[1] In Anglo-American measurement, 5 feet.

the rich take their turn . . . anyway we must finish the cloth we have begun to work on so as not to leave our mothers and fathers in poverty.

There was more draft evasion when repressive measures against those trying to escape from their duty were related. On the other hand, the victories of the Year II and the peace treaties with some of the allies in the coalition made some believe that the requisition—that "helping hand" that one owed to one's country—was no longer necessary. We hear from the district of Castelarrasin in May 1795:

> Of 400 men registered only 179 have presented themselves, of whom 36 have been rejected by the *procureur-syndic* for being over or under the legal age or for recognized and well-established infirmities. Of those going to the armies, 59 have departed as individuals, and 84 in four detachments.

When the commissioners of the Executive Directory conscientiously fulfilled their task, the requisitioned men would not answer the call. When they came, it was to quibble; they talked at length of their particular situation under the law or the exceptions that might apply to their case. When the commissioner finally exposed their "false and malicious logic," they or their parents bewailed "the damage done to their affairs or to their affections." They asked for more time. Time passed from one delay to the next, and in any case little could be done with only five gendarmes for an area containing a hundred communes.

The appearance of representatives of the law sometimes led to open revolt. At Mazères in the Ariège, from June 17 to July 12, 1795, there were continuous troubles in the town, of which the draftees were the cause. At Moulis in the same department, on July 25 of the same year, some draft evaders met armed force by gathering together and attacking the troops and the homes of local officials. In the Ardèche, on September 27, the mayor denounced the formation of a band of evaders in his commune. They acted like brigands, cut down trees of liberty, and set "a price on the head" of the mayor, who no longer slept at home and appeared by day nowhere but in his office. The commissioner of the Directory at Ille, in the Pyrénées-Orientales, declared in December 1795 that bands of young men, refusing to leave for the Army of Italy, had formed movable camps from which they threatened the authorities. In the Pas-de-Calais, at Magnicourt, Laventie, and Tincques, two hundred evaders held the field in January 1796, deployed in battle formation, and marched to the sound of a drum against the forces of order. Attempts were made to organize mobile search columns, but the citizens called upon to form such posses balked at the service.

Receiving fewer men than in the first stage of the requisition, the ranks of the military became thinner. The scourge of desertion was mainly responsible. The registers of battalions and demi-brigades show a rate of desertion, which had fallen to 4 percent in the Year II, rising again to 5 percent in 1795 and 8 percent in 1796 and 1797. The 42nd demi-brigade, in the Army of the North, which had 2,480 men in 1795, suffered from 454 desertions in 1796, or 18 percent of its effectives, while losses as a whole rose to 532. In fifteen months the 66th demi-brigade fell from 2,277 men present to 1,612, and of these 665 losses 450 were due to desertion. Deserters formed veritable small armies, not merely bands like those of evaders. A group of 1,500 men was reported from the district of Mauriac (in the Cantal), and there were said to be 10,000 deserters in the neighborhood of Lyon. The representative on mission Poultier announced that he was pursuing "12,000 young men who have deserted from the Army of Italy and are committing excesses."

The Revolutionary Government, for better or for worse, had assured the provisioning of the army. After its fall the camps were in a state of perpetual famine. In the Army of the Rhine generals Marceau, Bernadotte, and Kléber echoed each other: the soldier went barefoot, his clothes in rags, receiving neither food nor pay, and dreaming of flight and pillage. Royalist emissaries turned up in the camps to incite abandonment of the army. Priests wrote to their former parishioners to urge them to come home.

In the Year V a new military code, in the matter of desertion, renewed the laws issued by the Legislative Assembly and the Convention. Desertion to the enemy became punishable by death. Conspiracy to desert brought death for the leaders of the conspiracy. The years of imprisonment for desertion to the interior were multiplied. But the Directory was unable to apply this arsenal of judicial weapons. It no longer had, as the Convention had had, a network of civilian militants in the popular societies, who had assisted in reclaiming delinquents by education or coercion. Now the whole people protected the deserter, seeing in him a protest against a government that left the rural worker in poverty. In the Pyrénées-Orientales, for example, the commissioner of the Executive Directory wrote in 1797 that he had been threatened by wall posters ordering him not to pursue deserters. Overzealous commissioners found their vines uprooted and their olive trees destroyed. Gendarmes, as at Tarascon, made compacts with deserters and their families, and even ate and drank with them "to the sound of fiddles."

If caught, the deserter was not subjected to the rigors of the law, because he was too much needed in the army. Attenuating circumstances were found: simplemindedness was to desertion as drunkenness was to violence, an excuse often used to reduce or cancel the penalty.

Soldiers who remained faithful to their flag grew impatient with the soft-heartedness of the civil authorities toward men that they regarded as traitors. To them, desertion to the enemy or to the interior was much the same; in either case deserters were like émigrés and hence allies of the aristocrats. The citizen-soldiers retained a habit formed in the Year II of writing to municipal officers, and sometimes even to families, to urge them to bring deserters back to their duty. In the Years III and IV they still appealed to the patriotism by which every citizen should be motivated. In the Year IV they also issued threats: if deserters were not found and returned to the camps the army would intervene. In January 1796 placards could be seen on the walls of municipal governments like this one from the Army of Italy:

> Come back, young brothers of the requisition and all of you who have abandoned us! Liberty awaits you

And further:

> They must obey . . . if they hesitate we will swear implacable hatred against them! We swear now to bury ourselves under the ruins of the Temple of Liberty or see that these deserters are loaded with irons! We will do more. Sharing the indignation of the *Pères de la Patrie* [the government?] we will ask permission to march against these traitors; we will seize them, overwhelm them with curses, and commit them to the execration of future generations!

The time would come when legitimate authority was no longer invoked for action against those who, as in the Year II, were seen by the army as sympathizers with the Old Regime. A nation at war, and determined to win, had to reject all compromise with "vice" and combine all its springs of action. Once again the lesson of Jacobinism was not forgotten.

2. A BETTER-TRAINED AND BETTER-ORGANIZED ARMY

The proportion of soldiers from the former royal army continued to fall. By 1798 they formed only 3.3 percent of the total forces of the Republic. Many volunteers had by this time disappeared; they represented no more than 27.9 percent. The group originating in the levy of 300,000 in 1793 was less reduced, accounting for 18.2 percent. More than a third of the combatants were draftees from the Year II.

These men had developed a physical resistance without which it would have been impossible to put the new strategic precepts and the new tactics into practice. Soldiers' letters reveal their endurance. Sergeant Louis Primault of the 1st battalion of the Deux-Sèvres saw a march of seven hundred or eight hundred kilometers in a month as nothing to be afraid of. A fusilier of the 6th battalion of Bec d'Ambès recounted his troubles:

> We were at the siege of Lyon, then we went into Savoy and pushed back the Piedmontese as far as the top of Mont Cenis. After that we departed for Toulon, where we were to remain in garrison. Then we had to go to Arles, but received a counterorder to proceed to Nice. After an eight days' march we had to turn back and go to Perpignan.

Or let us follow the 39th demi-brigade in the Year IV. In May 1796 it left Tortona near Alessandria and in two months covered over three hundred kilometers, deep in the mountainous zone as far as Trent and Bolzano. We have Louis Valleyre to tell what this required of the men:

> For a week [he wrote to his father] we have not taken off our knapsacks or whatever else we carried on our backs. Always on the march, night and day; flitting about always in enemy country; overcome with sleep yet unable to rest for a moment; unable to eat when we wanted to, our bodies exposed to rain and bad weather, lying outdoors in the chill of night, resting on our guns, always on the back ready to leap up and depart.

To this physical endurance was added the instruction that continued to be given in the camps. An émigré observed:

> The French military system differs from that of all other powers in its practical application of the elementary science of tactical evolutions. Training and small-unit movements are not in themselves the objective in which the soldier is to reach the height of perfection; they are a means of arriving at results in war. They are indispensable vehicles for maintaining order and cooperation in the army, to teach the soldier to recognize the voice that is to direct him in major tactics. They also pro-

vide a common language without which the army would be
unable to move for lack of mutual understanding.

The soldier thus continued to learn to watch his platoon leader,
feel his neighbor's elbow, and stay close to the men at his right
and left. He was expected to recognize the friendly voice of an
older comrade and form part of a "working brotherhood."

Describing the campaign of 1796 in Germany, the historian
Daniel Reichel notes the military professionalism that the new tactics presupposed, as in luring the enemy by apparent weakness,
and firmly withstanding his assault while awaiting the moment for
all factors to come together for a counteroffensive, leading to destruction of the enemy troops. The French knew how to feel out
the adversary's position, judge its components, attack in columns,
and deploy in line or in a square. They achieved close collabora-
tion between line infantry and artillery, which in the case of a
square was located at the corners. This reciprocal understanding
between the arms, as to the different rhythms and effects of their
fire, was a consequence of successful training. It was training that
produced the capacity to pass flexibly from offensive to defensive,
to move calmly or precipitately at will, or to detach hundreds of
tirailleurs and reintegrate them with their supporting platoons. A
reorganized and remounted cavalry was trained for scouting, pursuit, or destruction of the enemy force. The artillery, technically
excellent, achieved greater firepower and mobility.

The infantry was reorganized in January 1796 by a new system
of brigades. The problem was to brigade the units that were still
independent, and to bring up to full strength the demi-brigades
that had declined into skeletons. The number of demi-brigades of
battle infantry was brought down to 110. Each process of brigading differed from the others in its details. The 1st demi-brigade
was simply reconstituted from the 3 battalions of a former demi-
brigade (the 131st), so that there was no fusion. But to form the
4th, so many men had been lost that it was necessary to take men
from 21 battalions from 8 different demi-brigades.

The army as a whole was divided into seven field armies. Those of the Rhine-Moselle and Sambre-Meuse were the most numerous, each with 103,125 men. The Army of the West had 82,137; the Army of Italy, 70,935; the Army of the North, 51,086. The Army of the Interior, together with the artillery schools and the coast guard, consisted of 94,236. In fact, the men present under arms were less numerous than these figures show, and the entire army had hardly more than 400,000.

3. THE COMMAND STRUCTURE: CONTINUITIES AND CHANGES

The second *embrigadement* made possible a new selectivity in the appointment of officers. By a law of 14 Germinal Year III (April 3, 1795), the principle of seniority in years of service was abandoned. It was replaced by seniority in existing rank. This new principle, combined with a requirement of four years in the rank just below the one to which promotion was to be made, was intended to make more difficult the advancement of men who had entered the army many years before but were lacking in demonstrated ability. The same law of Germinal Year III suppressed election by fellow soldiers. It revived the Girondin project for nomination by peers with choice by superiors. Election by peers was definitively suppressed by an article thrown as if by chance into the law of 10 Brumaire Year IV (November 10, 1795), by which election reverted to the Directory.

The Thermidorian Convention and the Directory did more than follow a policy initiated in the Year II, which was to gain a hand over appointments so as to obtain qualified personnel. Political motives were at work. At a time when the popular masses were rebellious it was important to take from the Jacobins and sans-culottes the greatest possible number of command posts, and to fill them with reliable men.

The Thermidorians, and then the Directory, rehabilitated hundreds of officers who had been imprisoned as suspects at the time of the Revolutionary Government. Men like a battalion commander named Gosse, who had been arrested at Landau for belonging to an "aristocratic conspiracy," were restored to the service, after taking an oath to defend a regime that had overthrown the tyrants "who drank the blood of patriots to introduce the triumph of virtue!"

The reintegration of suspects of the Year II was accompanied by a purge of the "anarchists." Chiefs of staff, and inspectors-general of depots, were ordered on November 2, 1794, to appoint an officer "of intelligence and probity" to examine the conduct and moral qualities of every officer. A number of officers were rejected after these inquiries. How many is difficult to say, because few of the relevant files have been preserved. Some information filters through in the correspondence of the secretariat of state and the records of military justice. Thus, we learn that a representative of the people, stationed with the Army of the Eastern Pyrenees, ordered "citizen Hilaire, captain of the 18th Dragoons, to be dismissed, disarmed, and sent back to his native commune. . . . He is an exaggerated terrorist."

Officers suspected of royalism were expelled in turn after the uprising of Vendémiaire. The minister ordered that those who had resigned after August 10, 1792, and then been reintegrated, should be dismissed. Relatives of émigrés were to remain excluded from all military functions, but the government made exceptions—General Desaix, for example.

The laws and decrees providing new criteria for promotion were disliked by the oldest officers, who had been allowed by seniority in years of service, as previously applied, to pass rapidly from the enlisted ranks to commissioned status. In their annoyance, some of them let their men disobey orders in the policing of popular revolts. The second *embrigadement*, in 1796, renewed their alarm. Because the new organization involved the suppression of many battalions, thousands of officers faced the prospect of going home with a reduction in pay, a reduction by a third or a half according to their seniority.

The "old timers" were all the more annoyed by the fact that appointment of officers and NCOs now went by seniority in rank.

An officer or NCO of the volunteers of 1791, having more than four years of service in his rank, would be promoted before an officer or NCO of the former royal army who had attained his rank in 1794. This concern was expressed by the NCOs of the 97th demi-brigade of the new formation:

> NCOs with fewer years of total service are made officers simply because they have more years in their rank as NCOs. [We ask] that the legislative body take action to restore our just rights and claims to higher rank on the ground of seniority in service. We point out to you that almost all the NCOs now in our demi-brigade, and in the whole army, were elected to their rank with farmer's tools still in their hands, at the time of formation of their respective battalions. Hence they now have five years in their rank. We have been soldiers in the same units for twelve, sixteen, eighteen, and twenty years. We have reached the same rank only since the war began, even if we were corporals before. Is it right that preference should go to these men to whom we gave the training they needed when they left the plow?

Such a statement was not accurate, since studies have shown that many officers and NCOs of the volunteers were in fact former soldiers. But there was tension within the army between "whites" and "blues." It produced more or less open revolts in some units. One group of officers wrote menacingly from the banks of the Rhine:

> You are doubtless not unaware of the discontent in the army produced by your unheard of ingratitude toward officers that your reform has exposed to the horrors of indigence and despair. . . . Unless you change your barbarous and impolitic attitude toward us, within two months, there will be no more army. . . . *O Patrie! O Liberté!* . . . Take care not to misunderstand the silence of the army. It is the dreadful calm before the storm of a general commotion.

Officers seeking reassignment poured into Paris. A ruling of March 30, 1797, in fact directed that vacant sub-lieutenancies should be given to officers made redundant by the reorganization. But these officers believed that they would obtain better results if they were on the ground in the capital, where their arrival coincided with preparation for the coup d'état of Fructidor. The government, being so dependent on the intervention of the army, reached an understanding with it. In March 1798 it issued an order that favored the displaced officers. In each demi-grade twenty-seven places would be created for "accessory" officers, who would take part in training and other ordinary duties. But in September the government felt strong enough to reverse this decision.

There was never complete obedience in the army to the orders of the central government on the filling of vacant posts. Some pretended not to know the law. Or, while knowing it, they intervened with authorities with requests to circumvent it. For example, Citizen Rumédon was indicated for promotion to battalion commander, but should not Captain Cornac, with perhaps the longest service in the whole army, be given preference? The regimental administrative councils, to push their own candidates, thought of methods that in some ways revived elections. Disregarding the law, they sent petitions to the government signed by both officers and common soldiers in their units. Failing to obtain satisfaction, they still got around the law. The law forbade election, so they ignored the law. Nicolas Forest thus became an officer in the Year VI.

The government, quite apart from its political aims, sought to eliminate officers who were over age. There were still men like sub-lieutenant Calvier or captain Ancel who held their posts although their age—over sixty—made them irregular in their duties. A sampling of the dossiers of infantry demi-brigades, consisting of more than a thousand cases, reveals that the officers were quite young, especially at the company level: 64 percent of the captains, 64.9 percent of the lieutenants, and 64.3 percent of the sub-lieutenants were under thirty-five in 1797. But the requirement of four years in a given rank checked the rise of the young madcaps called *sabreurs*. Where only 25 percent of the sub-lieutenants had been over thirty-five in the Year II, we find 35.7 percent in this group in 1797. In the Army of Egypt, almost 18 percent of the sub-lieutenants were between forty and fifty years old, where the average in the Year II had been only 10.5 percent.

These officers were experienced soldiers. Some 52.6 percent had served as privates, corporals, or higher NCOs before the Revolution. Volunteers of 1791 and 1792, who had been at war for five or six years, shared with them the positions as officers at the company level. Neither the volunteers of 1793 nor the draftees could have much chance of promotion among so many "technicians."

The level of theoretical instruction was judged to be good or adequate by the inspectors for 63 percent of the officers, but in practical performance only 36.4 percent were rated as satisfactory, 19.8 percent as moderately satisfactory, and 7.6 percent as passable. A little more than a third were judged to have insufficient theoretical and practical knowledge, though showing "zeal." Schauenburg, a severe inspector, declared himself content with the way in which officers led their troops. Some progress could yet be made in maneuvers, he said, for all too often they wanted to "learn everything at once," and "showed no tenacity in learning the details."

Officers were increasingly reproached for conducting themselves carelessly. Not that there were too many drunkards—they had been eliminated; but some commanders were blamed for taking on the airs of *muscadins*. They wore fantastic clothes, and were sometimes remiss in their work. The high command, encouraged by the government, tried to impose a new form of behavior. Earlier in the Revolution officers had been thought of as magistrates enjoying the confidence of citizens who were their equals, and as such had had to consider what they owed to the men over whom they were "administrators." Now they were to understand that the army was composed less of citizens than of soldiers, whose leaders would observe a moral code like that of notables of the Directory. The process by which an army officer would be considered a "notable" under the Empire had already begun in the Year IV. After 1796 an officer could be rebuked for "not knowing how to manage his private conduct," or for "compromising himself with subordinates," or for "being by nature a corporal and not changing with the change of costume." A stigma fell on those who had contracted "an unsuitable marriage with a woman without fortune."

But some officers remained Jacobins, along with their men, and they opposed this trend in hierarchic relationships. Their most cutting insult was to call an officer "worse than under the Old Regime." If they thought a superior incompetent, or arbitrary, or unfaithful to his promises, they acted as in 1793; they refused to obey him, and drew up petitions demanding his dismissal. Ferdinand Edelman, a hussar in the 5th regiment, shouted from his place in the ranks that "he had no respect for an officer who did not respect him, and that he had served in many units, knew the laws, and would teach them to him." The first tribunal chosen to judge a difference between an officer and his superior was still often formed by the troops themselves. Pestered by his brigade commander and unable to get satisfaction, a squadron leader in the 3rd Hussars waited for a review of the troops, then turned and addressed his men: "Hussars, I call you to witness that the brigade commander is the cause of all the trouble in this regiment."

This sort of direct democracy went on in some places into the years of the Consulate.

• • •

CHAPTER XI

The Occupation of Enemy Territory and Change in the Army Morale

Beginning in 1795 the army operated in enemy territory. No longer receiving supplies from the government, the troops formed the habit of living by pillage. What had been occasional in the Year II became systematic after 1795. The citizen-soldiers lost their respect for the "cottages" and ended up by scorning the local populations. On their return to France they adopted the same attitude toward their fellow citizens as toward foreign civilians—all of whom seemed to forget the sacrifices made by the army and view it with contempt. In the eyes of the army, French society was gangrened and corrupt. A gap opened between the army and the nation.

1. Privation and Pillage in Foreign Countries

A Lieutenant Michel wrote on 20 Prairial Year III (June 8, 1795): "We don't live, we just suffer. We have no bread. We are reduced for our daily food to two pounds of sprouting potatoes or three ounces of worm-eaten dry peas. A while ago we caught a cat. He had to go into the pot and we ate him with good appetite. We know that horses and squirrels may be good, too." With the fall of the Revolutionary Government, famine returned to the camps. From a letter written in 1796 by Captain Bernier of the Army of

Italy: "It is now the fifth day that the army has had nothing to eat but bread except for an ounce of oil yesterday. . . . If this happened only from time to time we would not complain, but it happens too often and results in much sickness."

When food was procured by private enterprise it was often spoiled. A sub-lieutenant in the 4th battalion of the Côtes-du-Nord wrote on August 18, 1796: "I have seen bad flour made into bread, rancid meat, and often moldy rice used in place of meat." Inspector Chaumont confirmed this allegation on September 21: "Bread is baked from spoiled flour which makes it very bad." In the Army of the Pyrenees men on their way to join the Army of Italy died of hunger on the road.

Pay in *assignats*, and later in "territorial mandates" that no one wanted, was not enough to buy food. The government decided, indeed, in April 1796 that part of the pay should be made in metallic value, but its order remained mostly without effect. In August 1797 the minister of war admitted that army pay was three million in arrears.

Grumbling was followed by revolt. In 1795, for example, there was a revolt in Belgium on June 13, when the 1st battalion of the 183rd demi-brigade refused to return to its barracks; the soldiers said there were magistrates in the town that they must go to see. The leaders were arrested, but within a half hour the whole demi-brigade prepared to free them: "They took arms, disobeyed their chiefs, marched off to the beat of drums, and charged across the town." At Groningen in Holland the commander was obliged to aim cannon at the men of the 24th demi-brigade who demanded more to eat. On September 2 the 3rd battalion of the 43rd demi-brigade assembled to prevent arrest of a soldier who demanded food and an increase of pay. The rebels shouted, "He won't go to the lock-up, or we all go. We should have had a raise a week ago." In October a revolt broke out again at Groningen. One of the soldiers, Bardin, urged his comrades to promise that if their demands were not met within two weeks they would seize the cannon, load them, and get justice done. "A seditious crowd went to the places of detention, where the guards let them pass, and the punished soldiers were liberated."

Revolts in 1796: In the Army of Italy on February 28 a part of Serrurier's division mutineed at Ormea. In the Army of the Rhine on March 19 Desaix noted the bad feeling of the advance guard, which was murmuring audibly. On the 25th the 35th demi-brigade revolted, on April 1 the 36th followed its example, and on April 10 the 86th. In May in the town of Zweibrücken, the 74th refused to obey orders. In June, after the breaking of the armistice, the 17th called attention to itself by frequent insubordination and two companies of the 84th rebelled. The same occurred in the Army of the Sambre-Meuse when a unit refused orders because of lack of food.

Revolts in 1797: In the Army of the West men of the 52nd demi-brigade protested that they were "ready to march against any enemy and that they loved and wanted to serve the Republic," but that they would not go by way of Belle-Ile, where everything was lacking; "they might be shot, but they would never change their minds." In January revolts occurred in the Army of the Rhine-Moselle (31st demi-brigade), in July in the garrison at Landau, in August at Metz, Strasbourg, Neufbrisach, Huningue, and Sarrelibre.

Seditions continued into 1798, principally in the Army of Italy. The 7th demi-brigade, for example, returning from Italy, camped near Marseille. In September it was ordered to recross the Alps back to Italy. The men had not been paid for five months, and remembered the privations that they had borne. They drew up in battle formation, with their officers at their head, and demanded money before they would depart.

More and more, to avoid revolts, commanders shut their eyes to marauding. Some officers even incited their men to pillage. The Germans in 1796, according to the historian Jacques Godechot, used the word *Kripper*, or robbers, to characterize the French. And, in effect, the French soldiers possessed sets of burglars' tools to search for hiding places for money, which they did while repeating, "Buggers. *Landsmann Wein! Landsmann Geld!* Hurry up, *oder kaput!*" In Franconia they pillaged houses and cellars. While drunk, they engaged in all sorts of brutalities, beating the men with their gun butts and violating the women. When complaint was made to the officers, they replied, "bagatelles." The officers themselves held places to ransom. An inhabitant of Baberach, near Mainz, wrote to a French friend, describing the extortions of a brigade commander named Delforty, and then added:

> When a general arrives, the whole town is busy with satisfy- ing the despotic demands of such a republican Sardanapalus. I am assured that the headquarters spends 1,000 livres a day on its table in the town where it finds itself. They say, "We are given no money, and yet we must live." Are these your laws, you French? They must be no stronger than spider webs. . . . The soldier lets himself go in disorder and pillage, and the officers cannot stop it.

Sometimes the troops were ordered to sack everything. This happened when a community tried to defend itself. Gilbert Gas- pard, a soldier in the 8th company of the 2nd battalion of the 42nd, wrote to his parents in June 1795:

> I will tell you that we took the town of Frankenthal, a sizeable town in Prussia [sic], very rich and full of merchants. We en- tered the town at shoulder arms, without firing a shot. They surrendered as good republicans, and they did as we did. We passed through another village where they revolted against us. We put it to fire and sword, and the village is burned down.

In 1797 Paul Laceta, when accused of stealing clothes at Ville- franche, said in self-defense that what was found in his quarters came from Italy, "where the commanding officers had authorized pillage and burning."

Generals in chief were troubled by such conduct on the part of enlisted men, officers, and sometimes even brigade commanders.

Davout, for example, did not hesitate to write to the minister of war, in the spring of 1795, to denounce the 86th demi-brigade for engaging in rapine: instead of assisting in requisition of food supplies and other necessities for the benefit of the Republic, it took them by pillage for its own use. It had sacked the village of Sept-Fontaines, fifteen kilometers from Luxembourg, and subjected the inhabitants to serious losses. General Grenier, in September 1796, in the region of Cologne, arrested some pillagers who sold the product of their thefts to merchants. As Colonel Maigret reported:

> He ordered an inspection of the soldiers' personal effects, and had burned in the presence of the troops all those recognized as coming from pillage, regardless of their value or usefulness. Beyond that, he ordered taken from the soldiers all their money in excess of 9 francs, and used it for an advance on two *decades'* pay for his whole division.

Hoche, commanding the Army of the Moselle, hoped to prevent pillage by obtaining a regular and abundant provisioning of his army. With this in mind, he levied requisitions and contributions on the richer classes of the country. Favoring a policy of establishing a Cisrhenane Republic, he ordered severe measures against extortion by the troops. As for Bonaparte, although he promised his men the wealth of the Italian plains, he was intelligent enough to oppose pillage that would compromise his program for the occupied regions. He knew, too, that to restrain the excesses of his troops he must assure them an adequate pay; from May 1796, thanks to war "contributions," half their pay was made in specie.

. To end "the reign of an unruly soldiery," the generals obtained from the Directory a new organization of military justice, which, under their control, became a powerful instrument of dissuasion against brigandage. Post commanders in the Army of Italy, under Bonaparte's orders, put up proclamations like this one:

Republican soldiers! In the name of the laws of the Republic: You are invited, in the name of your superior officers, to respect the poor and unfortunate inhabitants of small towns, villages, and open country. I also invite all troop leaders, by use of scouts and patrols, to prevent their men from doing any damage in any house in such places.

The complaints of rural inhabitants were thus heard, and efforts made to find and punish the guilty.

Nevertheless, privation in the army had led to invasion of humble cabins and seizure by force of what could not be had by asking. The inhabitants of occupied countries felt a mounting hostility to French soldiers. The French presented themselves as liberators from the feudal yoke, which they believed themselves to be. They appeared in the guise of oppressors. They came to consider all civilians in foreign countries as enemies. They soon transferred this hostility to civilians to French society itself.

2. In France: The Military and the Civilians

The soldiers saw an image of *la Patrie* as if in a broken mirror, in letters from civilian friends or from veterans who had returned home, in the reports of convalescents from the hospitals, and in the tales of comrades assigned for a time to the Army of the Interior. Their country seemed corrupt, disdainful, forgetful, and ungrateful. They had sacrificed all to the Revolution, and at one time the Republic had exhausted itself to support them. Now, they were begrudged a place at the table of Equality, and were refused even a proper share of the bread of Fraternity.

Was *la Patrie* corrupt? It was said in the camps that aristocrats returning from the emigration were subverting the nation and that the aristocracy of wealth was assisting them. Comrades returning from France described the theaters in which "gilded bellies" occupied the front rows and objected to the brave soldier who intoned the Marseillaise or *Le Salut de l'Empire*. At Dunkirk, by one report, some soldiers had tried to drown out the reactionary song, *Le Réveil du Peuple*, by singing the hymn of the Marseillaise; they were beaten almost black and blue, and they were the ones that the police arrested. Similar events, and similar repression, were reported from Rouen, Rennes, and Bordeaux.

The republican soldier had to defend himself, unaided, against *muscadins* and royalist agents. When taking a walk, or attending a spectacle, he had to keep his eyes and ears open; a brother in arms might call for help, and the holiday of the *décadi*, begun agreeably enough, would end in an outright battle. Soldiers on leave made their rallying cry *A bas les Chouans*! In Paris they had a meeting place in the rue Vivienne, where they chased away anyone not wearing the cockade. Another meeting place was the Palais Egalité (the former Palais Royal), where they would lie in wait for fops in black collars, then with a few twists of the hand remove their clothes and chase them, "with tumult and provocation," while bellowing out the Marseillaise as far as the Theater of the Republic.

Did *la Patrie* disdain them? Soldiers returning from home told that in the towns people avoided their company. They felt insulted. A year or two before they had been seen as the best of citizens; everything had been done to give them a few days of relaxation and care for their needs. Now, with empty wallets, they were refused credit. Grocers laughed at them, and citizens shunned their approach. They were regarded as brigands. Of course, one might meet soldiers "dressed like Mars for a fight and ready for a spree," who broke into a cookshop with naked sword and emptied the pot without paying. Some held retailers for ransom, or played with the exchange rates on money, or became protectors of prostitutes. In Paris, they gathered every evening at the Palais Egalité, according to police reports, and stopped women indiscriminately, treated them as whores, and stole their lockets and earrings. The Place de Grève was full of drunken soldiers who assumed the most indecent postures with "the servants of Venus." They threatened passers-by: "If the Parisians don't get in step, Paris will be put to fire and sword."

But why should the whole army be judged by the acts of a few deviants? Anyway, if such men behaved so badly, was it not because they were forced to by the inadequacy of their pay? And if citizens complained that they acted as if in a conquered country, how could they do otherwise when no one tried to relieve their miserable material circumstances?

In the provinces, as in Paris, the troops acted, by one report, "as if at liberty in an enemy country, taking to pillage on the pretext of having had no subsistence for a week." At Nanterre, near Paris, it was said, no day passed without robberies, scuffles, and even murders in which army men were involved. In the Haute-Loire, in January 1796, some hussars, "thinking they were in enemy country or on the frontiers, made a clean sweep of everything." As a local official reported, "This is enough to alienate from us the few patriots and peaceful inhabitants, who are outraged and revolted by such pillage." In February 1796 the commissioner of the Executive Directory with the local administration at Versailles announced that

> the immorality and indiscipline of some soldiers in the garrison at Versailles keep peaceful citizens in a perpetual state of alarm. Nothing is sacred for them; the laws are without force, the authorities without power, and the rights of society are degraded.
>
> The most respectable women cannot go out on their household errands without being outraged. The judge is menaced in his courtroom; dissipation, speculation, and every kind of vice are protected.

Early in 1797 a group of soldiers commanded by a sergeant appeared at Retzwiller. They were charged, they said, with arranging lodgings for the troops. The inhabitants were frightened by the prospect of having soldiers in their homes. The soldiers proposed a bargain: if they were given some money they would remove certain places from their billeting lists. At the same time dragoons from the 4th regiment were going through the neighborhood in search of forage. At Mornach they committed acts of violence and other excesses against the inhabitants. They ate and drank without paying, almost set fire to a house, burned a crucifix, seized a servant girl and played with her, and as a climax forced a man to drink urine. Everywhere the troops demand "lovemaking with threats of force." But to say "everywhere" would be to generalize too much.

Many soldiers who took no part in such outrages failed to understand the hostility that they met with, and were ready to think that their brothers in arms, rather than civilians, had the better case. At Draguignan, for example, when a soldier was arrested for stealing tobacco, his comrades demonstrated in his favor, and their officers denounced the municipal official who came to see them as "a dirty beggar and dirty scoundrel." They "didn't give a damn for his scarf, and they would pin back his ears."

As a contemporary said: "Such are the pretensions of the military chiefs and misconduct of many soldiers that peaceable and honest citizens are afraid of falling under the iron rod of a military government that will cut the throat of liberty with the sword of despotism."

As for the soldiers, they bitterly resented the disgust that they aroused. As a sub-lieutenant Chauvin wrote in 1796:

> It is hard to tell, in moving from camp to a billet for rest, whether or not you have moved to some extremity of the empire after having conquered somewhere else. Instead of consideration on the part of our fellow citizens we meet with nothing but scorn, snubs, and even insults. Anything can be borne except public contempt. We are lodged in the worst possible and most disgusting quarters. Should aristocrats be given the right to degrade us? If we complain we are always in the wrong before magistrates, who regard us as foreigners and always decide in favor of their constituents. The law regulating what a soldier should expect in his lodging should also prescribe the consideration and decency owed to friends and brothers.

The soldiers were unanimous in complaining that they were looked down upon everywhere. "At the beginning of the Revolution," they said, "it was not this way."

So *la Patrie* was not only corrupt and contemptuous but also forgetful and ungrateful. She showed no recognition for the sacrifices made. Officers and men were all the more convinced of these failures by two affairs by which the demi-brigades were much troubled: the matter of documents confirming promotions, and the "billion for the soldiers."

At the time of a vacancy in appointment as either commissioned or noncommissioned officer, the government could act in either of two ways: either by confirming the appointment by seniority, or by appointing a man of appropriate rank who seemed the most meritorious in the light of papers sent in by the regimental administrative council. But all too often the bureaucracy of the Directory was unable to reply as promptly as was expected. Such delays were an annoyance to all officers and especially to commanders, who meanwhile lacked the necessary number of responsible subordinates. This situation resulted because an officer temporarily replacing one of his comrades declined to do so for long, since he knew that at some time or other the position he filled might be taken from him. A vacancy blocked all promotions.

The quartermaster of the 118th demi-brigade wrote to the government in 1795:

> Your delay in replying to us makes it impossible to fill vacant positions. Kindly take into consideration, citizen, the deficit in officers of the demi-brigade caused by the failure of replacement since 1 Thermidor Year II until now. We call to your attention that in affairs that took place on 7 and 9 Messidor the demi-brigade lost four officers, plus ten dangerously wounded, and that it also lost a good many noncommissioned officers, with the result that the state of the service is very weak.

Officers and NCOs, once appointed, had to await receipt of the document, the *brevet*, by which their appointment was confirmed.

Without it, they could not be in the competition for new appointments, or collect the pay to which their new rank entitled them.
To obtain this document they had to assemble and forward to the
ministry a multitude of papers. When these had been sent off after
much trouble, the ministry kept silent for four, eight, or even
twelve months. A veritable debauch of writing was sometimes
necessary to get satisfaction; one quartermaster wrote every
month for almost a year!

The complaints became more numerous at the end of 1795. It
was known that the second *embrigadement* was approaching, with
its reduction in the number of posts. It was unlucky for the man
who, competing with another, could not produce his *brevet*. The
same alarm arose in 1797, when the announcement of peace with
Austria portended a thinning of the command structure. Without
his *brevet* a man would find himself on the streets with a meager
pension. Some officers remembered what their older colleagues
told them of the sad aftermath of the Seven Years War. Officers
waiting for their *brevet* concluded that the delay reflected some
concerted plan not to pay them. The administrative council of the
141st demi-brigade wrote:

> You will see that most officers are still without their *brevet*.
> We are absolutely ignorant of the reasons for the delay, for
> we transmitted to you all the necessary papers eight months
> ago, including all those that you required. Hence the officers
> have grounds for believing that the government does not de-
> sire to have the *brevet* sent to them.

Common soldiers felt the same anxiety about what would follow the peace. Miserable as their conditions might be, they nevertheless had what many civilians lacked: along with worn out
clothes, a bit of bread, and an occasional drop of wine, they had
the pride of belonging to communities of brothers before whom
aristocrats had once bent their knees. As civilians again, they
would have trouble in finding employment, when in some cases
for more than six years they had forgotten how to handle the
scythe, the plane, or the trowel. The exaltation of conquest and

adventure would be followed by the dreariness of daily life and the tedious search for a job. As one plain soldier wrote to the Directory in an unpunctuated letter:

> For those who have no trade (and how can they get one) three-quarters who will have neither father nor mother, who have no trade and not knowing what is to become of them will be forced against their will to act like brigands or else die of hunger on a dung hill, that is why it is important for them to be compensated for their labors and build hospitals to take care of the crippled and wounded that is the least that can be done for them for without them what will become of the Republic. . . . There are lots of bets that peace will be made with all the powers within a month. . . . Our poor people are suffering cruelly in every way. Half of them have no bread which is very expensive, wine and everything doubling since 1790 which is frightening, oh unlucky that I am what will become of us, good-bye. I embrace you with all my heart.

To relieve the distress of discharged soldiers there was the "billion in nationalized properties" promised in the Year II to the fighting men. *La Patrie*, through her organ of government, was bound to honor her engagements. The soldier took over from the sans-culotte the aspirations to own a small piece of property. One officer, Chauvin, made himself the spokesman for his men when he wrote in 1796:

> There is no happiness without virtue, and also not without a decent living. Why blame the military man for desiring it? It is to seek it that the Macedonians went into Asia and the Portuguese crossed the seas; this passion necessarily grows when property is acquired, and instead of extinguishing it you should wisely direct it. It leads us to equality or at least it relieves us of dependency. To be totally without property has never been more than a folly and hypocrisy of philosophers and monks.

An officer in the Army of the Sambre-Meuse echoed Chauvin:

> The law sends away supernumerary officers with nothing to live on, so that those who remain expect the same fate, or at least that is what they are led to understand. Why not give them something from the nationalized properties to assure their existence? Sacrifices should be made for those who have sacrificed so much.

The same declaration is heard at the level of the common soldier. Louis Guérard, a maimed veteran, explained in July 1797 that he was now the only one in his family alive, his father and brother having died in battle in the ranks of the 1st battalion of the Calvados. He was in poverty. Why were they waiting to give the promised billion to the defenders of the country? "My statement," he said, "is what all my brothers in arms would make. My petition would be covered with signatures if I had showed it to them."

But the politicians vacillated on the matter. The affair of the billion became a tool of propaganda and was used by the Babouvists in 1796 to penetrate the army. Two years later the "constitutional circles," in which the neo-Jacobins met, pressed the Directory for a distribution of land. In 1796 as in 1797 the government equivocated, relying on an opinion rendered by some of the generals, such as Belair, who thought effecting a land distribution would be difficult and sometimes impossible. It would necessitate the breaking up of operations that had long been combined in large farms and were more developed and more productive. Moreover, such an immense redistribution throughout all of France would rearouse the "shameful desires of the envious." Encouraged by the mere idea that division among fifteen hundred thousand defenders of the country was possible, "they would throw firebrands among the people to cause a general conflagration, spread the germs of interminable civil war, and give the signal for the most dreadful and deplorable anarchy by proposing changes in ownership."

The Council of *Anciens*, on February 19, 1798, prescribed a mode of payment. It announced that "the billion due to the immortal servants of the country will be paid in the form of a lifetime tontine annuity." It would constitute a sacred debt, subject to no withholding, and beyond seizure for any purpose. The maximum was set at 1,500 francs a year; the amount due to each soldier would depend on his years of service without distinction of rank. The share of the deceased would be added to the share of his survivors; when the combined payment reached 1,500 francs the annuity of the deceased would terminate, to the benefit of the state.

A sum of 1,500 francs was enough for a discharged soldier to live on in moderate comfort. The painter, tailor, or stonecutter in the provinces, with two or three francs paid for a working day, had less than this amount for a year. With half his annuity, in regions like the neighborhood of Toulouse, a man could buy a bit more than two *arpents*[1] of land; it was not much, but he could then live on his own and not have to ask for alms. But in fact the law was not applied. So much is evident in a letter written to the government by Captain Simon in 1799: "You promised a billion to the defenders of the country. You renewed the promise a hundred times, but the soldiers see it as a chimera."

With no billion, it was not until September 1799 that the government produced a complete reorganization of retirements for years of service or for infirmity. The new measures were less favorable than those of 1790. Although the law represented progress in the methods of application, it marked a clear regression in the scale of the pensions.

As it advanced ever further into enemy territory, the army became more cut off from the rest of the nation. The only messages that it received confirmed it in the belief that the social body rejected it. Gradually the army turned in upon itself. Its members began to conduct themselves less as citizen-soldiers than as professionals of war, ready to follow their leaders in the conquest of Europe. And

---

[1] Slightly more than two acres.

also, when the generals thought it desirable to lend aid to a state attacked from both the right and the left, the troops were willing to support them. The army exercised repression both on royalists and on popular revolts and neo-Jacobin movements. Did this prove that, from an early date, the military forgot the fraternity that bound them to the sans-culottes, to become no more than pretorians?

In fact, a study of sources in the national archives and the war archives shows that it was only gradually that the army became a docile instrument in the hands of the generals. Until 1797, some officers continued to question the justification of their orders, and notably those that invited them to turn their arms against the populace. The popular demands found many echoes among the troops.

• • •

CHAPTER XII

The Army and the
Suppression of Popular Revolts
In the Year III (1795)

The Thermidorians dismantled the Revolutionary Government piece by piece, and in returning to the free market they exposed the common people to poverty. Crowds rioted around the grain convoys. In the absence of an effective police, the movement of necessities had to be protected by the army. Famished crowds attacked the soldiers, barring the roads, forcing the unloading of merchandise, and dictating the prices. The soldiers found it hard to understand these disorders, the outcries against them, and the blows given and received. They said they were "provoked and harassed." Some began to execute their missions half-heartedly, despite threats of punishment by their officers.

1. Soldiers and Rioters in April 1795 in Paris

On 12 Germinal (April 1, 1795) workers from the faubourg Saint-Antoine burst into the Convention, demanding bread and the implementation of the Constitution of 1793, although the Convention had decreed on March 21, on the initiative of Sieyès, that any insult to the national representation should qualify as a crime. At the same time, when soldiers tried to disperse the lines forming at bakers' doors, women called out to them, "You have bread and the people have none. Throw down your arms! We want no soldiers when there is no bread!"

Handbills circulated among the troops, urging fraternization between soldiers and people:

> Republicans! Avengers of *la Patrie*, you have not fought for her in vain. It is not to benefit your enemies that you have struck down the hordes of foreign slaves. You have conquered liberty on distant shores. Will you let it perish within our walls, in your families desolated and starved by the ugliest of conspiracies? Will the chains you have so courageously broken be again riveted on the hands of your fathers, mothers, wives, children, and cherished companions? Will those ages of abhorrent servitude be reborn? . . . Two factions seem now to divide the fruit of your conquests. One rises from the debris of monarchist fanaticism. The other, more wily and deceitful, longs for a government by the selfish rich and the aristocrats. It does not present you, it is true, with ideas or images of former enslavement. But as a declared enemy of the rights of the people it wants liberty, enjoyment, and happiness only for itself. . . . Surely it was for yourselves, your brothers in arms, your friends, and relatives that you have withstood the rigors of winter, braved the heat of summer, and exposed yourselves to danger and exhaustion. Or was it for a handful of corrupt and cowardly idlers?
>
> Like us, you detest kings, aristocracy and servitude. Like us, you love the democratic constitution of 1793. We have all taken an oath to it. Like us, you will defend it. Like us, you will not allow it to be meddled with or defiled. Then help us as brave men to establish it firmly. *Salut, fraternité indivisible*.

Did the soldiers need such a reminder? They could remember that in 1793 they had received, as the people did, a minimum subsistence for living. Poverty had thereafter spread through the camps, as it did through the streets of villages and towns. They could say, as in an address by the officers, NCO's, and men of the 2nd battalion of the 60th demi-brigade, that they had witnessed "the atrocious sight of a miserable child dying at the dry breast of a starving mother," while "ambitious men grew fat on the privations of others, poisoned what they could not consume, and sterilized an earth shocked to bear such monsters on its surface." They continued to stigmatize the skulking rich who would not depart for the front. In the words of an officer named Laborie:

> I would like the government to require service in defense of the country of all those individuals in the Republic who are under forty-five years old, and who before the Revolution did not labor on the land or otherwise work at a trade for a living, that is, all those useless sluggards who in many cases own large properties, which those who have none are forced to go and defend for them.

In April 1795 the poor began to fraternize with the soldiers. They were convinced, as one of the insurgents of Prairial later testified, that "we had no need to be discouraged, because the army, the faubourgs, and the gendarmes were with us." The government was alarmed, for the alliance of the populace and the army was not confined to Paris or the Paris region. The authorities learned that "the embers of Jacobinism still stirred in the army." The government declared, in one of its circular letters: "A seditious and artfully contrived paper has appeared, of which the tendency is nothing less than to have the army intervene in favor of the terrorists against whom we have declared war to the death." When this letter from the government was sent to the Army of the Rhine, among others, the representatives on mission there, Bourbotte and Goujon, took the side of the insurgents and were guillotined as a result. From the Army of Italy the representative Matthieu Dumas, after the popular uprising, sent a report to the government on his investigation of terrorist addresses circulating among the troops.

As an immediate step, the government took care to send away

from Paris the units "corrupted" by the sans-culottes and Jacobins. It was moved to do so by reports of its agents, such as the agent assigned to the district of Paris, who wrote:

> The exaggerated disproportion between daily necessities and the falling value of money makes it impossible to oppose a disastrous outbreak of the people in despair. Alarmed by this threatening crisis, the government attempts at first to set up a dike. With the national guard failing it, it is obliged to resort to the military. The *chasseurs* are said to be unwilling, and there remain only the youth of elite units.

The government replaced unreliable troops with *carabiniers* and gendarmes. Both let themselves be won over by the people. On May 16, 1795, the Committee of Public Safety and the military committee sent away the gendarmes of the 29th division and isolated others in their barracks. The *carabiniers* left the capital; two divisions of gendarmerie took stations at the gates of Paris; and infantry battalions were concentrated within a radius of five leagues or less, along with squadrons of recently arrived cavalry. Before departing, the *carabiniers* announced that they were "forced to leave" for refusing to take an oath to defend the Convention in case of popular insurrection, and for having answered that they were part of the people and "would not kill men half dead with hunger if they rioted for bread."

Gendarmes at the Place du Carrousel used the same language.

2. The Army and the Popular Insurrection of 1 Prairial (May 20, 1795)

The people rose on the first of Prairial. They invaded the Convention; one deputy, Féraud, was killed, and his severed head was presented to the presiding officer, Boissy d'Anglas. "Bread and the constitution of 1793" was the cry. The Convention temporized and prepared for repression. On the 4th, at four in the afternoon, 3,000 cavalrymen pushed into the faubourg Saint-Antoine and put down the demonstrators by force. This action by men obeying the orders of their chiefs may seem to undermine the idea of an army sympathetic to popular demands. But who were these cavalrymen and who were their commanders?

All the officers of this improvised force had been dismissed or imprisoned in the Year II. One of their number, General Poissonnier-Desperrières, said in his memoirs: "What will seem unbelievable is that all the generals employed in the Army of the Interior were from the class of officers proscribed by a previous decree; that is, they were officers of the Old Regime." Among them, the commander-in-chief was Menou, son of a *maréchal de camp*, deputy of the nobility from Touraine in the Estates General. Those around him included Baraguay d'Hilliers, former cadet in the Alsace-Infanterie, arrested in July 1793 and liberated in 1794; General Dubois, a former "officer of fortune," suspended by Joubert; and General Berruyer, a lieutenant-colonel in 1789, arrested in the Year II. The dragoons were under command of Louis Antoine de Montgay, baron de Montchoisy, formerly of the royal bodyguard, a colonel in 1791, put under arrest in April 1793, and set free after Thermidor. At his side was brigade commander Saint-Germain, who had been arrested in April 1794 under suspicion of uncivic behavior. In this Paris that had known no military repression since July 12, 1789, these were the officers now commanding the Army of the Interior—it could be seen as the revenge of the aristocracy. It seemed that the bourgeoisie, which had overcome the aristocracy in alliance with the popular masses, was using this force to destroy the conquerors of the Bastille.

As for the troops, the presence in Paris is known of the 21st *chasseurs*, the 22nd cavalry, and the 3rd dragoons. The administrative files for these regiments are silent for this insurrectionary day. Kilmaine, freed from revolutionary jails on 21 Thermidor Year II, was in command of the 3rd dragoons. He asserts that his men followed orders without faltering. He reports that they said to him:

Under the royal despotism, when someone wanted to use us to oppress the people, it was our duty as citizens to take the part of the people against despotism. Today it is otherwise. It's a horde of brigands and murderers that want to revolt against the sovereignty of the people. This sovereignty is delegated uniquely to the National Convention, which is its sole depository. Whoever revolts against the Convention is in rebellion against the whole French people. We are here, at peril to our lives, to defend the national representation against Jacobins, brigands, and anarchists, and we will fulfill our task.

It is evident that the lesson had been intelligently given: it employed against the sans-culottes a theme in the Jacobin political education of the Year II, to instill obedience and unity behind the representatives of the national sovereignty, that is, behind the Convention.

Information is lacking on the infantry units that took part in the repression. The files on the Army of the Interior, at both the Archives Nationales and the Archives de la Guerre, contain nothing until eleven days after the uprising. On 15 Prairial, there were stationed at the gates of Paris or within the city the 1st and 3rd battalions of the 38th demi-brigade, the 3rd battalion of the 128th, the 2nd and 3rd of the 176th, the 7th of Yonne, and the 6th of Soissons. They came mostly from the Army of the North, and were made up of men from the rural West, Normans, Bretons, and Vendéans, but with a nucleus of Parisians. Their company officers were of mature age (from thirty-six to fifty-six), almost all of them career men who had served under the Old Regime. Among them was one, Grisel, who would later betray Babeuf. In social origins they resembled the army command in general, with artisans like Captain Cheloux and sub-lieutenant Grolleron, along with peasants such as Captain Robert who had been a vine grower in the Yonne, and bourgeois such as Brisson, who had taught in a college.

Some of these men revolted in the weeks following the *journée repressive*, 4 Prairial. It might be open rebellion. In the 6th Soissons battalion, which was in dire need, when the men began to scrounge in all directions and an officer tried to stop them, four companies assaulted him by throwing stones and lumps of grass. Possibly it was a revolt prompted by hunger, without political significance. In any case, there was a more covert form of opposition, namely desertion.

A study of the troop registers of units involved in the repression shows a sharp rise in desertions in Prairial and the first *décades* to follow it. In the 21st mounted *chasseurs* there had been only one desertion per month before the repressive action; there were then twenty-five in Prairial and thirteen in Messidor. The 176th demibrigade had no deserters from Pluviôse to Prairial, then suddenly five in Prairial and seventy-five in the first *décades* of Messidor. In the 6th battalion of Soissons there was no deserter until Prairial, then abruptly ninety-seven who disappeared.[1]

It may be objected that none of these desertions had a political cause, that being in Paris created an opportunity to desert when a man was near home and could lose himself in the Paris crowds. But the researcher cannot be assured of the correctness of this explanation, because he knows from the reports of departmental administrators that desertion did have a political motive at this same time. The legal officer of the Drôme wrote to the Committee of Public Safety:

> From the information that reaches me it seems possible to identify the cause of the extraordinary defection of the national volunteers: in principle, it is attributable to hardships in the volunteer battalions . . . others think they see the result of maneuvers by the terrorists.

Is it too much to see in this motive at least a partial explanation of the recrudescence of desertion in the Army of the Interior, during

---

[1] The sequence of the republican months, each of three *décades*, was: Vendémiaire, Brumaire, Frimaire—Nivôse, Pluviôse, Ventôse—Germinal, Floréal, Prairial—Messidor, Thermidor, Fructidor.

the days that accompanied and followed the popular insurrections? Were not some of these deserters imitating the patriotic gendarmes, of whom eighteen were guillotined after declaring that we "will gladly fight on the frontiers but will not fire on the people?"

What is well attested is that the rest of the army was by no means insensible to the drama that played itself out in Paris. According to a report from the commander of the 2nd battalion of the Nord, in Germinal, a volunteer in that battalion, Citizen Lesage, found himself on the 24th of that month at the Place Boppart, near the Rhine, when he received some papers from the Convention. After reading them he shouted that no one was now guillotined in Paris except the patriots, that he would die like them willingly, and that it made no difference to him whether he died on the scaffold or on the battlefield. He admitted to all the facts of which he was accused, "except for saying 'shit on the Convention,' by which he meant to refer only to the largest number of deputies in the Convention at present."

Shortly after the Germinal uprising, on April 26, 1795, at Foix, the commander of a detachment of the 1st regiment of hussars cried out at the head of his troops, *"Vive la République! Vive la Montagne!"* and took pride in the nickname of "the Marat of the Midi." In May 1795, when "frantic terrorists" were being hunted and forced out of the army units, the captain of the 18th regiment of dragoons, a Citizen Roussel, called Saint-Hilaire, was among a number of officers dismissed for this reason by the representative of the people at the Army of the Eastern Pyrenees.

On May 23, 1795, Jean-François Bénard, aged twenty-two, a lieutenant in the 9th sappers, ostentatiously paraded in Dunkirk in the sans-culotte costume of trousers and jacket. With others, he systematically provoked *muscadins*, or "dandies." The police had him labeled as a pronounced terrorist. Simultaneously at Loudun, scuffles broke out between some citizens and "terrorists" of the 11th hussars. On May 31, 1795, a former aide-de-camp of General Labourdonnaye, named Vallée, was accused by the municipality of Dax of being "one of those terrorists who hope to bring back the regime of the Year II."

Sometimes such sentiments were collectively expressed. On May 24, 1795, a battalion commander in the 15th infantry demi-brigade wrote to the general commanding the Army of Italy that his men were becoming more and more undisciplined, regretted the end of the price controls and the rule of the Jacobins, and cried "*Vive la Montagne*," while their officers circulated petitions tending to sanctify Robespierre and "resuscitate Jacobinism."

On July 14, 1795, the 3rd battalion of the 117th demi-brigade (Army of Italy), formed mostly of men from the Drôme, arrived at Sisteron and loudly manifested their liking for Robespierre and the Montagne; they announced themselves also as defenders of the system of the Terror. They took some old Robespierrists in the municipal government under their protection. General Keller-man, apprised of these facts, ordered the arrest of the command-ing officer, the first captain, the first lieutenant, the first sub-lieu-tenant, and the first sergeant of the battalion, to subject them to questioning and purge the unit of seditious elements.

Addresses were sent in from the armies in support of the insur-gents of Prairial. Representatives of the government, such as Chaudron-Rousseau, Paganel, or Bousquet at the Army of the Western Pyrenees, claimed that they were fabrications made by conspirators to destroy the republican government. What we know of the spontaneous character of the Prairial insurrection throws doubt on this assertion. In the armies of the Pyrenees, as in the Army of Italy, there were soldiers sympathetic to the Paris sans-culottes, and who thought that 1793 should be reborn.

Did anyone take up arms in favor of the insurgents of Prairial? We have evidence in Thermidor and Fructidor of some revolts in the armies of the North and the Sambre-Meuse, and among troops stationed in the Batavian Republic, but it seems impossible to distinguish between lack of subsistence and political action as causes of these revolts.

On the other hand, nearer to Paris, there was collusion between army men charged with the requisition and escort of grain and insurgents in town and country. Thus at Nogent-le-Rotrou, when revolt broke out in neighboring villages and soldiers were dispatched to restore calm, they took sides with the people. We find soldiers among the demonstrators at Rouen, as at Reims shortly before; they joined the rest of the people in demanding the right to existence. In April 1795, according to the representative Albert, soldiers sent from the Army of the Sambre-Meuse to protect grain convoys were attacked by hungry assailants and were increasingly reluctant to fulfill their mission. This attitude on the part of the troops, which sometimes brought "terrorists" bent on re-igniting civil war into the camps, was to be found again after the insurrection of Prairial. Thus, at Orléans and in its neighborhood, as we hear from a report of a commissioner of the executive power attached to the civil and criminal courts of the department, the two hundred soldiers stationed in the city, far from repressing the demands of the crowd, participated in them actively.

Having little confidence in the feelings of the army toward them, the Thermidorians issued many addresses to the troops to present their version of the facts in the capital. They amalgamated "terrorists" and "royalists," who, they said, had combined to overthrow the legitimate government of France and had misled the people, the better to exploit them. Had they succeeded, there would have been everywhere "massacre and pillage of family possessions." Fortunately for France, the mass of the citizens had recovered their senses and befriended the soldiers, who had well understood who guided the movement and what its aims were. The zeal of the military and of honest citizens had saved the Convention and France itself. It would henceforth be possible to live under orderly conditions in internal peace. This peace, "a basic source of the prosperity of empires," would finally "bring back to this unfortunate land the happiness that has so long eluded it."

In the absence of official instructions, the representatives of the people with the armies, in the first days following Prairial, were obliged to improvise. In their proclamations to the army, first of all, they contrasted an unworthy populace with a virtuous soldiery that accepted sacrifices with abnegation. If bread was scarce in Paris, they pointed out, it was scarce everywhere and especially in the army. The people should imitate the steadfastness of soldiers who fought without shoes or proper clothing and sometimes went without bread for five days. The question of subsistence, in the view of these spokesmen, was only a pretext used to manipulate the people. The manipulators were "bold and bloody men." The terrorists, as in the past, wanted only to turn the Republic— a Republic founded on the blood of its defenders—into their personal "appanage." The leaders of the insurgents, under cover of the Terror, meant "to organize pillage, multiply proscriptions, and renew the bloody scenes that besmirched the Revolution under the tyranny of Robespierre."

Then, when orders came from the government, they were to portray the insurgents to the army as "no more than a horde of vandalisers—marquises, priests, and assassins—the infected residue of the privileged classes—the hirelings of Pitt."

They all had a common interest in dissolving the Convention. A deluded crowd, demanding bread and the constitution of 1793, was only a kind of framework for this horrible plot, a protective cover for the conspirators.

On the whole, the Thermidorian propaganda achieved its purpose. Some soldiers, without news from the interior except what came from the authorities, believed in a royalist plot, whose end and consequences came in the counter-revolutionary insurrection of 13 Vendémiaire Year IV, or October 5, 1795. Sergeant-major Dumey wrote to his family: "At last the agitators have been undone! Neither terrorists nor royalists have been able to succeed in their anarchical projects." Battalions of the 2nd and 9th of Jura, and the 3rd of Hérault, wrote on June 13 to the Convention "to express their most energetic feelings of attachment to the national representation." The representative with the Army of the North, Pérès, affirmed five days after the Prairial uprising that columns of soldiers were ready to march to the rescue of the Convention. At the same time the representatives with the Army of the Pyrenees said they had troops ready to move in defense of the Republic if it was menaced in Paris.

Some army men were intelligent enough to observe that at the source of the insurrection was the problem of subsistence, for which the government had some degree of responsibility. Also, if the people were duped by enemies of the Republic, it was from lack of political education. "The people must be fanaticized," said Lieutenant Audouin a little later, for in no village of France could the language of patriotism any longer be heard. To revive it, it was necessary to send throughout France commissioners who were "honest, educated and patriotic," and who

> would exert themselves to arouse the public spirit, encourage citizens in republican virtues, have patriotic hymns and songs sung in all communes of the Republic, see that newspapers were read on every street corner, inform citizens of the progress of our armies, publicize acts of valor and civic virtue, and finally restore some degree of ease if not abundance.

By amalgamating royalists with terrorist sans-culottes, and invoking the creed of unity and obedience to the Convention, the governing elements managed to hold the support of the great majority in the army, which then remained loyal to them at the time of the royalist insurrection of Vendémiaire. But there still remained numerous militants for whom repression of popular uprisings presented cases of conscience. Some, both those stationed in France and those far away who learned about conditions at home from newly arriving draftees, or from men returning from leave, or from letters from their families, were inclined to wonder about the contradictions between the principles and the practice of men in the government. The unity of the country supposed an equitable sharing of sacrifices by all citizens. The government of the Year II had acted on this principle. Its successor demanded more from the poor and from the soldiers than from the comfortable classes of society.

• • •

CHAPTER XIII

The Army in the Year IV:
From Attempted Royalist Subversion
to the Projects of Babeuf

Seventeen ninety-six was the year of victories for the Army of Italy under General Bonaparte. Its successes have hidden from many historians the profound malaise from which it suffered—the empty stomachs, the tattered clothing, the comrade dying for want of care, the widow and orphan left without relief at home, and above all the pervasive feeling that the soldier was not respected. These thousand miseries of his daily existence accumulated until they burst out in rancor against the authorities. Royalists took the occasion to infiltrate and influence the army. At the other extreme, some Jacobins, along with the Equals gathered about Babeuf, also tried to exploit these bitter feelings. Both failed. The army withdrew into itself, while its generals gained control of its organizational mechanism, to use for their own advantage the legacy of the Year II that still existed in the army.

1. A Disheartened Army in 1796

For no other time does the investigator find in the archives such cries as those uttered by the army in 1796. Breaking its law of silence, the army sent a continuing stream of addresses to the Directory. We can do no better than to produce these documents of despair in their raw state and at length:

> A soldier [wrote one of them] complains without result that the aid granted to wives and children in poverty, or who have been reduced to poverty, does not exist or is insufficient or is not paid.
>
> And that the soldier who has been hospitalized for a long time, and so has not touched the smallest piece of metal money, sees his wife reduced to begging bread for her innocent little ones and obliged to pay taxes in hard silver on a little wretched dwelling (better called a shack), when neither she nor her husband has received any metal coin from the government for three years.
>
> Pay in silver! None of your old small change! Real silver! Or else in the name of the government that you defend your wife will be put in jail, and if charitable friends don't get her out, your poor little hut will be sold.

And another:

> You want the soldier to do everything for you, to abandon his father, mother, wife, and children to protect you, and when you have risen to the height of grandeur you forget him. You arrange to have yourselves paid in myriagrams,[1] but give him nothing but a miserable piece of paper that makes him rebuffed everywhere and wouldn't pay for a glass of water.
>
> Do you think the soldier will keep quiet when forbidden the pleasure of seeing his relatives, and when he can't correspond with them because of the enormous fee for carrying letters? A convalescent soldier, or someone leaving a hospital

---

[1] In view of anticipated inflation, the constitution of 1795 provided that Directors and members of the two legislative chambers should be compensated in myriagrams of wheat. The metric system, then being introduced, originally provided for *myriagrammes, myriamètres*, etc.—that is, ten kilograms, ten kilometers, etc.

far from his unit, used to be able to take a public coach, but now you ask him to pay 100 livres a league. Yet this soldier was wounded in combat defending your liberty, while you enjoyed the tender embrace of your wives and children.

Some wondered what they were fighting for:

The poor armies are reduced to a fragment of bread, sleeping on straw, badly clothed, without shoes, marching in snow-covered mountains, while citizens live in abundance, on good beds, well dressed, in warm houses, with all that their hearts desire, and so do not feel the sufferings of the poor defenders of the republic at the front.

What have we been fighting for? We are told it is for our liberty, but on the contrary we are more slaves than ever in the past.

And another adds:

The worthy founders of the Republic are reduced to despair. There is no respect except for those who insult the public misery by scandalous luxury.

Speculators are allowed to get rich, who "openly scoff at whatever bears the imprint of the Republic." They are supported by moderates "who are too weak to display the noble character of a republican."

Promises were made to the fighting men, but the reality is

generosity to enemies and ingratitude to your defenders. Is this justice? The more republican the army is, the more is required of it. It is exhausted by efforts that should have won it better treatment.

To have been victorious and yet be in want of everything! Spare your pocketbooks, and expend our blood! Great God! Are the defenders of the country only cheap instruments to be flattered when needed and thrown away when no longer useful?

The army is embittered, even demoralized. It should be attached again to *la Patrie*. Eulogies are not enough; we want some benefits, and that the Revolution should not all be for intriguing idlers, but part of it for defenders of the country and their indigent families. Justice imperatively demands this much.

The rich keep their sons far from the army. Show no mercy to those dandies who fill up the civilian bureaucracy. They are

all the very pillars of cafés, brothels, and the theater, while as for me, poor soldier, I am on maneuvers every day, and learning every day to defend my liberty and my country. If I am thirsty I go to a pump while these gentlemen go to a cabaret. Tired out in the evening, with a morsel of dry bread, I lie on the ground while they recline on downy couches. I eat what I have and wear old clothes while they are dressed as if before the Revolution, in silk stockings, trousers of varied colors, with damask vests and handkerchiefs, and boots in the English style. When ordered to depart I travel with my gun and pack on my back; but when these gentry go from one town to another their wardrobe goes in a carriage and they ride a lively horse that covers you with dust in summer and mud in winter, and, besides that, you have to yield to them the narrow paths made for pedestrians. Is that Equality for us poor slobs?

And finally, a warning:

In the end injustice produces independence. If it is to try our patience that you expose us for the last three months to committing excesses, forced by need, you should know that our patience is at an end and that it will be dangerous to keep trying us. Do you mean to mock us by telling us every day of millions that never come? If you are trying to arouse our appetite you may soon find that empty stomachs have no ears.

2. The Royalists and the Army in the Year IV (1796)

After their failure of Vendémiaire (October 1795) the royalists felt the need of working on the army, whose material and moral con- dition in 1796 seemed favorable to their enterprises. They turned first to some of its higher commanders. Thus they established contact with Pichegru, who had suppressed the troubles of Germinal of the Year III. They hoped through him to corrupt the spirit of the Army of the Rhine-Moselle. Entering into these counter-revolutionary plans, Pichegru began by checking the advance of his troops and treacherously allowing the Austrians to retake Mannheim. The loss of Mannheim gave a pretext for retreat, which turned into a rout. He put his men into very uncomfortable quarters for the winter of 1795–1796, and by emphasizing their privations tried to make them more amenable to royalist propaganda. Royalist agents like Fauche-Borel circulated freely in the camps, distributing money and clothing, as well as tracts like "The Tragedy of Louis XVI," "The Story of the Siege of Lyon," and "The Great Malady," all of which contained invitations to treason.

After Pichegru left his command, his successor, General Moreau, was also contacted by the royalists and compromised by them. They tried also to develop their propaganda in the Army of the Sambre-Meuse, where they "spread pamphlets written in a style calculated to please soldiers and incite desertion." There were so many cases of fraternization between French and Austrian officers that Joubert was obliged to intervene. Even some generals within France were won over by the royalists; one of them, Ferrand at Besançon, tried to subvert the 8th Hussars. Police reports in Paris indicated that "*chouans*" were on the lookout for army men every day and on the pretext of paying for drinks were turning their opinions toward a restoration of royalty.

The royalist propaganda had its greatest effect in the Army of the Rhine-Moselle, from which there were numerous desertions. Some deserters on returning to France made themselves agents in turn for the Bourbon cause. Thus Dupuichot, a *chasseur* of the

21st demi-brigade of light infantry, became a propagandist at Buix, where he concluded by loudly insulting the authorities: "Shit on the Republic! Long live the king! I am a soldier of the king!"

But the royalist efforts had less success than they hoped for. Discouragement among the troops might impel some to a passing revolt, a kind of military *jacquerie*, or others in an excited moment to shout a few ill-sounding words against the regime, but most remained attached to the Republic, which for them was "first of all the blood of brothers." Of what use were royalist pamphlets compared with that bible or holy book of the soldier, the control register of his unit, to be opened on the occasion of solemn reviews and in which the names of the dead were prominently displayed? What use were the words of a royalist agent when you remembered the "brother" dying in your arms, and crying *"Vive la Patrie!"* as he expired?

To counteract royalist propaganda and maintain the ties between the government and the army, the authorities organized civic ceremonies in the camps, as in the Year II. For this purpose the Thermidorians had already used the occasion of acceptance of the new constitution by the army. The Directory arranged ceremonies to commemorate the death of the tyrant Louis XVI, and for the swearing of eternal hatred of royalty, the celebration of victories, or expression of the national gratitude to defenders of the country. Most such *fêtes* were rather contrived and lacking in warmth. At the Army of the Rhine-Moselle, for example, the men were hastily assembled, speeches were delivered "breathing hatred of kings," and a few salvos of artillery were fired "to announce to the Austrians the inveterate hatred of the soldiers for kings." Then the men broke ranks. The *fête* had been simply one of their duties.

In other places such *fêtes* sometimes took on the appearance of those of the Year II. At Auch, for example, the soldiers were brought together in the Champ-de-Mars, where, in the presence of the multitude, they swore on their weapons an oath of eternal hatred of royalty and unswerving love of the Republic. They planted a tree of Liberty and sang "the sacred hymns that strike terror in the soul of royalists and act so powerfully" on the hearts of soldiers fighting the enemies of the Republic. The ceremony concluded with a dancing of the farandole.

Municipalities were urged to multiply these celebrations as a means of uniting the people and the army behind the representatives of the public power. At Chinon, on May 29, 1796, the military and civil authorities paraded through the streets to the town square, where the 6th Hussars were assembled. Fathers and mothers of soldiers from the commune marched with the official procession. To the sound of martial airs and republican chants, the parade passed around the tree of Liberty, then mounted a platform bearing a statue of Liberty and an altar of *la Patrie*. The commissioner pronounced a discourse on the undying recognition owed the French soldiers. Silence followed, and a magistrate read the names of men of the commune who had died for their country, enumerating the wounds they had received and the civic crowns they had been awarded. Citizens who had several sons with the colors were cited as examples to be admired. The parade reformed, and proceeded to the Place de la Prairie, where a bonfire was lit and cannon were fired. Republican songs were sung. The presiding official put together fourteen laurel branches as a symbol of the fourteen armies, and presented the resulting bundle to the officer in command of the 6th Hussars. A "republican ball" terminated this festival of Unity and Indivisibility of the Republic and its Army.

A recurrent theme marked these official speeches: "The army is the unshakable pillar of our constitutional edifice." But was the purpose, in these *fêtes*, to exhibit the union of the people and the army, or to demonstrate to the people that the government in power could count on military support? In the background of these commanded events, for the bourgeoisie, there was not only the haunting specter of royalist subversion but also the fear of reviving popular protest. The "anarchists" were at work, agitating the people and attempting to penetrate the army. It was no coincidence that most of these civic festivals occurred on May 29, 1796, hardly more than two weeks after Gracchus Babeuf had been arrested.

3. THE BABOUVISTS AND THE ARMY

It is well known that Babouvism involved an abrupt mutation. The Jacobin and sans-culotte ideologies were characterized by attachment to property based on personal labor. In Babouvism the abolition of property was to transform the conditions of social life; poverty, fanaticism, and moral perversity would disappear. Resources should be put in common, and commerce and money would be suppressed as sources of inequality. To bring about this distributive communism, Babeuf attracted some old Jacobins to the Pantheon Club. When the club was closed by Bonaparte on February 28, 1796, on orders from the Directory, Babeuf set up a secret Directory of Public Safety to prepare an insurrection of the popular masses and a seizure of power.

As a militant sans-culotte in the Year II and employee of the subsistence administration, Babeuf had drawn two lessons from a close observation of the role of the army at that time. First, that at the immediate level of revolutionary practice the Conspiracy for Equality had no chance to succeed except in alliance with the army. Second, in the longer run, for the new political and social system that he planned to establish, the army would serve as a school for young citizens, as one of the privileged places for civic education of new men, who would know nothing of selfishness, duplicity, ambition, or pride and be wholly devoted to the collective interest.

From among old army officers Babeuf and his friends chose five military agents, whose function was to coordinate the work of agitation and penetration in the army. They were Jean-Joseph Fion or Fyon, who was to make contact with retired soldiers at the Invalides; Germain, to work with the Police Legion, a force of repression created by the Directory and recruited from the army;

Massey, for the detachments stationed at Franciade (the former Saint-Denis); Vanneck, for other troops; and Grisel, for those at the camp of Grenelle adjoining Paris. To these five were soon added Massard and Rossignol. The latter, who had been a militant sans-culotte and a general in the Vendée, still had influence in popular circles of the Faubourg Saint-Antoine by which he could assure liaison between the people and the army. Much could also be expected from General Fion, a Belgian refugee in Paris from an early date, who then served in the French army from 1792 and won the rank of general by his bravery. He had helped in repression of the royalists in Vendémiaire.

The principal task of these Babouvist agents was to observe the officers of both subordinate and superior rank, in the various units stationed in the neighborhoods of Paris, and to identify those who were "most able to assist in the march of the movement" and fill responsible posts. They were to take note also of officers who might be able to obstruct "the development of the energy inspired by good principles and regenerative ideas." The agents were urged to form discussion groups along the boulevards, at the Tuileries, at the Palais National (the Louvre), in the smoke-filled rooms of the Beaubourg, and in the cafés called the Café Chrétien and the Bains Chinois. Conversation was opened in such places on the material and moral condition of the troops, their inadequate pay and subsistence, and the increasing severity of their discipline. Then the fate of the soldier was associated with that of the people. After talking for a while, it was recommended that the agents withdraw. As a group broke up, its members would find distributors of tracts and journals along their way. These distributors might be soldiers who knew almost nothing of the conspiracy, and who had been paid with a drink to hand out such materials to the public. The military agents also used women who haunted the cafés, such as Sophie Lapierre, who declaimed verses calling for insurrection and sang equalitarian songs for which the drinkers took up the chorus. Women of the people also offered Babouvist writings at the gates of barracks. Others went along with food sellers into the camps to spread the propaganda. These women continued their activities even after the arrest of Babeuf. Until June 1796 the Babouvist tracts and journals were easily sent to the armies; a clerk in the war ministry, won to their cause, used the minister's seal to dispatch them.

Most of these Babouvist writings intended for the army stressed the danger of a return of the royalists, and denounced the culpable indulgence toward them of a government that acted like the worst of tyrants toward the military and ordinary civilians. They emphasized the vanity of promises to the soldiers concerning aid to their families and the billion decreed for the veterans. They asserted that those called "anarchists" by the government only wanted justice and sacred equality for the soldiers, their brothers, and the citizens with empty stomachs. They usually ended with an assertion often heard in conversation in the cafés—the soldier would never fire on the people.

There is little evidence that allows us to judge the extent of Babouvist penetration of the army. The files on military justice, still in process of classification at the Archives de la Guerre, should provide more information than we have until now. An important source is the list of subscribers to Babeuf's journal, the *Tribun du peuple*. Giving the name, rank, and place of residence of officers who were subscribers to this journal, the list makes possible an investigation in the individual personnel records of these officers at the Archives de la Guerre.

The first on the list was a divisional general, Laronde, a Canadian born at Quebec. A man of forty-five, he was an old soldier, who had fought in the War of American Independence, then become a lieutenant in 1789. He took part in the wars of the Revolution, campaigned against the *chouans*, and was transferred to the Army of the Sambre-Meuse as general commanding the district of Givet. He was not included in the reorganization of general staffs in 1795, and so ceased his functions on June 19. He took part in the repression of royalists on 13 Vendémiaire, in the ranks of the 2nd battalion of the patriots of '89. He was restored to the service in October 1795, but authorized to take his retirement in February 1796.

The second, Jean-Baptiste Gardon, was commander of the 9th infantry demi-brigade. Son of a merchant, he had enlisted in the 3rd battalion of volunteers of the Nord in 1791. He was the immediate superior to the third man on our list of subscribers, Augros, head of the 2nd battalion of the 9th demi-brigade, who came from an artisan family; his father was a tanner. He married a grocer's daughter. Enlisting very young in the infantry, at the age of only seventeen, he was a sergeant-major by the time of the Revolution, in which he rose to battalion commander. He gave proof of bravery in all the campaigns in which he was involved.

On the next name on the list, Honoré Desplaces, the archives furnish little information. A soldier in one of the royal regiments in 1791, he was elected quartermaster-treasurer in 1792, and remained in this rank until 1796. Nothing is known of his social origin except that it enabled him to obtain the usually solid education needed by a quartermaster. Later, under the Empire, he became auditor in the court martial of the Kingdom of Italy. As a sergeant-major, first class, he went on half-pay like many others at the time of the Restoration. By 1825 we find him requesting award of the cross of Saint-Louis.

The last man, Jean Favre, was a picturesque character. In 1789 he was a Swiss guard, thirty-five years old. In the revolution of July 14 he joined the rioters who captured the Bastille. The new municipality made him head of an armed detachment to protect the grain convoys that supplied Paris. He entered the paid guard of Paris, and when it was dissolved went to war in the 102nd regiment of the new formation. He won the rank of lieutenant. From the Army of the Moselle to that of the Rhine, from the siege of Lyon to the invasion of Spain, from the Pyrenees to the Army of the Alps, he was involved in various affairs that produced more wounds than pecuniary advantage. In 1796, with his body cut by scars, he returned to his native place, Thonon in Savoy, where his father was a bourgeois. He led there the life of a retired soldier who reminisced on his campaigns and insisted on his continuing attachment to Jacobinism. He took part in pursuit of draft evaders and was especially impatient with the sons of well-to-do peasants. He was thus unpopular in some quarters. "Some respectable persons" denounced him to the authorities in 1796 for his "tyrannical and arbitrary ways." He retorted that a cabal of "royalists and a riffraff of priests" had formed against him. We find him later, during the Hundred Days, at Napoleon's side on the general staff of the 19th division.

To this list may be added other individual cases to show that the Babouvists had been able to reach influential military men. A certain Fonque was a staff officer in the defenses of Paris. A captain La Roche, prosecutor in the criminal court of the Doubs, was also "entirely won over to the anarchists, who consider him especially useful because in his position he can influence the judicial police of the department." It appears also that much was expected of a quartermaster Gauthier, and of a sub-lieutenant in the Gers-Gironde demi-brigade, both of whom circulated petitions in their units in favor of the Conspirators for Equality.

Beside these individual cases there were collective efforts, first of all in the Police Legion of Paris. On learning of Babouvist influence in this body, the government ordered two of its battalions to leave the city, but they mutinied and set up a committee to get in touch with the Babouvist secret directory through someone named Germain. The mutiny was stopped by dismissal of the suspected elements. It is evident, as shown by Jean Tulard, that the insubordination was limited in extent, and that the two insurgent battalions were motivated as much by fear of departing for the front, and by chagrin at seeing certain financial misdoings exposed, as by any real attachment to the Babouvist cause. But the Police Legion was not the only armed force in Paris to be penetrated by the Babouvists.

On each *décadi* the troops stationed in or near Paris furnished more than 2,000 men to act as sentries for the legislative assemblies and as guards at the bridges, the Palais de Justice, the Argenterie, the Trésorerie Nationale, the powder works at the Thermes, the prisons, the ministries, and the entrances to the city. These sentries were approached by agents of the Equals, who found a timely moment to talk with them in local grog shops. It was these soldiers that the police reported as "corrupted by the anarchists" shortly before the arrest of Babeuf. "They loudly declared that they hoped for a great change very soon." Threatened with being transferred to some point far from Paris, they said that "we have all sworn not to have done to us what was done to the Police Legion. We will not leave Paris before slicing off seven or eight hundred heads, and after that the people will triumph, and we will be called the saviors of France." From February to July 1796 the commissioner to the Army of the Interior, Lefebvre, and generals Laubadère, Duvigneau, and Foissac-Latour, commander of the first division, repeatedly alerted the government to the dangers of agitation and insubordination because of the bad material condition of the troops, from which "malevolent elements sought to profit by lighting brands of discord" at the camp at Grenelle.

Food shortage and "anarchist" propaganda combined to produce at Grenelle a desertion rate that soon rose to 10 percent. An inquiry launched by Foissac-Latour revealed that deserters were joining a group at Rueil supposedly formed on orders from General Hoche and commanded by a certain sergeant Jourdan. This man, who came from the Midi, had been a soldier in the pre-Revolutionary Bourbonnais regiment and a drum-major in the paramilitary "revolutionary army" of the Year II; then he managed to get into the Police Legion and become a sergeant-major there. "His own friends," reported Foissac-Latour, "accused him of being a Jacobin."

Early in May 1796 the police arrested Jean-Baptiste Meunier. He was a young man of nineteen who had served for seven months in the Gravilliers battalion when it operated in the Vendée, and then had been assigned to the former Marat legion as a sergeant-major. On his return to Paris the Babouvists contacted him, and he distributed for them on the boulevards such tracts as "The People Enlightened," "The Police Legion to Itself" and "The People of Paris to the Police Legion." He was brought into court on May 4. He pleaded drunkenness as an excuse; he had been made to drink, and some papers were then slipped to him to distribute. Who had done this? He did not know. But twelve days later he retracted his statement. He now said that he was part of the conspiracy, and had been present at a gathering of soldiers at Versailles, "outside the chateau, not far from the lake." Here the Babouvist Félix Lepeletier had made a speech in the presence of various generals and officers. Meunier said he had recognized a sergeant from the 21st *chasseurs*, stationed at the Grenelle camp, with whom he had once been a fellow prisoner. He himself had acted as messenger for Lepeletier. He was sentenced to prison, and was later to appear at the trial of Babeuf and attempt to say as little as possible against the accused.

The Babouvists, then, had succeeded in gaining allies in Paris and in the Army of the Interior. Did they have similar success in other demi-brigades?

When the Army of Italy invaded that country, some Italian patriots accompanied it from Nice. They were adepts of the Equals. In addition, one of the commissioners of the Directory attached to the Army of Italy was Saliceti, a friend of Philippe Buonarroti, the companion of Babeuf. Using Saliceti as an intermediary, the Babouvists were able to carry on their propaganda in the Army of Italy. The government became concerned, and ordered an investigation. The commissioner Garrau reported that the spirit of the army was not contaminated: "The defenders of liberty belong to no faction."

In the Army of the Rhine-Moselle, a few days before the arrest of Babeuf, there were still to be found officers, like a lieutenant Paul, who petitioned for a return of the Terror, to be exercised especially against the rich. It was also to denounce the "gilded bellies" that some volunteers at the Grenelle camp sent a letter to the Directory well after Babeuf's arrest. The Jacobins continued to work on them according to their general, Foissac-Latour. On August 11 he had collected all the "anarchist" tracts and ordered them burned. Like other officers in the Army of the Interior he was willing to act as an apostle of the government. He repeated the old theme already used in 1795: the "anarchists" were allies of the British, and to follow them was treason. In the night of September 9–10, 1796, some Jacobins came to the Grenelle camp to precipitate a revolt. The government had been warned of their attempt two weeks before. It let the agitation proceed so that the guilty men could be arrested. They were very few in the ranks of the army.

If the Conspiracy of Equals failed in the army, it was not only because of lack of means or of time, but also because the army for a year had been withdrawing into itself, and had fallen completely under the thumb of its generals.

CHAPTER XIV

• • •

The Army and the
Coup d'État of Fructidor,
Year V (1797)

While the civilian commissioners of the Directory lost their authority over the troops, the prestige of victory and stability of command strengthened the empire of the generals. One by one, they took over the institutional mechanisms of the army. They fed and paid their men. They knew how to use the language of the militants of the Year II. *La Patrie*, they told their subordinates, had fled into the camps. The generals provided the government with the gold needed to keep the state alive, and to a large extent they dictated the foreign policy of France. In 1797 they intervened to break up a political majority elected by the notables to sit in the two legislative chambers.

1. THE ARMY ENTIRELY IN THE HANDS OF ITS GENERALS

From 1795 to 1797 military justice and administration passed under the generals' control. A new law on military justice was promulgated by the Convention on September 18, 1795, that is, about three months after the insurrection of Prairial and a few weeks before the royalist uprising of Vendémiaire—a date possibly not accidental. The law marked an early phase in the abandonment by the state of its authority over the army. Where previously the courts martial had been composed of civilian judges, with juries made up half of military men and half of civilians, the new law provided councils made up only of military men, of whom no especial judicial competence was required. But these courts were not yet entirely subject to the army chiefs. They retained a slight touch of democracy: three common soldiers sat along with three NCOs and three officers. The soldiers took an active part, even denouncing the generals in 1795, the better to defend their comrades and obstruct the proper course of judicial proceedings. Some had the audacity, according to higher officers in the Army of Italy, not to take the word of officers making charges against a particular soldier; they even demanded witnesses! They should, according to the generals, "rely blindly on what officers have written or caused to be written, whatever the grounds of the indictment." The generals continued to make such complaints in 1796, finding the military courts too slow and the penalties too light, so that in November the courts were replaced by permanent councils established within each division of the army. These councils revived the earlier pattern of a court with a fixed composition regardless of the rank of the accused. They were composed entirely of officers, except for one NCO appointed by the division commander. The commander had the power, in the interests of the service, to change the membership of the council, all or in part. The whole regulation recalled the similar councils of the Old Regime. In its reactionary character this law carried forward the trend set by the law of September 1795. It put the soldiers in a stricter dependence on their generals.

There were soldiers who denounced both these laws. One of them wrote:

> The critical state of affairs has brought an alarming legislation for the army. With excessively severe penalties, arbitrary procedures, and too much power in the hands of the generals, the soldier has almost as much to fear from justice as from the weapons of the enemy.

Soldiers at the Grenelle camp protested in 1796:

> We are told that there will no longer be any volunteers, but only officers, in both the administrative and military councils. Allow us to make a few observations. We have believed you worthy of hearing the naked truth, which has never been hated except by tyrants. As we are sworn enemies of lying and base adulation, we are finally making an end to a culpable silence. From now on our councils will be like those in the days of the kings. No more need be said; it remains only for us to be punished with the flat of the sword as under the Old Regime. That is what is already happening to the people.

As these soldiers pointed out, it was not only the military courts but also the administrative councils that were being restructured. The administrative council had been a victory of democracy for the troops. By it, the soldier could make his voice heard in his battalion. Henceforth the generals dominated the councils. For promotions, they nominated whom they pleased to the Directory, which always ratified their nominations. They could thus enlarge their own following, and rid themselves of "anarchists" who wished to perpetuate in the army the habits of the Jacobins of the Year II.

The generals—Hoche and Bonaparte in particular—were impatient of the control over them still exercised by the civilian commissioners of the Directory. They obtained their suppression in December 1796. The Directors—La Reveillière, Reubell, and Barras—alarmed by the political success of royalists disguised as moderates, knew that in case of internal danger they would need the support of the troops. To sacrifice the civil commissioners was to please the generals. It was a measure heavy with consequences, for the commissioner, present in the army, was the ear of the civil power, and represented a government to which the soldier always had recourse in the event of abuse of authority by his superiors. Henceforth the soldier would know no other authority than that of the generals. These latter, disembarrassed of the commissioners, were free to carry on requisitions and "contributions" in the conquered countries as they saw fit. To leave to their discretion the use of the gold thus accumulated was to provide them with a means to win favor with their troops, to whom they distributed gold pieces as supplements to their pay.

The recall of the commissioners also left the generals free to play the diplomatic game. They accepted or rejected peace terms as they chose. Indefinite pursuit of conquest gave the soldier a security against the poverty that would follow demobilization, and so assured the generals of possessing a more amenable instrument. In the end, as Mme de Staël observed, the policy of conquest was to lead to military government. At the moment, as noted by the royalist journalist Richer-Sérizy, the soldier saw nothing but "his general who led him to victory, shared in his glory and dangers, blamed all his troubles on higher authority, relieved his sufferings, attended to his feeding and clothing, and often paid him with gold won by his conquests. He might have added, "and transferred the cult of *la Patrie* to the general's person." In fact the generals, and notably Bonaparte, employed a whole arsenal of psychological propaganda to gain a firmer hold on their men's hearts and minds.

The Directory unintentionally helped Bonaparte to develop the cult of personality in his army. On the initiative of Carnot, it created a military press. The *Journal des défenseurs de la Patrie* was meant to unify the armies and put them on guard against adversaries of the government. But in form and content it presented the army no longer as a force whose mission was to achieve victory, but as a body apart from the Nation or at least attached to it only through the medium of the Directory. For the bonds of fraternity that in the Year II had joined citizens and citizen-soldiers, the *Journal des défenseurs de la Patrie* substituted a dependence of the army on the executive power. "Under the reign of the Thermidorian bourgeoisie," as the historian M. Martin has written, "the prime civic and military duty was obedience." The guarantee of discipline was in the commanding officer, and the source of discipline was the admiration in which he was held. The Directory, in its press, gave the highest place to the principal commanding generals as go-betweens between the State and the soldiers. It recounted their acts and deeds, attributed victories mainly to their merit, recommended a strict obedience to their orders, and pushed praise to the point of eulogy and adulation. The net image of Bonaparte given by the *Journal des défenseurs de la Patrie* was not only that of a victorious general but also of an heir to the philosophy of the Enlightenment, a diplomat, and a man of government, as well as an eminent strategist.

Bonaparte lost no time in spreading this image. In two journals that he caused to be written in the summer of 1797, the *Courrier de l'armée d'Italie* and the *France vue de l'armée d'Italie*, the soldiers were invited to the diplomats' table to see their general debating the destiny of Europe, and gained access to the secrecy of cabinets or the gossip of salons, so they could hear the questions put to their general and the replies that he made. The State was eclipsed, leaving only the general to be seen as the incarnation of the Nation. Bonaparte's journals gave the impression of a national unity against a "party of Clichyans"[1] in which royalists were concealed. The army was thus prepared psychologically for Caesarism. As mandatory of the Nation, it was to urge its commander to intervene to save the Republic from the henchmen of kings.

To strengthen his hold on the army entrusted to him, Bonaparte used other methods also. As in the year II, the letterheads of battalions were adorned with emblematic devices. In the foreground had figured *la Patrie, Liberté*, and *Egalité*. But now the general appeared alone, prancing among his troops with banners streaming to announce his military successes. The flag, which had symbolized the unity of army and Nation, now became a sign of attachment of the army to its general. Bonaparte changed the flags of units in the Army of Italy. They became alike in their arrangement of colors, but each carried, with its unit number, a motto

---

[1] The Clichy group, formed of constitutional monarchists, met at the townhouse of the former secretary of state, Bertin, which was at Clichy.

telling the deeds accomplished under its commander's orders: "I was not worried; the 32nd was there." There was a new encouragement of esprit de corps and emulation among the demi-brigades. All were to remember that their glory had been won under the orders of Bonaparte.

The new flags were distributed with great pomp. Their delivery gave a chance for personal contact and an exchange of words between the men and their commander. Whether spontaneous or contrived, some of these occasions allowed the soldiers to manifest an attachment to their chief that had formerly been reserved for the Nation. At Milan, on July 14, 1797, while the army paraded before General Bonaparte, a corporal of the 9th demi-brigade approached him and said, using the *tu* of familiar address:

> General, you have saved the Republic. Your men, for whom it is glorious to belong to this invincible army, will make a rampart for you with their bodies. Save the Republic! and may the hundred thousand men who compose this army close ranks to defend liberty!

The citizen-soldiers thus gave up their destiny into the hands of a providential leader who identified himself with *la Patrie*.

Bonaparte also used military celebrations to anchor this spirit more deeply in his troops. They were in some ways like the celebrations of the Year II. They were *fêtes civiques*, recalling the great principles for which comrades in arms had given their lives: liberty, equality, and unity of the Republic. As *fêtes civiques* they expressed also the association of army and people. At Vicenza and Padua, the local Italian authorities and citizens liberated from the yoke of aristocracy were invited to attend the military ceremony. Everywhere the image of the chief was displayed. At Vicenza, for example, the *fête* of July 14 took place in a field arranged to resemble the Champ-de-Mars. At the entrance was set up an arch of triumph "of simple and antique construction," and Bonaparte, with his hand on a trophy, surveyed the scene "with a calm and satisfied eye."

These festivals always ended in a fraternal banquet in which the generals, the demi-brigade commanders, and some old campaigners chosen for their merits took part together. Two themes were heard when the toasts were offered: the crimes of aristocrats and their allies, and the army as the regenerating force for society. The army must be ready not only against the foreign foe but against the enemy within. The commander of the 12th light infantry, brandishing his glass, proposed a toast "to the union of French republicans; may they imitate the Army of Italy, and with its support regain the energy that is proper for the foremost people of the earth." So within a few years the spirit of the troops was subjugated by the generals, and most especially by Bonaparte. As an officer named Drouault of the 33rd demi-brigade recognized, "In Italy we have neither law nor government! The generals are the sovereigns!"

2. THE ARMY BREAKS ITS SILENCE

The elections of 1797 for the renewal of a third of the chambers produced a victory for the "party of order," that is, a majority of more or less disguised royalists. The combined chambers then took measures announcing the political line they would follow. They abrogated the laws of 3 and 4 Brumaire, Year IV, which had excluded returned émigrés, deportees, and seditious persons from future elections. Returned émigrés and refractory priests became more visible in the provinces, where they threatened persons who had purchased the confiscated properties. In some places, in the west and southwest, republicans were murdered.

The Directors finally took alarm. La Reveillière, Barras, and Reubell turned to the troops, arousing their fear of the dangers of royalist subversion. The armies hardly needed such a call. They replied with messages not only to the government but to the departmental authorities. Disregarding article 275 of the constitution prohibiting political deliberation in the army, and article 364 forbidding collective petitions, the army spoke.

In the Army of Italy this was done, at least partly, at the instigation of its commander. We have a letter written by the 4th division artillery, addressed to Bonaparte:

> General, we have received this morning your letter of the 26th of this month, and we make haste to reply for our unit. You are a republican, Citizen General, and so are we; and we renew to you our oath to defend the constitution of the Year III against all enemies whatsoever, acting with you, and unto death. *Salut et respect.*

In his proclamation of July 14 Bonaparte had sketched some ideas for the men under his command, who now recopied them. The more the counter-revolutionary cries were heard, they said, the more it became the sacred duty of good citizens to show themselves. If the brave did not face the cowards, the efforts of conspirators might trouble France, bring back the days of anarchy, wear down the weak, exasperate the strong, and reproduce within families the scenes of bloodshed and revenge. Royalism was raising its head and multiplying murders in the departments; brothers in arms returning from Italy to France were being killed. This must be ended. For example:

> The Army of Italy is ready to return over the Alps bearing thunderbolts. [The royalists] will be annihilated, and France purged of its cruel enemies.

Or again:

> Speak out, Citizen Directors, and soon the rascals that defile the soil of liberty will exist no longer. We have the power of life and death over them, and their pardon depends on our bayonets.

Some addresses made additions to the sketch proposed by Bonaparte. Those from the 5th division drew a parallel between attacks on the republican government and those directed against Bonaparte. Those of the 1st cavalry division saw peace as an Austrian maneuver to gain time and sow discord within the Republic. Several addresses associated the Army of Italy with the other armies in its will to punish. "The Army of Italy," wrote its 4th and 5th divisions, "is a sister to the others, and joins hands with them across the separation by space, mountains, and rivers."

While Bernadotte's division sent in addresses in a more moderate style, the 2nd division of the Côte de Nice, the 8th division, the 4th demi-brigade, and the 6th battalion of sappers addressed the Directory in language verging on an actual warning. As one expressed it:

> What use is it for us to have brave generals and drive off the satellites of the allied tyrants? What difference does it make to defeat kings, if we are defeated by weakness and apathy that will bring a new enslavement? Republicans are oppressed, assassinated, or put to flight, and the government seems unmoved or recoiling before the factious. . . . Do you want to go back? Or to stop before reaching the goal of the course we are now in? . . . Or share the crimes of those usurpers of the mandate of the sovereign people who dishonor the national representation by their factions?

Or another:

> We want the constitutional laws to be respected and executed, and for the law to strike the enemies of our just cause without pity. It is time to put an end to their excesses of infamy. Let there be no more indulgence or half measures.

And again:

> Renounce if you can that mistrustful spirit that is contrary to morality, that pernicious system of balance and counterweights between parties that can be upset by a trifle, and which makes the public peace and social well-being depend on next to nothing. See the harm done to us by the inconstancy and changeableness of your administration, which is

the consequence of these false principles. Put your confidences in the founders of the Republic. It is high time.

And still again:

Remember that we are your first offspring and that you exist only by us. . . . Decide at last to support the Republicans, or else fall victim to your own weakness and vacillation.

These addresses, many of which came from Augereau's division, revived the style of the Year II in contrasting "frank, honest, virtuous republicans" to "émigré scoundrels, monsters of furious and menacing mien, avid for blood, frenetic, cunning, perfidious, and cowardly." To the opprobrium poured on the aristocracy of birth, they added ignominy for the aristocracy of wealth: "Those who by the most shameful methods have sucked the blood of the people and grow fat on its remains."

The Army of the Sambre-Meuse was slower in sending in addresses. Its commander, Hoche, on the anniversary of August 10, pronounced a speech glorifying the army for having "alone" enlarged the territory of the Republic and helped foreign peoples to throw off the yoke under which they labored. He thus prepared his army for a possible intervention against "fanatics and rebels against republican laws." General Ney (then with this army) called attention to himself by an attack on the Clichyans when the toasts were offered. "Great politicians of Clichy," he said, "please have the kindness not to force us to order the charge." The addresses from the Army of the Sambre-Meuse resembled those from the Army of Italy in depicting the internal situation of France as menaced by royalism and in invoking the shades of dead comrades to justify military intervention. They differed from those of the Army of Italy in their constant concern to link the fate of the army with that of the people; they held that royalists in attacking the constitution were attacking the citizens as a whole, and especially the buyers of nationalized property, and the citizen-soldiers.

Similar themes were taken up in an address from the Army of

the Alps, dated August 27, and hence not arriving until after the Fructidor coup d'état. The 23rd demi-brigade accused Kellerman of having forbidden such addresses. As for the army of Moreau, it sent no addresses, except for a few soldiers of its right wing.

The armies of Italy and the Sambre-Meuse wrote also to the departmental authorities. A few complaints were addressed to the legislative chambers. The army was supposed not to "deliberate." It did so, as reflected in these addresses containing thousands of signatures. Was this not a sign of military dictatorship to come?

3. THE COUP D'ÉTAT OF 18 FRUCTIDOR, YEAR V

The constitution of the Year III provided no solution in the event of a conflict between the Directors and the legislative chambers. Only force could resolve it. The royalists made preparations to use force. But they did so badly. They could count on bands of "Chouans" in Paris, which were in contact with Pichegru, president of the Five Hundred. They hoped also for aid from Moreau and his army. Of the five Directors, Barthélemy inclined to the royalists and Carnot rejected the use of force against the chambers, but the three most threatened by the royalists, Barras, Reubell, and La Réveillière, called Hoche and Bonaparte to their aid. Bonaparte promised money but sent none. Instead, he sent to Paris one of his chief subordinates, Augereau. Intent on legitimating his personal policy in Italy, Bonaparte waited upon the turn of events. He was in touch with both camps, with Barthélemy, and with Carnot through his envoy Lavalette. Carnot, believing he could maintain legality by playing on divisions among the royalists, advised Bonaparte to wait.

The first to act therefore was Hoche, commanding general of the Army of the Sambre-Meuse. On the pretext of transferring some of his troops to Brest for an expedition to Ireland, he had them march on Paris. In mid-July some of these troops approached the "constitutional cordon" around Paris, within which no armed force was allowed to enter. On the 14th the "triumvirs" appointed Hoche as minister of war. He had to resign on the 22nd, being not of the constitutional age, and subject to attack in the chambers. His troops continued to invest Paris. A majority in the chambers drew up an accusation against the triumvirs and sought the support of Carnot. But Carnot refused; he had just learned of the treason of Pichegru through some papers of a royalist agent, the Count d'Antraigues, which Bonaparte had seized in Italy. Augereau took command of the Paris division, and one of Hoche's generals, Chérin, took that of the Director's guard. On the night of 17–18 Fructidor (September 3–4) Paris was occupied by the army, which found allies on the ground in the hundreds of detached officers who had come to the ministry in Paris to seek new assignments.

These officers were used by the triumvirs. The files at the National Archives contain a "list of officers present on the day of 18 Fructidor, on whose requests the Directory had yet to act." It includes twenty-seven names, a very small sample of the detached officers taking part in the coup. In the absence of other documentation, we think the information in it is not to be disregarded.

Of the twenty-seven officers, twenty-one had been in the army of the Old Regime with an impressive total length of service. Hallez, a captain in the gendarmerie when the Revolution began, entered the Gardes françaises in 1792. He was made battalion commander by drawing lots. When a representative on mission in the Year II disapproved of this manner of appointment, Hallez was suspended from his command and since 1795 had haunted the streets in the neighborhood of the ministry. Of the twenty-one from the Old Regime, nine had been present in the army for from thirteen to seventeen years, and nine others from eighteen to twenty-seven years.

These veterans were mostly of subordinate rank: two noncoms, three lieutenants, and thirteen captains. Among the nine of higher rank we note the presence of a brigade commander and former noble, Dejean. He had been a cadet in the 18th infantry regiment in 1777, then a dragoon in the Legion of Condé. A battalion chief in 1793, he received command of the 7th demi-bri-gade in 1796. Since then he had had no appointment. Among these higher officers, three had belonged to the Police Legion, which had been infiltrated by Babouvism. The Babouvist General Fyon, who had taken part in the repression of royalists in Vendémiaire, was post commandant on 18 Fructidor for the area comprising the Gravilliers, the Barriers, and the region between the rue Antoine and Le Roule. Of the same kind were captain Renaudin, Captain Massuet, and Battalion Commander Hallez, who had been with Bonaparte in helping the republican government to put down the royalist rising of 13 Vendémiaire.

Further information is furnished by a list of officers relating to the faubourg Antoine. On the day of 18 Fructidor three hundred men from the faubourgs, with two cannon, came to offer their services to the Directory. They were commanded by unassigned officers. Such were captains Lefaure, Poilpré, and Massuet, and sub-lieutenant Crevôt. Some, like Massuet and Poilpré, had been chiefs of the Paris cannoneers and had friendly relations with the sans-culottes.

Among the actors on 18 Fructidor there were, then, citizen-soldiers who, by their presence, marked the continuity that military men wished to see between early days of the Revolution and the time of the Directory. But these officers got no reward from the Directors. Only one was reintegrated, six others saw their cases left open but delayed, and all the others remained without employment.

After 18 Fructidor the armies—now including the Rhine-Moselle—again dispatched addresses to the Directory. Most of them resembled those that preceded the coup. Thus the Liège division wrote:

We have paid for the Republic by six years of fatigues, privation, and misery; we have cemented it with our blood; we wish it to remain intact. Let them appear—those fanatical priests that wave brands of discord and light the fires of civil war. Let them appear—those wild anarchists who want to swim again in blood. We shall be ready for them.

Despite their allusion to "anarchists" almost all these military addresses called for Terror against conspirators:

There must be no grace for conspirators. Indulgence toward them is atrocious, clemency is parricide. Let the axe of the law strike them like lightning. . . . We will not have triumphed against the phalanxes of despotism only to become the laughingstock of nations.

Several addresses, notably those coming from Moreau's troops, called for a prompt purging of the civil administrations and the army.

Very noticeable in these addresses is how the army persisted in seeing itself as the watchful guardian of the Revolutionary legacy. As such, it engaged in a continuous and open scolding of men in the government. The 30th demi-brigade of the Army of the Interior wrote, still using the familiar or patronizing *tu*:

We might today, as passive witnesses of the progress of royalism, reprimand the public patience and perhaps your indulgent attitude. . . . We speak to you frankly in assuring you of our attachment to the Constitution. You know the danger to the Republic, and you wish to save it; remember then that there can be no transaction with crime, and that the law must either be cleansed of its stain or declare itself impotent. . . . In that case our battalions, though widely dispersed, will quickly rally to the flag of Liberty, avenge it with lightning speed, and leave to our armies at the front only the task of mopping up the bloody traces of a severe punishment.

The first two battalions of the Indre-et-Loire, in addressing the administration at Tours, expressed their desire to see the earliest possible purge, to chase away the "gilded youth," and be everlastingly vigilant against *ennemis de la Patrie*. They said they were well informed of what was happening in their home department, and were ready to intervene against traitors if stern action was not taken soon enough against them.

The idea of the vigilant citizen, the citizen examining the acts of his mandatories and intervening with them if necessary, the citizen executing a prompt vengeance against the lukewarm and the vicious, was an echo of the lesson learned in the Year II, which the army now recited to justify its interference in the civil city.

It will be said that the army intervened on appeal from men in the government, that these latter had intended and controlled what the military did, and that the state remained in the hands of civilians. True, but not the whole truth. The army had spoken, and it took action against a freely elected national representation. It declared aloud that it would intervene again if necessary. The cuirass of the pretorian was concealed ever more awkwardly under the toga of the statesman. The coup d'état of 18 Fructidor marks a capital date in the relations between the state and its army.

CONCLUSION

• • •

The Army and Bonaparte's Coup d'État of 18 Brumaire, Year VIII (1799)

After the peace of Compo Formio, concluded with the Austrians on October 18, 1797, the "second" Directory entered upon a policy of expansion that disturbed all Europe.[1] In 1798 the free city of Mulhouse was annexed, and Geneva became the chief town of a new French department of the Léman. The Batavian Republic was reorganized and bound more closely to France. The same happened in the Helvetic Republic, which replaced the old Swiss confederation. The Cisalpine Republic was obliged, on February 21, 1798, to sign a commercial accord and treaty of alliance. After a riot in Rome on December 28, 1797, a Roman Republic was created and the pope deported to France. The King of Sardinia had to accept a French alliance, and the French occupied Turin. Four French departments were set up on the German left bank of the Rhine. Austria expected to receive compensation, which the French refused, thus pushing Austria toward England. A Second Coalition was formed against France (April to December 1798),

---

[1] By the "second" Directory are meant the five Directors in office after the ouster of Carnot and Barthélemy in the coup d'état of Fructidor. They were more inclined than the "first" Directory to keep up the momentum of the Revolution.

composed of England, Austria, Turkey, the Kingdom of Naples, and Russia.

The second Directory, to provide manpower for this expansionist policy, obtained the enactment of conscription in the Jourdan law of September 5, 1798. Compulsory military service became a permanent institution for young unmarried men of ages twenty to twenty-five. To avoid a new revolt the Vendée was exempted. Elsewhere there was lively resistance. Insurrection broke out in the Flemish provinces of Belgium. In other departments the first levy failed to produce the expected numbers: of 203,000 conscripted only 143,000 were found fit, only 97,000 really departed, and only 74,000 arrived in the camps. A law of 28 Germinal Year VII (April 17, 1799) allowed conscripts to assemble in advance to choose volunteers, fill the contingent by drawing lots among themselves, and enable those drawing unfavorable lots to purchase replacements. The army received 57,000 men in this way.

The law thus tended toward a militarization of society as desired by career soldiers. It also revived in the army the popular character that it had had in the Year II. The conscripts, assigned to the existing demi-brigades, were surrounded by men who gave them their military, and sometimes a political, education.

The Jacobins benefited from the coup d'état of Fructidor by spreading their propaganda in what were now called "constitutional circles." They made new efforts to influence the army. They invited soldiers to the civic festivals and banquets that they organized. They supported requests submitted by soldiers to administrative officials. They demanded payment of the billion for veterans. To finance compensation for the troops they called for the sale of confiscated émigré properties and new taxes on the rich. After the coup d'état of 30 Prairial Year VII (June 18, 1799), and with the foreign menace again looming over France, they brought about a decree of a new *levée en masse*, forced taxation of the rich, and the law of hostages.

The army remained dominated by its generals, who continued to use its republican spirit for their own purposes. The Directory attempted to control the generals by reviving the office of civil commissioners, who were to have the sole power to levy contributions and make requisitions in the occupied countries. Conflict between generals and commissioners followed immediately: Amelot against Joubert in northern Italy, or Faipoult against Championnet when the latter governed Rome as an absolute ruler. In Paris, as George Lefebvre observed, there was formed a veritable party of generals who duped the Jacobins by claiming to oppose the commissioners because they were *ci-devants* and aristocrats. The Directory as re-formed after 30 Prairial became more and more captive to the generals, and again suppressed the commissioners in September and October 1799. The civil powers, in the words of Jacques Godechot, thus lost "the only means to prevent the army from intervening in politics, the soldiers from issuing 'pronouncements,' and the generals who manipulated the soldiers from playing at being the government." In addition, Bonaparte had just disembarked from Egypt.

Political leaders grouped around Sieyès took alarm at the action of the neo-Jacobins and a new radicalization of the Revolution. They wanted a *revision* of the constitution, with installation of a power strong enough to stabilize the Revolution and ward off the perils from both "anarchists" and royalists. With some aid from financial circles, these "revisionists" made preparation for a parliamentary coup d'état. To keep order in the streets they needed a "sword," a general with enough prestige to have the army behind him and hold the Jacobins and the counter-revolutionaries in check. They thought that they had found such a man in Joubert, who however was killed on the battlefield. The revisionists then turned to Moreau, but police reports raised suspicion of his alliance with royalists. They then thought of Bernadotte; but might not Bernadotte, who listened to both the revisionists and the Jacobins, simply use them both the better to establish his personal power? They then turned to Bonaparte, just arrived from Egypt, as their best recourse.

Despite his setback in Egypt Bonaparte preserved all the glory of his Italian campaign. An astute propaganda, orchestrated by him and his brother Lucien (who was president of the Five Hundred, the lower legislative house), presented him as the savior that France awaited. Very adroitly, he made himself appear as "the most civilian of the generals." Putting aside military accoutrements, wearing bourgeois attire to receive politicians that came to seek his advice, scarcely going out in Paris except to attend sessions of the Institute, of which he was a member, he pretended to be no more than a simple citizen, a kind of Cincinnatus ready to defend the Republic without personal ambition. He outwitted his civilian visitors and built up a military clientele. He renewed his ties with officers and soldiers in the garrison at Paris through his brother Louis, his son-in-law Eugène de Beauharnais, his brother-in-law General Leclerc, his future brother-in-law Murat, and such Corsican friends as Sebastiani. As commander of the Army of the Interior in 1795 Bonaparte had attracted officers of the gendarmerie and adjutants of the National Guard to himself. All now came to put themselves under his orders. Thus, even before receiving a new command, Bonaparte controlled a part of the troops in the capital: the dragoons under Sebastiani, the 21st *chassuers* in which Murat had once served, and the 6th, 76th, and 96th demi-brigades of infantry which contained a good many soldiers formerly in the Army of Italy.

When the political coup d'état seemed to be going badly on 19 Brumaire, and Bonaparte was denounced by the deputies as a conspirator who should be outlawed, he owed his success to the intervention of soldiers led by Murat. The *coup d'état politique* became a *coup d'état militaire*. As First Consul, a little later, he tried to hide the facts. To overcome the fears of military dictatorship felt by the notables he gave his reassurances:

> In every country force yields to civilian qualities. . . . I predicted to certain scrupulous soldiers that military government would never take hold in France. . . . I do not govern as a general, but because the nation sees in me the civilian qualities suited for government.

He promised a government of social defense, friendly to order, respectful to property, and committed to peace.

The war carried on by Europe against the Revolution had generated a power that, while safeguarding the gains of the bourgeoisie and the peasantry, also imposed itself upon them. The military had gradually become distinct from civilian society. In the military society we see a blend of the military ethic born in the eighteenth century with the moral spirit of the Revolution. In the eighteenth century a new military ethic replaced the old warrior's code. The new ethic praised such physical qualities as sturdiness and endurance, but it put a value also on cool conduct, discipline, and a spirit of sacrifice. The honor of the soldier consisted in accepting the discipline of the unit to which he belonged, and in developing his powers to repress anguish at the moment of combat; it lay in going beyond himself and in a readiness to accept death as well as inflict it. These qualities were expressed differently from one regiment to another. Each unit was animated by its own esprit de corps, which produced emulation but might also result in sanguinary brawls. The Revolutionary Government of the Year II had tried to suppress such esprit de corps, but it reappeared under the Directory. A man was of the "Army of Italy" or the "Army of the Sambre-Meuse"; he belonged to the "Unstoppable 57th" or to the 32nd of "proverbial assurance in battle." There was trouble for anyone who derided such claims or risked provoking a comrade to a fight. In 1796, at Orléans, when a soldier of the 2nd battalion of the Gard was killed in a duel by a cavalryman of the 21st, a hundred men were chosen by each unit to do battle. The generals often shut their eyes on such actions; esprit de corps gave them a more reliable following.

But above this esprit de corps and traditional ethic there was now and henceforth, among all soldiers, the pride of being sons of the Great Nation. They thought of themselves as the vanguard of a France which, by them and through them, had imposed the Rights of Man and Citizen on the kings of the earth. Sacrifice was accepted in the name of the principles expressed in this Declaration. Every victory proved for them that men who were free and equal were superior to the mercenaries of kings. In the art of war, according to officers of the Old Regime, only those could excel who combined experience with birth. Now combat carried on by an army of "cobblers," led by officers originating in the people, proved that the former masters were in no way superior, that they could be made to kneel before the democracy in arms. Those men were the sons of an egalitarian Revolution, and well into the Consulate and Empire, at the moment of the charge, it was still the hymn of the Marseillaise or a song of the sans-culottes that drove them forward:

> To the nobles we present
> The precious boon of Liberty.
> Let the buggers now consent
> To bow before Equality.
> A thousand gods! Together we
> Will fire our guns and break our chains,
> Until by all our strife and pains
> The whole world can at last be free.[2]

This military society no longer recognized itself in the civil society from which it had issued. It saw citizens who, doubting the destiny of the Nation, and so ignoring the sufferings of departed comrades, were seeking compromise with the adversary. In France, as it seemed to the military, everone thought only of himself and was plunged in a mad pursuit of profit. Civilian society, in their judgment, was a society of "immorality and filth." It was unstable and disorderly, harsh and competitive, unlike their own society in which the individual knew how to forget himself for the common good. In the army, they thought, one found courage, devotion, probity, and mutual helpfulness among friends. Outside it were fear, refusal of personal sacrifice, dishonesty, and incessant

---

[2] Freely translated or adapted. For the original, see Appendix II.

rivalry of all against all. Where was the unity that republicans owed to each other?

Many soldiers thought a regeneration of civilian society by the military to be necessary. As a certain Captain Simon wrote in a published pamphlet of 1799:

> In a conquering people the military spirit must prevail over other social conditions. Youth must burn to join the warrior host. By these well-known but seldom observed principles, public positions should only be given, as rewards, to those who have fought several campaigns and to fathers of defenders of *la Patrie*. Then the young will learn that unequivocal proofs of patriotism must be given before employment can be obtained. They will learn to respect and esteem those who have so often offered their lives in combat for the glory and defense of their country. Then, too, the men in the army will sense their own dignity.

In addressing private persons, or the local administrations or the government, the military affirmed the purity of their intentions. If they wished to assist citizens in recovering what they owed to themselves and to the Republic, they claimed also to have no desire to dominate or take over the state. But in such protestations there was a restriction. Captain Simon went on to say: "With no desire for military government, let us recall our fellow citizens to their own best interests. Let us remain strong in our virtues and sacrifices, *but*[3] never suffer ourselves to be led to a disgraceful death or to humiliation." It was disgrace and humiliation to forget the revolutionary meaning of the struggle or compound with the adversary. The generals gave out that this was what some men in the civilian society were ready to do. Against them the power of the army must be employed.

The army had become a parallel power, or a counterpower, to the state. Since the Year VI it possessed in itself all the apparatus

---

[3] Italicized by the author.

of the state of which it should have been only one element. It controlled its own military justice, and if it did not itself make the laws by which it was ruled, its chiefs interpreted them with the widest latitude. Living on its conquests, the army was mistress of its own finances, and, even more significantly, it provided an increasing portion of the finances of the state. Commanders of the different armies conducted their own diplomacy and sought to control the states that they created. The Directory wished to return Lombardy to Austria in exchange for annexing the left bank of the Rhine. But at the preliminaries of Leoben, Bonaparte disobeyed the Directory and obliged Austria to recognize the Cisalpine Republic, which was his creation. Hoche in Germany attempted to found a Cisrhenane Republic on the left bank of the Rhine. His death ended this project. Joubert tried to become a chief of state in the Batavian Republic, then in the Cisalpine in 1798. At Naples General Championnet, against instructions from the Directory, set up a "Parthenopean" Republic.

Over five years and more the army had developed a remarkable body of administrators. In every battalion were at work officers and NCOs who had learned to read the text of laws, decrees, and regulations. They sorted, classified, and resolved the problems that arose in their units, as in a small city. In correspondence with the ministries they were annoyed by the slow and bumbling replies that they received. They lost patience with what they saw as ever increasing mismanagement. The army was far from deracinated. It had antennae that reached the political and administrative life of France. These antennae were precisely those administrators required by their duties—doubtless more than any other Frenchmen—to read official communications. They imparted to others in the army their distrust of a civil power that could no longer always get itself obeyed by its own immediate subordinates.

Administrators in the army were by no means found in the quartermasters' offices only. Every officer had at some time or other to act as an organizer. Occupying important parts of Europe, needing to provide for its own security and subsistence, the army assigned certain officers to administrative functions that co-incided with those of civilians. From the level of lieutenant and captain to that of general, from the echelon of government of a country to that of a town or village, the army had learned to ad-minister or supervise the powers that it found in place. Thousands of officers acquired the habit of dealing with problems that were more civilian than military in their nature.

Within France itself officers were required to work with their home municipalities in matters of civil status, requisition, con-scription, draft evasion, and desertion. They thus obtained infor-mation from home of a kind that was of interest to their generals. In any case the generals had other sources of information espe-cially through the gendarmerie, which was often recruited through their patronage. The heads of the administrative military divisions within France possessed a network of political intelli-gence. The commander of the 14th division in 1799 knew all about the activities of neo-Jacobins and royalists in his area and was not the only one to establish files on the subject.

The military hoped for a strong government, able to restore the unity of France, which they saw as essential to victory over the aristocracy. They thought they had obtained such a government by their intervention in Fructidor of the Year V. Their disappoint-ment was all the greater in the following years, as they were per-suaded of the permanent ineptitude of the men in the govern-ment. Those in the government enjoyed a brief respite, due to division among rival generals. But when the generals reached a temporary agreement, they swept away the men in office. "The military," said Napoleon, "are a kind of Freemasonry. There is a certain understanding among them, which means that they can recognize one another unfailingly, find one another out, and reach an agreement."

Bonaparte needed time after the coup d'état to rid himself of rivals among the generals or establish his control over them, to purge and remodel the army, and do his own "thing." The army was now not merely the protective shield for consular and imperial

France; it served also the purposes of Napoleon Bonaparte in his building of a new society. Conscription, which was more successful than has been said, made it possible, by mixing Frenchmen from different regions, to carry on and improve the efforts at national unity undertaken by the Revolution.[4] The officer corps was a crucible for the society of notables that Napoleon envisaged. His aim was "to unite the parties," to bind and associate with his regime the older elites—the aristocracy of the Old Regime—and the new elites produced by the Revolution. First in his lycées, then in his military schools, and finally in the ranks of the army itself, the sons of pre-Revolutionary nobles and those of notables who had been born as commoners would learn to know one another and forget the hatreds born of the revolutionary tempest. In a society based on money, and divided by conflicting self-interests, the officer corps would instill in the sons of notables, and through them in society as a whole, the principle of honor, or civic virtue, as a mainspring of the New City. As in former times, honor meant courage and respect for one's word, but it meant also acceptance of the supreme sacrifice, forgetting of self, and concern for the good of the Nation and the State as incarnated henceforth by Napoleon.

While never making the State a mere preserve for the military, Napoleon gave army officers assurances of a favorable place in the society of notables. Officers on active duty received material and financial advantages and a legal status that allowed them to maintain their rank. In retirement, they could simultaneously draw their pension and receive a salary as civil officials. By a decree of 1811 military men even received priority for appointment to places in the civil administration of the Empire. Even before that date former army officers were to be found among the subprefects, mayors, and deputy mayors of the prinicipal cities of France.

Forming the most numerous cohorts in the Order of the Legion

<hr>

[4] See Isser Woloch, "Napoleonic Conscription: State Power and Civil Society," *Past and Present* 111 (May 1986): 101–29.

of Honor, filling the ranks of the nobility of the Empire, enjoying after 1805 a special place in official ceremonies, marked out by "honors and precedences" that attracted public attention, the military made their imprint—and would long do so in the history of France—on the society that arose from the Revolution.

APPENDIX I

• • •

A Note on Archival Sources

In 1907 the ministry of war ordered the garrison commanders throughout France to set up research teams to be composed of their officers. These teams were to locate and make copies of all documents relating to soldiers of the Revolution. The purpose was to obtain a basis for evaluation and comparison to clarify the debate over a professional versus a national army. It was thought possible to find, in the archives thus assembled, materials that might be of use in the education of the conscripts then being prepared for a war of retaliation against Germany.

The improvised teams not only examined the departmental and municipal archives but in some cases private archives also. They read and transcribed the registers of the general councils of the departments and their subdistricts, the enlistment rolls, the records of meetings of the popular societies, addresses presented by militant sans-culottes of the provinces, and the correspondence between the municipalities and the central government and military authorities. Soldiers' letters and in some cases marching diaries were brought to light. The opening of these files reveals a vast swarming of provincial activity. The enthusiasm and energy of militant Jacobins in calling their fellow citizens to the colors, and in arming, clothing, and feeding them, all appear again. We can see also the dissension, incompetence, and indecision of some local leaders, against which the representatives on mission had repeatedly to act. To sum up, we can hear the incessant dialogue between those who fought and those who struggled on the home front to bring a new world into being.

When to this documentation is added that supplied by the *Archives parlementaires*, the *Actes* of the Committee of Public Safety, the papers of the military committees of the Assemblies, and those of the Secretariat of State and of Military Affairs in the National Archives, it is possible to grasp the process of formation of the army of the Revolution. The files of the *Correspondance générale des armées* and of the *Justice militaire* yield additional information on the combat experience, sufferings, and mentality of the army of the First Republic. In the files of the *Justice militaire* we find interrogations of the accused; we see at first hand the attitude of soldiers toward civilian populations, toward their comrades in battle, and toward their chiefs. In their dialogue with the examining magistrate they express their difficulties, joys, and hopes.

What kind of men were they? One source gives answers to this question. It consists of hundreds of troop control registers deposited in the *Archives de la Guerre*.

The First Republic was heir to a military administration that had been improved by the Old Regime. Between the general renewal of the registers in 1786 and the inauguration of those of the consular and imperial period, the troop registers took on a form that changed very little until the second half of the nineteenth century.

The registers were meant to draw their information from the enlistment rolls. These rolls were initiated by the municipal governments at the time of the levy of volunteers in 1791 and 1792. The information in them was usually limited to family name, given name, age, and sometimes place of residence. It was the same with the levies of 1793. Then at the time of the *levée en masse* the government required the district administrators to prepare four rolls giving a complete description of the draftees: one copy to remain with the district, a second sent to the department, a third to the battalion commander, and the fourth to the ministry of war. In practice only the first two rolls were usually produced.

Their absence retarded or made impossible the keeping in complete form of the registers ordered by the Convention. Well before the amalgamation, the Convention sent registers to the volunteer battalions in two copies, one signed by the chief of the fourth division and intended to remain with the battalion, the other to be transmitted to the ministry. The same was done at the time of formation of the demi-brigades.

As soon as the copies reached the administrative council of the demi-brigades, the officer detailed for this purpose was expected to put aside all other duties and turn to completing and filling out the register. After one copy had been dispatched to the ministry, this officer continued to enter in the copy held by the demi-brigade the names of new recruits and subsequent incidents in their careers. He received printed forms from the ministry in which such changes were to be recorded. At the end of each month these were to be sent to the war department, signed and certified by the battalion commander and the quartermaster.

If in form these control registers were a legacy from previous times, the principle governing their contents during the Revolution was entirely different from what it had been under the Old Regime. Of course there was the desire for more accurate knowledge of an army that had become enormously larger, so as to avoid excessive differences in numbers from one battalion to another. As in the days of the monarchy, the government wanted to identify men who skipped from one unit to another, or "billiarded" as they said, and to detect false hospital papers, by which dead men were reported as living as a way of getting more money. There were a thousand other erratic devices, such as pretended assignments, by which to cause deception and pocket undeserved pay. But above all, by insisting on an exact keeping of the registers, the government showed its desire to establish and maintain a tie between the soldier and his family. In particular, the register allowed the soldier's relatives to obtain the financial aid provided by the state, because it offered proof of the existence of a son or husband in the army. In the years II and III the ministry repeatedly reminded the administrative councils of the demi-brigades:

> The Convention having authorized aid for the fathers and mothers, wives and children, of military men so long as they are in the service of the country, it is necessary for such persons to furnish certificates of the existence of their relative in a military unit. Many citizens of both sexes appear before the commission to obtain such certificates, but the negligence of administrative councils makes it impossible for the commission to satisfy their requests.

Such carelessness led to the creation of little private enterprises that, for a fee, offered to assist families by performing the desired researches. Battalion commanders were quick to agree with the arguments of the ministry, and willingly showed their registers so as "to procure the aid granted by the law to families of their brave comrades." They were under pressure from their men. At first the volunteers of 1791 and 1792, thinking of themselves as citizens enlisted for a campaign, and then for a war that they hoped would be short, resisted the reporting of their names, fearing that they would be considered as career soldiers. But in the end they understood that the register provided a tie with their families. And as they finally accepted their lot as professional soldiers they became aware that the register was the sole guarantee of their right to promotion because it recorded the details of their career. There was another advantage, in that the register became the memorial to sacrifices undergone, the expression of the patriotism and honor of the battalion. Long before Bonaparte the covers of the registers began to display distinguished individual or collective actions. The First Consul generalized the practice.

But though most registers were zealously maintained, there were still many gaps in them. The reason lay in the often absurdly exaggerated bureaucracy of the Revolutionary Government. Within a few months the military units were swamped with paper work. Their administrative councils were still protesting in 1795 against bureaucrats who knew nothing of the realities of war. The council of the 60th demi-brigade wrote:

To expedite the receipt of commissions needed by our officers it is necessary to submit:

1. A copy of the record of formation of our brigade. This is possible. . . . I will have it done.

2. A report, by company with the number of each company, and by battalion, of the situation of officers of our demi-brigade as they have been placed in our formation. . . . This is possible, and I will see to it.

3. A general summary of the service of all officers both before and since the Revolution. . . . This is a bit difficult, but I will see to it also.

4. The minutes of election of officers in the two volunteer battalions to the grades they held before formation of our demi-brigade, as well as the certificates of their service if any in the former Line army, and their birth certificates. . . . The last two are easy, but the minutes of elections! Oh! That is absolutely impossible. Because I have only those of the 8th battalion of the Côte-d'Or. The 12th of Anjou lost everything in the Vendée. . . . And what has become of the men who wrote the minutes? Where are the authorities for whom these minutes were composed? . . . The Revolution has consumed paper and devoured men.

5. Finally, to complete what is needed for the former battalion of the 30th regiment, and supposing (what is true) that some officers are not provided with the commissions for their grade, you ask for documents specifying the vacancy, with supporting papers. . . . Good God! Where can I turn to penetrate this labyrinth in which I shall certainly be lost? The commander of this battalion and a succession of its quartermasters were all lazy. My queries and searches today? *Vox clamans in deserto!* What shall I do?

I call upon the enlightenment of the commission. I beg it to show me the course I should take. . . . Otherwise our commissioned officers will remain without their commissions in writing; the good ones will have reason for vengeance against the bad; but revenge is so odious that we will not use it; and yet justice would not be done to those that deserve it.

The work of keeping the registers was encumbered and delayed by inquiries concerning the moral qualities and patriotism of the command structure, questionnaires to fill out in several copies on men who had disappeared, or were in the hospital, or on detached service, and by situation reports and accounts of the demi-brigades. Men qualified for such multiple tasks were hard to find. Any officer with enough education for such duties soon tired of a post that meant a dead end for his career, and soon took steps to obtain command of a company or a battalion.

And above all there was the war. How could such a task be accomplished with the enemy only a musket shot away? If there was a truce, how could one find a place to do the work? With no tent, no shelter, and paper so wet it stuck to the pocket, there was hardly a moment of peace even for ordinary correspondence and other daily details. At best, one might draw up a list of men who disappeared in the heat of combat without finding out the names of their father and mother and the exact place of their birth. Could one ask the commanders who had escorted these men to the frontiers? They were dead without leaving a register. And if nevertheless the job was done, the enemy might seize the fruit of one's stubborn labors. The speed of movement and change of camp grounds made it impossible to keep records up to date. It is not surprising that the 116th demi-brigade of line infantry, for example, took more than a year to send in its copy of the register.

The government was often for a long time without knowledge of the situation of a particular unit. The 7th battalion of the Jura, for example, was thought by the ministry to have been amalgamated since 1794. But by the hazards of war the *embrigadement* had not been effected. The agents of the ministry were late in learning the facts.

The existence at the Archives de la Guerre of more than a thousand registers for the Revolutionary period therefore testifies to an extraordinary achievement by the citizen-soldiers. It is exceptional to have no information, as in the case of some of the national volunteers, not only because they rejected true military status for a while, but also because some believed that anything written on paper might be used for magical practices against them.

Let us then open the registers and, as statisticians, excuse omissions, which were due less to negligence than to the vicissitudes of a struggle carried across Europe by the fighters for Liberty.

The spelling of names was unstable. A soldier named Haguenau of the 182nd demi-brigade of battle infantry becomes Agneau in the 68th of the 2nd formation. Many soldiers did not know their mother's maiden name.

Under the Old Regime the noncommissioned officers often gave nicknames to new recruits so as to recognize them more rapidly. So each company had its *fleurs d'amour* or *la tulipe*. We still find these picturesque nicknames in the battalions of the Republic, but in smaller numbers, and only the older soldiers had them. In the years of the constitutional monarchy the desire to express political convictions produced new nicknames. Some of these became embarrassing, like the name "Lafayette" taken by the volunteer Dumelin, a soldier in the 66th demi-brigade (no. 3364). After that, we find "Liberty" and "Equality" standing next to "Have-a-drink" and "No-quarter."

Age is expressed in the registers by date of birth. It is a sign of authenticity. But there are many errors. If men are traced from one register to another it is evident that age can vary by four or five years, or sometimes more. Thus a certain Bajard aged by six years from one register to the next. Most often the fault arose because the man did not know his age, but sometimes it was deliberate, because if seniority was equal it was the older soldier who was promoted to corporal or sergeant.

By comparing age with date of enlistment, it is possible to identify, where it is not explicitly stated, those that were called the "boys of the company," or even children that the volunteers brought with them. Some municipalities enlisted children in order to fill their contingents. They would then be discharged "for lack of age."

Birthplace is indicated by commune, district, and department. This information begins to appear in the registers of 1794. It was sometimes given in addition to the *généralité*, the administrative area of monarchical times. Spelling of names of villages and towns was phonetic, and the same man is said successively to have been born at Bilibiret and Viliberveg for Bilisberg in the Pas-de-Calais. Names given to places by the Revolutionary Government, such as *Ville sans Nom* and *Commune affranchie*, were respected in 1794, and such places regained their earlier names only under the Directory.

Physical appearance is given by height, shown until 1796 in feet, inches, and lines. The new republican measures were ignored by some quartermasters until 1801. Complete description (by color of hair and eyes and by facial features) was generally omitted. It is found in only a dozen of the registers.

As under the Old Regime the officer in charge often gave a confused account of occupation, and the term "no occupation" signifies, as in former times, that a man was a day laborer or journeyman. The words used to designate trades constitute an extremely varied catalog, and it is still difficult today to determine the social status of a given individual. A *laboureur* may be a comfortable farmer in one region and a simple manual laborer or a kind of servant in another. When by chance we can follow the declaration of the same man from 1794 to 1801, we can see him calling himself an artisan and then transforming himself into an agricultural worker. He may be one of those poor peasants who earned wages both from agricultural labor and from some other trade; or he may be one of those soldiers who called themselves farm workers to get a temporary leave of absence. Other soldiers concealed their true occupation because it "smelled" of the Old Regime and aroused the suspicion of their comrades. Thus a gendarme named Paderno, in asking for papers verifying his birth, gave a warning to his mother: she should avoid calling his father a "domestic coachman" and present him as a merchant trading in grain and wine; she should not forget that "the other designation is not in season."

The vocabulary employed is thus imprecise, and as in other sources of the period it may use the same word for different social realities, the employer and the wage worker, the small owner and his journeyman, the street stall and the shop in which men shared in the same joys and pains, and in the pay scale allowed by a "manufacturer."

The name of each soldier is followed in the control registers by the number of the company and battalion to which he belonged. This allows us to reconstruct the process of amalgamation by revealing whether *embrigadement* meant only the juxtaposition of battalions or involved a closer union between soldiers of the royal regiments and the volunteers. It may happen that a company is identified not by a number but by the name of its captain. This was a carry-over from the Old Regime; as under Louis XVI, there were captains who wanted to show that they regarded their company as their property.

Dates of enlistment and the first unit in which the soldier served are recorded. The dates are not certain; some volunteers, eager to obtain the grade of lieutenant by seniority of service, gave as their date of enlistment the time when the municipal rolls were opened and not the time of official formation of the battalion. Men raised under the *levée en masse* did the same. In most cases the quartermaster settled the matter by respecting the wishes of the ministry against those expressed by the soldiers.

The soldier is designated in the registers by the term *volontaire*, still used in the Year II to mean the *requis*, or men requisitioned under the *levée en masse*. The word *requis* was late in appearing, and was replaced in the Year VI by the official term, *conscrit*.

The soldier's destiny is shown in the last column. The register employed formulas reflecting the uncertainty of combat. As causes of disappearance from the demi-brigade, we may read "dead or prisoner of war." Many men thought to be dead reappeared in their villages after the Empire.

Dates of discharge, with or without military compensation, and with or without a note of pension awarded, along with the dates of departure of veterans, are also included. Some particularly well-kept registers show also the departing man's physical condition, with a notice of the wounds or amputations that he may have suffered. It is thus possible to form an idea of the physical deterioration that in some campaigns could turn a youth into an old man. We can also, from this information, reconstruct certain armed clashes and judge the use and effects of firearms or edged weapons.

Desertions also appear in the last column. But care must be used in interpreting this word, for the deserter sometimes was only a man in the hospital. Carried off the battlefield to a hospital with which communications were difficult, the wounded man might lose contact with his battalion for months on end. The hospital was often also a place from which desertion was easy, and a quartermaster, uncertain of a man's fate, would simply note "hospitalized or deserted." Penalties for desertion were not always recorded, so great was the habit of pardoning those who returned.

Finally, it is in this last column that we can sometimes trace cases of "billiarding." Men passed from one unit to another without authorization because they knew that the welcoming battalion behaved better on the field of battle. Or they got tired of remaining too long with the same troop. This was the reason given by one Desbrières, who thought he had stayed too long in one place.

Toward the end of the Revolution, feats of arms received a special recompense. The hero was distinguished from his comrades by the bearing of an *arme d'honneur*, the award of which was sometimes noted in the register, with the courageous action summarized in a few lines.

An American friend of mine, Samuel Scott, was working on the registers of the former royal army while I was engaged in research on the volunteer battalions and the registers of the demi-brigades for the Year II and the Year IV. A survey of 2 percent, chosen at random, of all men inscribed in the registers enabled us to know the age, height, and military and regional background of the enlisted men, as well as the procedure of their amalgamation. An exhaustive study of several dozen registers was necessary for collection of information that only they could provide (occupational background, reasons for disappearance). The officers were studied in two other sources of information. The first was a printed source, to be found in the administrative files of regiments and demi-brigades (series Xb or Xc of the Archives de la Guerre), and giving the form of organization before the amalgamation. The other was the result of the extensive inquiry of the Year II by the Committee of Public Safety, of which the findings are deposited in the Archives nationales (AF II 360 to 400). They contain, with the identity of each officer, his age, birthplace, occupation before entering the service, sometimes that of his father, his level of education, his tactical talent, and his patriotism. Wanting to reconstitute groups of officers who had lived together for several years, in order to judge their degree of homogeneity and the possible quarrels among them, notably in matters of promotion, we produced a sample drawn from dozens of monographs concerning more than 10,000 battalion commanders, captains, lieutenants, and sub-lieutenants of all arms. In this sample we made allowance for two factors: the greater or lesser number of officers in each army, and the greater or lesser numerical importance of officers in the former royal regiments, the volunteer battalions, and the forces raised by the requisition. We had been able to make these distinctions in the analysis of the amalgamation.

To collect and deal with this information, we used a new method in computer technology, developed by M. Couturier at the Ecole pratique des hautes études. The method makes it possible to enter the data on a tape recorder in a language not very different from ordinary speech. Transcription of the data to data-processing cards is avoided. Transfer of the data to an electronic device for processing is almost direct.

The researcher should not forget, in using these modern methods, that his subjects were men of flesh and blood whose own words should be heard in other sources, as provided in the archives. It is to be hoped that this study will not betray men who were so exalted by the adventure in which they took part.

APPENDIX II

• • •

Originals of translated verse:

On pages 139–141:

> Un soldat de la liberté
> Quand il est par elle exalté
> Vaut mieux à lui seul que cent esclaves.
> (From a song by Théodore Rousseau,
> *Sur les succès de nos armées)*

> Au combat ainsi qu'au bal
> Je cours comme au carnival.
> (By "the brave patriot corporal")

> De ces guerriers chers à la France . . .
> Vois-tu flotter les étendards?
> C'est à l'autel de la Patrie
> Que l'amour dirige leurs pas;
> Tous vont à leur mère chérie
> Se dévouer jusqu'au trépas.
> (From the *Journal de Paris*
> September 20, 1793)

De aristocrates les crocs
Sont tout juste bons
A faire trembler les marmots.
   (From a song by Théodore Rousseau)

Du salut de notre patrie
Dépend celui de l'Univers. . . .
Ennemis de la tyrannie
Paraissez tous, armez vos bras
Du fond de l'Europe avilie
Marchez avec nous au combat.
   (An unidentified song)

Que le monde pour souverain
N'ait qu'un peuple de sans-culottes.
   (From a *Hymne aux républicains*)

La liberté n'est qu'un piège
Tant que le mot privilège
Blesse la Sainte Egalité.
   (Théodore Rousseau,
   Le tromphe de l'egalité)

Par ses talents, son savoir
Non son avoir
Tout mortel doit s'élever.
   (*Les principes du vrai républicain*)

L'avare et l'égoiste
Ont recours à l'obscurité.
On saura percer leur repaire
Où sur leurs trésors attachés
Ces traitres se tiennent cachés
Déchirant le sein de leur mère.
   (Verses by Citizen Dorli of the
   Section Montagne in Paris)

Le vieux bandeau de l'ignorance
Est déchiré par la Raison.
　(From a *Hymne à la liberté*)

Cessez trompeurs et vains oracles
Qui nous soumettiez à vos lois,
La Raison a repris ses droits.
　(Verses by Citizen Dorli)

Du mensonge profane
Renverse les autels
En tous lieux elle (la Raison) brise
La chaine des erreurs
Et partout pulvérise
Nos sanglants oppresseurs.
　(*Le voeu de tous les peuples qui
　veulent être libres*)

On page 348:

Au noble dans sa giberne
Présentons la Liberté.
Que le bougre se prosterne
Au nom de l'Egalité.
Sacré mill' dieux, tous ensemble
Tirons et brisons nos fers
Que dans le fracas, tout tremble
Pour affranchir l'Univers.
　(From a song of the sans-culottes)

APPENDIX III

• • •

A List of Relevant Books in English

Translations are available for the general histories of the French Revolution by the leading historians of the French Revolution mentioned in the Historiographical Introduction—Jules Michelet, Albert Mathiez, Georges Lefebvre, and Albert Soboul—but not for their more specialized studies. The general history written by Jean Jaurès has not been translated. The following is a list of books in English that bear on the military history of the Revolution.

Best, Geoffrey. *War and Society in Revolutionary Europe, 1770-1870.* New York and Oxford, 1982. Shows the impact of the French Revolution in the long run and in various countries.

Kennett, Lee. *The French Armies in the Seven Years War: A Study of Military Organization and Administration.* Durham, N.C., 1967. Illuminating for the army on the eve of the Revolution.

Lynn, John A. *The Bayonets of the Republic: Motivation and Tactics in the Army of Revolutionary France, 1791–1794.* Urbana and Chicago, 1984. An intensive study of psychology, training and combat in the *Armée du Nord.*

Phipps, Ramsay W. *The Armies of The First French Republic and the Rise of the Marshals of Napoleon I,* 5 vols. Oxford, 1926–1939. A leisurely, old-fashioned, and posthumous work; the author was born in 1838.

Quimby, Robert S. *The Background of Napoleonic Warfare: The Theory of Military Tactics in Eighteenth-Century France.* New York, 1952. Contents indicated in the title.

Ross, Steven. *From Flintlock to Rifle: Infantry Tactics, 1740–1866.* Rutherford, N.J., and London, 1979. Shows details of firepower, battlefield movement, and so forth.

Ross, Steven. *Quest for Victory: French Military Strategy, 1792–1799.* South Brunswick, N.J., 1973. On high-level operations in the wars of the First and Second Coalitions.

Rothenberg, Gunther. *The Art of Warfare in the Age of Napoleon.* Bloomington, Ind., and London, 1978. A general view concerning both France and its adversaries.

Scott, Samuel F. *The Response of the Royal Army to the French Revolution: The Role and Development of the Line Army, 1787–1793.* Oxford, 1978. On the regular army in the crisis of 1787–1789, and until its merger into the Revolutionary army in 1793.

Wetzler, Peter. *War and Subsistence: The Sambre and Meuse Army in 1794.* New York, 1985. A very intensive study of the provisioning of a single army for a short and desperate period.

Wilkinson, Spencer. *The French Army before Napoleon.* Oxford, 1915. A useful older general study.

Woloch, Isser. *The French Veteran from the Revolution to the Restoration.* Chapel Hill, N.C., 1979. On assistance to disabled and retired soldiers, especially but not exclusively at the Invalides, from the late Old Regime to 1814.

For a comprehensive classified bibliography of books, articles, guides, and bibliographies, in French, English, and German, see Ross, Steven T. *French Military History, 1661–1799.* New York and London, 1984.

INDEX

. . .